⌐STUDIES IN⌐
IMPERIALISM

general editor John M. MacKenzie

When the 'Studies in Imperialism' series was founded more than twenty years ago, emphasis was laid upon the conviction that 'imperialism as a cultural phenomenon had as significant an effect on the dominant as on the subordinate societies'. With more than fifty books published, this remains the prime concern of the series. Cross-disciplinary work has indeed appeared covering the full spectrum of cultural phenomena, as well as examining aspects of gender and sex, frontiers and law, science and the environment, language and literature, migration and patriotic societies, and much else. Moreover, the series has always wished to present comparative work on European and American imperialism, and particularly welcomes the submission of books in these areas. The fascination with imperialism, in all its aspects, shows no sign of abating, and this series will continue to lead the way in encouraging the widest possible range of studies in the field. 'Studies in Imperialism' is fully organic in its development, always seeking to be at the cutting edge, responding to the latest interests of scholars and the needs of this ever-expanding area of scholarship.

At the end of the line

At the end of the line

COLONIAL POLICING AND THE
IMPERIAL ENDGAME 1945–80

Georgina Sinclair

MANCHESTER
UNIVERSITY PRESS
Manchester and New York

distributed exclusively in the USA by
PALGRAVE

Published by Manchester University Press
Oxford Road, Manchester M13 9NR, UK
and Room 400, 175 Fifth Avenue, New York, NY 10010, USA
www.manchesteruniversitypress.co.uk

Distributed in the United States exclusively by
Palgrave Macmillan, 175 Fifth Avenue,
New York, NY 10010, USA

Distributed in Canada exclusively by
UBC Press, University of British Columbia, 2029 West Mall,
Vancouver, BC, Canada V6T 1Z2

British Library Cataloguing-in-Publication Data is available

Library of Congress Cataloging-in-Publication Data is available

ISBN 978 0 7190 7139 3 paperback

First published by Manchester University Press in hardback 2006

This paperback edition first published 2010

Printed by Lightning Source

CONTENTS

GENERAL EDITOR'S INTRODUCTION

On a visit to New Delhi, I found myself caught up in the (very imperial) celebrations of India's national day. The processions, ceremonies and bands were sufficiently intriguing to lead me to stand on the lower part of the plinth of a monument to get a better view. Along came an Indian policeman carrying that emblem of colonial policing, the 'lathi' (a long baton) which he wielded against me and others who had taken up the same vantage point. Officious as I thought his attentions were, I was nonetheless fascinated by the postcolonial implications of the action: an Indian policeman 'persuading' a European to act with more decorum. The heritage of 'invented traditions' represented by the ceremonies of the day, together with this tiny incident, gave some food for thought.

Of the many continuities from the imperial to the post-colonial periods, the police constitute a central phenomenon. As Georgina Sinclair points out throughout this book, the police were a key instrument of colonial control, but they also posed a major dilemma. The British Empire was generally in the business of exporting 'Englishness' and British politicians and administrators often deluded themselves into imagining that they successfully did this even through such a fraught institution as the police. The English and the Irish models seemed to offer some contrasts for external emulation, but the reality was that even the points on the spectrum represented by these differing cases were insufficient. The concept of 'policing by consent', allegedly the English ideal, simply did not work, and various state-controlled 'paramilitary' forms were found, at different times, to be more appropriate. Yet models are never fixed. Thatcher's manipulation of the police during the miners' strike of the 1980s (not to mention the changed role of the police during more recent terrorist attacks) indicates the manner in which British policing remains fluid in its character.

To a much greater extent, colonial policing represented different models both simultaneously and in sequence. The police had a variety of different functions, ranging from the suppression of what most would regard as 'crime' through support for traditional authorities and supposedly 'holding the ring' in the face of communal strife, to aspects of civil control in times of labour strikes, political agitation, or major insurrection. This range of duties became more pronounced during the turbulence of the decolonisation period. Yet we should not forget that there were many inhibitions to this complex exercise of imperial state power. One was fiscal parsimony, which led to the police being often undermanned and ill-equipped. The other was confusion as to whose interests were being served. Clearly policy-makers operated within an imperial mindset, but when they began to recognise that 'modernisation' was essential, they were never clear about the perspective from which that modernisation should be approached – from the points of view of the departing power or inheritor governments, from the standpoint of the people of varied ethnicities being policed, or from the interests of certain sectors of society (traditional authorities, specific ethnic groups, the bourgeoisie, the new political elite). Policies of localisation or indigenisation were obfuscated by these confusions.

Georgina Sinclair sets out to unravel these many complexities in the era of decolonisation. Her range across the many different territories of the British Empire is striking, as is her detailed examination of many specific cases of personnel recruitment and training, as well as the multiple moments of tension and violence in the decolonisation process. Not only has she used a striking range of sources and archives, but she has also collected some 400 interviews of surviving police officers which place future historians in her debt. She has also rightly pointed out that influences in policing were not all one-way. The experience of policing the empire also had an effect upon domestic policies, not least in the decolonisation and post-decolonisation years. This is yet another of the many ways in which the British were affected by their experience of Empire. Sinclair offers us much opportunity for further reflection on the complex roles and purposes of the police.

John M. MacKenzie

LIST OF ILLUSTRATIONS

ACKNOWLEDGEMENTS

There are many people who offered their support – intellectual, personal and practical – during the preparation of this book.

My fascination with post-war security and intelligence grew during my time as an undergraduate at Reading University. It was there that I met Philip Murphy, who was instrumental in developing my interest in colonial policing. In supervising my undergraduate dissertation, and then my doctoral thesis, Philip provided continuous academic support and encouragement over a six year period. His research and writing has fuelled my own enthusiasm for the history of decolonisation and will always be a source of inspiration. Philip has read various drafts of this book, always offering scholarly insight and guidance in the most sympathetic manner and with a great deal of humour. I will be forever indebted to him.

The research and writing of this book was completed as a graduate student and then as a member of the School of History at Reading University where I was surrounded by wonderful colleagues. In particular, I would like to thank Roy Wolfe, who has not only been a colleague but a great friend. His tireless searching has provided a wealth of material for my bibliography. Our frequent conversations, as I 'journeyed' around the empire, allowed for many of my embryonic theories to develop into practice. Moreover, the generous support of both heads of School during my time at Reading; Ann Curry and Nick Atkin, allowed some of the breathing space to prepare this book.

Mention of Reading University would not be complete without a big thank you to Tank Waddington. Tank has been a font of knowledge for all things policing. Over numerous lunches and cups of coffee, he has patiently answered questions and allowed me to develop my ideas. Outside Reading University, I would like to thank Clive Emsley, Chris Williams, David Killingray and Tony Kirk-Greene for their generosity in sharing their views on policing and the empire, which has helped to shape my own opinions. In Belfast, Chris Ryder has been a constant source of information in relation to both the RIC and the RUC and has been kind enough to allow me access to his own vast collection of material.

This book would not have been completed without the ongoing assistance of so many former members of the colonial police service and colonial administration. I would like to extend my deepest gratitude to Derek Franklin, Ted Eates, Neil Hadow, Jimmy Lindsay, Ted Horne and Robin Mitchell. They helped me not only to build up contacts, but an extraordinary collection of primary source material that will be useful to scholars researching colonial policing in years to come. In the course of preparing this book, I would like to thank: Paddy Anderson, Harry Anderson, David Angus, David Bailey, Ernest Barraclough, Bob Bradney, George Briffet, John Burton, Joe Bryant, Don Cartwright, Martin Clemens, Leong Chee Who, David Christie-Miller, Graham Clark, Don Clark, James Colquoun, Leon Comber, Adrian & Mary Davies, Jack Dean, Roger Dracup, Ted Evans, Tom Finnerty, James Foster, Martin Gee, Courtney Gidley, Jim Godsave, John Gold, Donald Gray, John Hanley, Peter Hewitt, David Hewson, Gerard Hogan, Michael Jack, Harry Jassy, Cherie Jelf, Geraint Jones, John Kearney, Charlie Kennedy, Michael Koo, Peter Kingsley-Heath, Peter Lapage, David LeClair, Colin Limb, Keith Lomas, John Martin, Avtar Matharu, Rick May, James Mcfeat, Philip Milton, Howyl Parry-Jones, Ronald Postlethwaite, Gerry Paxton, Hugh Phillips, Fred Punter, Dick Ray, Norman Reader, Peter Robinson, David Rowcroft, John Rymer-Jones, C.L. Scobell, Ivan Scott, Bert Selley, John Standring, Bill Stewart, Eleanor Thompson, Alex Thomson, Graham Tudor, Rex Wait, Ted Wells, Greg White, Percy Wild, Dave Willis, George Willis, Bobbie Winser and Lady Young. I am only sorry that John Biles, Dick Craig and Sir Richard Catling are not here to see the finished book.

In considering the 'theory' of colonial policing, I have spent considerable time at the National Archives at Kew, the Public Records Office in Belfast, and, Rhodes House Library in Oxford where the library staff have always been more than helpful, making every visit fruitful. I am particularly grateful to all the library staff at the National Archives of Canada in Ottawa and at McGill University Library in Montreal for bending over backwards to supply mountains of photocopies in a very short space of time. Also to Hugh Forrester of the RUC museum in Belfast, who provided access to fascinating material regarding the training of colonial policemen in Northern Ireland.

In preparing this book, I have had the constant support of Jonathan Bevan at Manchester University Press. I would like to thank him for bearing with me during the end stages of this book when time was of the essence.

Over the course of the past few years, my research and writing has often taken me away from spending time with friends and family. My friends have always offered their encouragement and simply by asking me how 'the book was going' was proof enough of their continuing support. My love and thanks are particularly due to Jules and Peter Morrow, Liz and Peter Paulden, Linda Vintcent, Triona O'Sullivan, Ross Wordie, David Long, Julian Watkins, Marina Kuechen, Elmar Krekeler, Thierry and Pascale Surun, Martin and Pun Baker, Libby Hilling,

ACKNOWLEDGEMENTS

Sarah Emes, Jackie and Ted Howard-Jones, the Hood family and Angie Murphie.

My husband James has also been brought into direct contact with this project. He has always been the technical person behind the scenes and without him this book would never have reached the editor in any reasonable state. More than this, he has so often put up with my complete absence from the real world, continuing to offer love and encouragement.

My only sadness is that my father has not been around to see this book come to fruition. Our conversations often centred upon the history of post-war security and it was he, who laid the foundations for my passion for history. My mother's support and belief in my pursuit of history has continued this legacy. I dedicate this book to her and to the memory of my father.

Georgina Sinclair

ABBREVIATIONS

ACPO	Association of Chief of Police Officers
ADC	Assistant District Commissioner
ASP	Assistant Superintendent of Police
BCC	British Columbia Constabulary
CPA	Colonial Police Advisor
GSU	General Service Unit
ICAC	Independent Commission Against Corruption
IGCP	Inspector-General of Colonial Police
IZL	Irgun Zvai Leumi
KIC	Kenya Intelligence Committee
KPR	Kenya Police Reserve
LHI	Lochmei He'rut Israel
MCP	Malayan Communist Party
MCS	Malayan Civil Service
MOCSDA	Malayan Overseas Chinese Self-Defence Army
MPAJA	Malayan Anti-Japanese People's Party
MRLA	Malayan Races' Liberation Army
NA	National Archives, Kew
NAC	National Archives Canada
NAP	Native Authority Police
NWMP	North West Mounted Police
OPA	Overseas Police Advisor
PPMF	Palestine Police Mobile Force
PRONI	Public Records Office, Belfast
RCMP	Royal Canadian Mounted Police
RHKP	Royal Hong Kong Police
RHL	Rhodes House Library, Oxford
RIC	Royal Irish Constabulary
RUC	Royal Ulster Constabulary
SAS	Special Air Service
SLO	Security Liaison Officer
UDI	Unilateral Declaration of Independence
UMNO	United Malays National Organisation

Introduction

A police force has been established as an armed semi-military force and is employed for the prevention and detection of crime, the repression of internal disturbances, protection against fire, the defence of the colony against external aggression and any other duties prescribed by the Governor in Council.[1]

This was how the Colonial Office described the role of the British Guiana Police in 1938 and how it would serve the interests of the British Empire. Defending the Empire became part of the bread and butter of colonial policing, alongside crime prevention and detection. This process was typically overseen by comparatively few gazetted expatriate officers who commanded a locally recruited rank and file. The numbers of colonial constabularies fluctuated with the changing shape of the Empire: independence in a colony led to the disbandment of a police force. With the onset of decolonisation following the Second World War, many expatriate police officers sought employment elsewhere; a significant number stayed on within the police forces of the newly independent states or moved to other Commonwealth police forces.

What was the function of these colonial policemen? They themselves describe their role not only as police officers but also as soldiers, administrators, magistrates, sheriffs, welfare officers, prison wardens, veterinary officials, teachers and more besides. The job of a colonial policeman involved many different duties and responsibilities reflecting the complex administration of the Empire. Yet many were recruited for this task with the barest of educational qualifications, being judged principally on their 'general educational attainment and suitability'.[2] Certainly the majority of colonial police forces did not expect a university degree and were more interested in an applicant's flair for sport than for the classics. While the upper age limit for the top police forces was 26, the forces of British colonial Africa and the Caribbean set an unofficial limit of 35.[3]

An examination of policing within the imperial context raises all kinds of problems. In the first instance, what do we really mean by 'colonial policing', as distinct from 'English' policing? As independence neared, did the former evolve into the latter as the Colonial Office hoped it would? And then how do we translate this broad theoretical framework into the practice of policing the end of Empire? Before answering these questions, I must first say something about the emergence of the *colonial* and *English* models.

Coercion or consent?

Britain quite clearly had a need for colonial police forces when the size of its regular army and the scale of its imperial activities are considered. In 1715, having colonised over 500,000 people in North America, a large part of the West Indies, coastal settlements in India and outposts in the Mediterranean, Britain's army was no bigger than the King of Sardinia's. By 1850, the home-produced army was still conspicuously modest by comparison with those of Russia and France, or even of Prussia.[4] This army was certainly not capable of maintaining day-to-day order and the defence of Britain's expanding colonial possessions on its own. Police forces provided part of the answer. As David Arnold notes, in a colonial context the distinction between political and criminal duties is largely false, because for the colonial regime the two were largely inseparable: 'The police were born out of the developing needs of the colonial state and they were expressly intended to be state servants and not public servants.'[5] This was particularly the case during the early stages of formal colonisation, when there was a need to impose the authority of the coloniser. Thereafter, the nature of colonial policing was multi-faceted, involving semi-military policing, civil police practice and extraneous police duties dependent on the requirements of the territory in question. As Michael Macoun, a former Inspector-General of the Colonial Police (ICGP) noted, each colonial force could aptly be described as 'an armed constabulary with a limited Civil Police capability'.[6]

Sir Charles Jeffries, as Deputy Under-Secretary of State for the Colonies from 1946 to 1956, had a specific theory about the development of colonial police practice. Jeffries posited three broad phases 'with very varying tempos of change in different places'. First, the police secured law and order within a colony, essentially through the use of force. Second, a semi-military police force was established 'with a view to the suppression of crimes of violence and mass outbreaks [*sic*] of the peace'. (This became general practice throughout the second half of the nineteenth century and the early part of the twentieth century.)

It was only in the third phase that the conversion from a semi-military to a quasi-civil police force could begin, once the need for internal security was outweighed by that of the prevention of crime.[7] Ultimately, however, the ideal, whether in the short or the longer term, was a ' "civilian" police without para-military functions', along English lines, which could be attained only when the conditions within a colony allowed for *community*-based rather than overtly *political* policing. Theoretically, phases one and two relied on coercion while phase three utilised the principle of consent. In practice, however, there was a great deal of overlap between the two during the turbulence of the post-war years.

Police models

Colonial rule was achieved through a system of law that incorporated some indigenous practices while delegitimising others. An essential feature of the colonial state was that it was an imported concept 'built on the surface of indigenous society'.[8] Power was generated from within the imperial centre, London, and was handed down to the colonial administration in each territory.[9]

The question of how policing operated under these conditions has generated a somewhat insular historiography. The only broad survey of the colonial police was published by Jeffries in 1952 and focused on the history of individual forces rather than offering a comparative analysis. Up until that time, few books on individual colonial police forces had been published;[10] thereafter, autobiographies of colonial police, memoirs and force histories gradually appeared.[11] Academic interest in colonial policing was revived in the 1970s with Tekena Tamuno's work on the Nigeria Police and David Clark's research into the policing of Bengal, Palestine and Cyprus.[12] This was followed by a programme of archival research, initiated by the Oxford Development Records Project, which operated between 1978 and 1984, gathering written testimonies and private papers of colonial officials who had worked overseas, primarily in Africa. Almost seventy former colonial policemen contributed to this project, with their responses and papers now housed at Rhodes House Library in Oxford.[13] This was really the starting point for the publication of a small number of articles on the nature of colonial policing.[14] More recently, two collections of essays, edited by David Anderson and David Killingray, have provided a real starting point for research into colonial policing prior to and during decolonisation.[15] This has generated renewed interest in the field, although the material has tended to focus on African territories.[16] Further research within this area will enhance our understanding of the machinery of Empire.[17] A study of colonial policing will allow the processes of decolonisation to be viewed in a more sharply delineated context.

A quick backward glance at how the term 'police' came into existence provides additional clues to the evolution of colonial policing in its broadest sense. The word has been around since ancient times and would appear to be connected with the ancient Greek *polis*:[18] the words *polis*, 'politics' and 'police' are found to share similar roots, indicating that there was a link between 'police' and the 'political world' – for the Greeks, *politeia* referred to the general instruments of government within the wider administration of the state. The British tradition of policing developed in part from Anglo-Saxon beliefs that the law reflected the will of the people, which every *free* man had an obligation to uphold. In contrast, the Roman tradition developed a centralised force 'at the disposal of the administering power to maintain public order by pragmatic action rather than worrying about accountability to the community as a whole'.[19] By the eighteenth century, 'police' (or *la police* and *die politzey*) encompassed administration, welfare, protection and surveillance within continental Europe. This was adopted to some degree in England where the first official use of 'police' came during the reign of Queen Anne, when she appointed 'Commissioners of Police' to undertake general administrative functions throughout the country. The word did not come into general use, however, until later in the eighteenth century, as it 'smacked of absolutism, and in particular of Bourbon spies and of the military *maréchaussée* which patrolled the main roads of eighteenth century France'.[20]

While there was a connection between police and social control, an identification with the local community provided the embryo for the later *British* policing models. As Britain moved into its age of imperialism in the nineteenth century, it developed a colonial policing model based on the idea that the police force would be a colony's first line of defence, as well as the providers of law and order, a model adapted from the British experience of keeping Ireland under quasi-colonial subjugation. In a similar vein, elsewhere in Europe a state-controlled, centralised, *gendarmerie*-style of policing materialised – the basis for the so-called 'continental' model.[21] However, regardless of the *model* that may be present, 'the police have developed in modern societies as the specialist organisation charged with the maintenance of order, and entrusted with the capacity to deploy the legitimate force that states monopolize'.[22] In essence the police became one of a state's key institutions, part of its political backbone. As P. A. J. Waddington reminds us, policemen '*exercise authority* founded upon the monopoly of legitimate force [which is] essentially *coercive*'.[23]

[4]

It is only through an understanding of *who* is policed, the *context* within which people are policed and the *means* by which they are policed that differences can be found between the various models. Waddington further argues that the use of coercion, which has been common to all police forces, is less of an issue within authoritarian societies where the police are openly an arm of government and hence free to 'exercise naked coercive force'. So '*how* that authority is exercised reflects the relationship between the state and the citizen'. This is a crucial difference between British and colonial styles of policing. Within a democracy like Britain, the emergence of the 'new' police must be understood alongside the development of civil and political elements of citizenship in the nineteenth century.[24] In that situation elements of police coercion were camouflaged by a veneer of legitimation.

There are core issues within policing that allow a deeper understanding of the models. Robert Mawby noted how policing could be 'distinguished in terms of its *legitimacy*, its *structure*, and its *function*'. *Legitimacy* refers to how the police function within society, on both a theoretical and a practical basis, with a government's backing; *structure* implies that the police comprise an organised body with a degree of professionalism and a code of practice underpinning policing activities; the *function* of policing typically revolved around the maintenance of law and order, and the detection and prevention of crime, activities that have evidently extended to other duties – for example, in the context of colonial policing, a paramilitary role.[25] Legitimacy, structure and function are particularly pertinent when attempting to disentangle the various policing models and establish differences as well as similarities. More generalised questions of accountability, impartiality and independence repeatedly crop up throughout this book. Policing the end of Empire was fraught with difficulties, bringing these issues to the fore in times of emergency.

Method and sources

This book is not a complete history of the police forces of the British Empire in the vein of Charles Jeffries's *The Colonial Police*. While using some of Jeffries's early work as a springboard, what I aim to provide are historical snapshots of the end of the Empire. The central thread weaving through this narrative explains how the theory of colonial policing – which centred on leaving a legacy of *Britishness* – collided with the realities of policing the end of Empire. The emphasis here, therefore, is on policing conflict rather than the application of British law and crime-fighting in an imperial context.

In explaining the origins of professional policing in Britain, it is possible to reach a greater understanding of the wider imperial dimensions. Certainly, the Irish model spread rapidly throughout the Empire, from India to Canada and on to Palestine and so on. By the same token, attempts were being made as early as 1864 in the Ceylon Police for example, to replicate the Metropolitan Police rather than the Irish Constabulary. The overlaying of these contrasting *British* styles of policing can be considered with the emergence of policing in Canada. In continuing this theme, I have noted how these influences affected the policing of the *old* Empire and subsequently the British Commonwealth. While the array of national, provincial and municipal police forces, which make up the policing of Canada, have borrowed from both the French and American models, their nineteenth-century influences were predominantly Irish–colonial and metropolitan–English. This can still be seen today in the traditions of Canada's best-known police force: the Royal Canadian Mounted Police.

Having considered the evolution of nineteenth- and twentieth-century British policing models, the book turns to the history of postwar colonial policing. Following the inauguration of the Colonial Police Service in 1936, concerted efforts were made to bring standardisation to all colonial police forces. It was not, however, until after the Second World War that real attempts were made to initiate reform. Even then, this was essentially a reaction to the spiralling colonial conflict that followed Britain's withdrawal from India in 1947. Britain's colonial headaches were only just beginning. In February of the following year, there was serious rioting in the Gold Coast, followed by the withdrawal from Palestine in June and the onset of colonial conflict in Malaya the same month. Colonial police forces were brought into the line of fire, making reform a matter of urgency. Having appointed the first *official* colonial police advisor in 1948, ostensibly to bring a degree of Britishness to imperial policing, the Colonial Office then clashed with colonial governments and their police chiefs over the implementation of such policing. However, attempts to export *Britishness* to the older established colonies, notably areas in the British Caribbean, had been going on for rather longer. Within this perceived backwater of the Empire, similar principles of reform through reorganisation, training and the importation of police officers from the home forces had been applied since the nineteenth century. Indeed the British Caribbean appeared almost as a testing ground for *proactive* rather than *reactive* reform. Inconclusive these attempts may have been, yet there were no efforts made to learn from the lessons of the Caribbean and apply these to the wider concerns of the Empire. In the Mediterranean, the Middle East, Africa and Southeast Asia, the British

Government was pressured into police reform as a result of the end of the Empire. The book considers whether English *and* colonial styles of policing could be accommodated within these areas. The perceived *English* areas of reform included the role of a roving police advisor and the secondment of senior members and personnel to serve in the colonies with a view to installing a different style of policing. In essence, this was a theoretical approach to policing the end of the Empire which fell short of the realities. As the shadow of decolonisation lengthened, so police forces reverted to their traditional roles as semi-military outfits operating at the beck and call of colonial governments. With increased tensions throughout the Empire, police powers escalated and the police developed new intelligence and counter-insurgency units. The policing of end of the Empire has more commonly been associated with 'dirty war' than with the English style of policing by consent.

The steady opening up of material in the National Archives (NA) has greatly assisted this research, enabling it to bridge the gap between the theory and the practice of policing. While undertaking research for both my doctoral thesis and this book, I have had access to a variety of source materials. The first has been the slow trickle of police memoirs; the second, and most valuable source, has been my personal collection of over 400 oral and written testimonies of former colonial policemen, administrators and members of the armed forces. These respondents not only provided a back-up in some cases of names, dates and places but have also been an invaluable font of all kinds of information relating to the day-to-day policing of the Empire. Many of those interviewed were exceedingly generous in providing access to hitherto unseen private papers; diaries, letters, memoirs, police handbooks and extraordinary collections of colonial police memorabilia. In bringing together the official and unofficial documentation, I have sought to move closer to an understanding of, as opposed to theoretical guesswork about, the realities of policing the end of the Empire.

Notes

1 'Particulars of the Office of Detective Superintendent of Police', Guiana Police – Establishment and Vacancies, 1938, National Archive (NA), Colonial Office (CO) 111/751/2.
2 'Eligibility for appointment/qualifications for the Colonial Police Service 1952/53', NA CO 1017/262.
3 'Junior Station Inspectors applying for appointments in the Colonial Police Service 1937', NA, Metropolitan Police Records (MEPO) 2/2796.
4 J. A. Houlding, *Fit for Service: The Training of the British Army 1715–1795* (Oxford: OUP, 1981), pp. 7–8.
5 David Arnold, *Police Power and Colonial Rule, Madras 1859–1947* (Oxford: OUP, 1986), p. 3, p. 233.

6   Quoted in Gerry Northam, *Shooting in the Dark; Riot Police in Britain* (London: Faber & Faber, 1988), p. 129.

7   Sir Charles Jeffries, *The Colonial Police* (London: Max Parrish, 1952), pp. 32–33.

8   David K. Fieldhouse, *Black Africa, 1945–80, Economic Decolonization and Arrested Development* (London: Routledge, 1986), p. 55.

9   The table in Appendix 1 shows the layout of a typical colonial establishment. The colonial police, alongside other departments, were directly accountable to the colonial governor.

10 See G. K. Pippet, *A History of the Ceylon Police* (Columbo: Times Publishing, 1938), Vol. 1; Robert W. Foran, *A Cuckoo in Kenya the Reminiscences of a Pioneer Police Officer in British East Africa* (London: Hutchinson, 1936).

11 See in particular: E. A. Burton, 'The Policing of Bermuda from the Earliest Times', *Bermuda Historical Quarterly* (1955); A. C. Dep, *A History of the Ceylon Police*, 2 vols (Columbo: Times Publishing, 1969); Robert W. Foran, *The Kenya Police, 1887–1960* (London: Robert Hale Ltd, 1962); Derek Franklin, *A Pied Cloak: Memoirs of a Colonial Police (Special Branch) Officer* (London: Janus, 1996); Edward Horne, *A Job Well Done: A History of the Palestine Police Force 1920–48* (Tiptree: Anchor Press, 1982); Colin Imray, *Policeman in Africa* (Lewes: Book Guild, 1997); *A Policeman in Palestine* (Bideford: Edward Gaskell, 1995); Michael J. Macoun, *Wrong Place, Right Time: Policing the End of Empire* (London: Radcliffe Press, 1996); William P. Mathieson, *A Chequered Career* (London: Janus, 1994); Geoffrey J. Morton, *Just the Job: Some Experiences of a Colonial Policeman* (London: Hodder & Stoughton, 1957); W. A. Orrett, *The History of the British Guiana Police* (Georgetown: Daily Chronicle Ltd, 1951); Peter Gibbs & Hugh Phillips, *The History of the British South Africa Police 1889–1980* (Melbourne: Something of Value, 2000); W. R. Shirley, *A History of the Nigeria Police* (Lagos: Lagos Government Printers, 1955); Tim Wright, *The History of the Northern Rhodesia Police* (Bristol: British Empire and Commonwealth Museum Publishing, 2001).

12 See: Tekena N. Tamuno, *The Police in Modern Nigeria, 1861–1965* (Ibadan: IUP, 1970); David J. Clark, 'The Colonial Police and Anti-Terrorism, Bengal 1930–36, Palestine 1927–47 and Cyprus, 1955–59', unpublished DPhil (Oxford University, 1978).

13 Anthony Clayton, *The Thin Blue Line: Studies in Law Enforcement in Late Colonial Africa* (Oxford: Oxford Development Records Project, 1985); and RHL MSS, Afr. s. 1784.

14 See: Mike Brogden, 'The Emergence of the Police: The Colonial Dimension', *British Journal of Criminology*, 27, 1 (1987); David Killingray, 'The Maintenance of Law and Order in British Colonial Africa', *African Affairs*, 85, 340 (1984); John McCracken, 'Coercion and Control in Nyasaland: Aspects of the History of a Colonial Police Force', *Journal of African History*, 27 (1986).

15 David M. Anderson & David Killingray, *Policing the Empire: Government, Authority and Control, 1830–1940* (Manchester: MUP, 1991), and *Policing and Decolonisation: Politics, Nationalism and the Police, 1917–65* (Manchester: MUP, 1992).

16 See: P. T. Ahire, 'Policing Colonization: The Emergence and Role of the Police in Colonial Nigeria, 1860–1960', PhD (University of Cambridge, 1985); Hamish Morrison, ' "Quis custodiet ipsos custodes?" The Problems of Policing in Anglophone Africa during the Transfer of Power', unpublished PhD (University of Aberdeen, 1995); Emmanuel K. Rotimi, 'A History of Native Administration Police Forces in Nigeria, 1900–1970', PhD (Obafemi Awolowo University, 1990); K. Rotimi, *The Police in a Federal State: The Nigerian Experience* (Ibadan: College Press, 2001).

17 See: Georgina S. Sinclair, "Settlers' Men or Colonial Policemen? The Ambiguities of Colonial Policing, 1945–1980', PhD (University of Reading, 2002).

18 The Greeks interpreted *polis* as issues revolving around the state.

19 Macoun quoted in Northam, *Shooting in the Dark*, p. 132.

20 Clive Emsley, *The English Police: A Political and Social History*, 2nd edition (Harlow: Longman, 1996), p. 3. The *Maréchausée* was a military police force whose

origin was the royal bodyguards at the time of the Crusades. The *Maréchausée* patrolled provincial France. Reorganised in February 1791, with the title of *Gendarmerie Nationale*, its role was to supply sentries and guards for courts, prisons and the National Assembly, as well as acting as provost: Philip John Stead, *The Police of France* (London: Macmillan, 1983), p. 35.

21 While the use of the British, colonial and continental models seem perfectly acceptable as a starting point for interpreting any history of policing, matters are open to a more complex interpretation. Alan Wright, for example, has considered police strategies, which he terms models, specifically within the realms of public order policing. He refers to: the 'civil police model', the 'state police model', the 'quasi-military police model' and the 'martial law model' drawn on an escalating scale. Simply put the civil police model operates where a constitution sets out a clear separation of powers and duties between the military and the police. The British model of policing operates within this context. In the state police model, once again there is a clear distinction between the legitimate functions of the military and the police. Here the example is of France and Germany; the 'continental model'. The quasi-military police model appears in states whose constitution dictates that the police and military share power and responsibilities. In its extreme, for example in totalitarian states, it is noted that the police need not legitimate their actions through the rule of law. This model type was seen as operating in Eastern and Central Europe up until 1990. The final model, marital law, is described as being present when the state is in total political control. Here there is no separation between the powers and duties of the police and the military. Police come under military command and control and are subject to military law. Wright claims that this form of policing was apparent in British colonial rule and cites the emergencies of Malaya and Kenya as examples: see Wright, *Policing: An Introduction to Concepts and Practice* (Cullompton: Willan Publishing, 2002), pp. 63–67.

22 Robert Reiner, *The Politics of the Police*, 3rd edition (Oxford: OUP, 2000), p. xi.

23 P. A. J. Waddington, *Policing Citizens: Authority and Rights* (London: UCL Press, 1999), p. 20.

24 Waddington, *Policing Citizens*, pp. 21, 26.

25 Robert Mawby, *Comparative Policing Issues: The British and American System in International Perspective* (London: Unwin Hyman, 1990), p. 3.

CHAPTER ONE

Towards an understanding of colonial policing: exploring policing models

Understanding policing models is particularly frustrating for historians. While it is possible to make sweeping theoretical generalisations, there are clear inter-country variations in the practice of policing arising from the historical timeframe and its context and the *type* of population policed. In the case of the colonial police model, the colonial population varied considered from colony to colony. The only common factor was that typically policing was about dealing with people of *colour* rather than *white* people. At the Imperial Conference in 1898, Joseph Chamberlain boasted of 'the traditions of the Empire, which makes no distinction in favour of, or against, race or colour'.[1] That was simply not true. In reality, issues surrounding *colour*, and indeed the colour bar, were present in all colonies: 'White people were of importance simply by being white. It was an inescapable fact of colonial life.'[2] This belief shaped the attitude of the colonial authorities towards the colonised and thus, of the policeman towards the citizen. In colonies like Kenya and Northern Rhodesia, the presence of white settlers complicated policing patterns still further, producing a three-tiered system between the European community, the police and the local population. Despite inter-colony variations, it is useful to consider the emergence and development of the colonial model alongside the English model to reach a deeper understanding of patterns of similarity and contrast.

It has been argued that accounts of the emergence of policing in Britain in the nineteenth century must take stock of the wider context of British colonial policing. Michael Brodgen's view was that the colonial police forces and nineteenth-century British policing differed only marginally, rather than being at opposite ends of the spectrum.[3] In the broadest sense, overlap occurred simply because policing across all systems displayed some basic similarities. Any police force has been and always is intrinsically linked to the state within which it operates: a police force is in reality an agent of the state. So 'colonial policing functioned to legitimate central rule from Westminster. Colonial police work, and perhaps also to some extent British police work, was pre-eminently missionary work to legitimise external governance'.[4]

An English policing model?

The police system that emerged in Britain in the early part of the nineteenth century was distinctive. Prior to this period, there had been no dominant policing model.[5] In theory these new policemen had the job of improving the prevention and detection of crime, while ensuring public order. In practice, they were encouraged to provide society with an acceptable face of policing, wiping away memories of incidents like Peterloo. This came at a time of reform and the police became 'one of the nineteenth century inventions which underpinned modern civilization and democracy'.[6] Revisionist accounts of the new police have tended to focus upon the police as a by-product of the British State and its changing class structures.[7] The police essentially protected the property and rights of the middle and upper classes, and in this sense they could be seen as similar to colonial police forces who gave preferential treatment to European expatriates at the expense of the local population.

Traditional accounts surrounding the evolution of the new police held a different view. Charles Reith stressed that service to the public was enshrined within the role of the new police. Reith noted nine essential principles: the prevention of crime and disorder; the maintenance of public respect; co-operation with the public; the recognition that the police are the public and the public are the police; the use of minimum force; the use of maximum force as a last resort; impartiality; effectiveness; and a strict adherence to police–executive functions represented all that was new in police tradition.[8] Indeed many of the Reithian historians focused upon the rise of urban crime during the early part of the nineteenth century. While one of the central duties of these new metropolitan constables was undoubtedly the prevention of crime, the novelty, as Emsley has pointed out, centred upon this large group of uniformed men brought under the direction of the Home Secretary.[9] These new policemen had to win back their legitimacy by presenting themselves as unarmed, non-military figures – Bobbies. They had a somewhat different approach when it came to the maintenance of order. It was within this sphere that Sir Robert Peel imported ideas from his earlier creation, the Irish Constabulary, developed during his time as Chief Secretary for Ireland from 1812 to 1818. There he saw 'a police which should tend not only to punish crime, but to prevent it . . . by habituating the people to obey the law [which] might probably in the end have the effect of attaching them to it'.[10] This necessitated the use of force. Indeed, in London, cutlasses and pistols could be carried by certain officers if a beat was considered dangerous, which rather went against the grain of these so-called Metropolitan police principles. Some county police forces, notably Essex, even adopted a military model of policing after 1839, deeming it to be more effective.[11] In essence, the policing of Ireland became as much an influence on the 'English' as it did the 'colonial' police model.

In his creation of the Metropolitan Police, Peel's idea was of a force that could tackle crime as well as public disorder. However, social conditions were not as compatible with a civil unarmed police force as the Government may have hoped. England was faced with serious internal disorder throughout the 1830s and 1840s. Often, the 'new' police constables were drafted in from outside the capital and sometimes even deployed alongside the military.[12] The military style of the Irish Constabulary was reflected in the appointment of Colonel Sir Charles Rowan in 1829, who had served in the French Wars and with the army on public order duties in the midlands and Ireland. Members of the community came to describe the role of the police as paramilitary rather than civilian at this time, characterised by a military model of organisation and by the drill employed. Cries of 'Down with the Raw Lobsters! No Martial Law! No Standing Armies!' at one public demonstration in 1830, and the use of the term 'Jenny Darbies', an anglicisation of the French gens d'armes made this all too apparent. Early protests against the new police considered that they were simply no better than an armed force.[13] The development of a civilian police force was tinged with Irishness.[14]

Real contrasts that emerged between the police forces of Ireland and Britain came in the form of their accountability to government. The Irish Constabulary came under the auspices of Dublin Castle, but the question of whether the Metropolitan Police should come under parish, county or central control remained a source of political debate until the 1850s. In the event the legislation of 1835, 1839 and 1856, the Parish Constables Act of 1842 and Superintending Constables Act of 1850, gradually moved the power from the periphery to the centre.[15]

There is, therefore, a problem in making a clear-cut interpretation of the English police model. What appears to have been in evidence were three different police structures in England and Wales following the 1856 County and Borough Police Act. The first was that of the Metropolitan Police, which was the largest force and the only one directly accountable to the Home Secretary, and more urban in nature.

Then there were the borough forces answerable to watch committees appointed by local councils. Third, there were the county forces responsible to police committees and later, to standing joint committees. Overall, the London model simply did not correspond to the needs of many rural constabularies. Gloucestershire and Staffordshire even recruited Irish policemen into their senior ranks, preferring *their* expertise. Following the 1964 Police Act, two police structures emerged: the Metropolitan, under the auspices of the Home Secretary; and forty or so provincial forces responsible to the new police committees and the Home Office.[16] Hence there were two closely linking police models emerging within the nineteenth century: the Metropolitan–urban and the English–rural model, both of which would impact upon the development of the colonial police.

The diffusion of ideas between English and colonial policing goes back to the early days of the new police. For example, the first of many appeals for assistance in police organisation was made to the Metropolitan Police Commissioners in 1834 from Barbados. Having abolished slavery, the local government requested 'a Police Force rendered necessary by the change in the condition of the Negro Population'. The Commissioners despatched Inspector Francis Mallalieu, who spent several weeks advising on the reorganisation of the Barbados Police.[17]

The overlapping between the Irish–colonial and Metropolitan–English policing models was noticeable throughout the British Empire. Colonial governments, during the early part of the nineteenth century, requested details of the structure of the Metropolitan Police and permission to replicate this within their own colony. There was a request, for example, from the Mauritius police in 1836 'to obtain from the Commissioners of Police information of organization to enable the Government to organize police on the same principle, details to include pattern of uniform'.[18] Indeed, during the 1830s information and sometimes, small numbers of Metropolitan Police officers, were sent out to Jamaica, Ceylon, Canada, Australia and South Africa. While Reith has argued that the 'principles and ideals' of the London constabulary were successfully exported throughout the British Empire and there constituted a part of future policing traditions and practices, the reality of policing was far removed from the image of the bobby on the beat.

A colonial policing model?

Policing models are shaped by the socio-political structure of a given state. Certainly, the police forces that developed within Western and Central Europe in the nineteenth century were different from the English model. By the same token, as Britain expanded its Empire, a different style of policing was needed to facilitate colonial rule. And so it is to the policing traditions of Ireland that we must turn to understand the history of colonial policing.

Historical research has pointed to Ireland's *colonial* characteristics. Even with the passing of the Act of Union in 1801, the Irish administration retained a colonial outlook, with 'efficiency in government being valued above the liberty of the subject and the sanctity of property.'[19] The proposed creation of a centralised, armed and bureaucratic police force, as early as the mid-eighteenth century, reflected this need for control. A paid police force came into effect from 1784. In rural areas, baronial constables, or 'barnies' as they became known, were appointed by the administration and operated along lines similar to those of the London watchmen. On his arrival in Ireland Peel made the maintenance of order his first priority. The genesis of the Irish Constabulary came with an Act for the Better Execution of the Laws in Ireland in 1814. This Act was prefaced with an explanation that 'disturbances have from time to time existed in Different Parts of Ireland for the Suppression Whereof the ordinary Police hath been found insufficient'.[20] This allowed the Lord Lieutenant to appoint paid magistrates, and officers responsible to them, in designated 'disturbed' areas to ensure adherence to the law. Known as 'Police Preservation Forces', these magistrates and their officers were effectively the strong right arm whose function was to assist with law enforcement. Wherever disturbances occurred, this Act permitted the appointment of a chief constable who could raise a police force. Peel had created a novel police system, in place of the army, for use in suppressing disorder. However, it was essentially military in nature, from the ranking system to the uniforms, armament and the recruitment of ex-soldiers. This concept of policing would remain as a permanent fixture of the laws of Ireland. Peel thus created the foundations for a semi-military police force rather than the more civilian style of policing which emerged in London some years later.

The Constabulary Act of 1822 removed the network of baronial constables in each of Ireland's thirty-two counties and a police force was established broadly on the lines of the Peace Preservation Force. An 1836 Act modestly sought to 'Consolidate the Laws relative to the Constabulary Forces in Ireland'.[21] From this time an Irish Constabulary was in existence, amalgamating the Peace Preservation Forces and the county constabularies under the executive command of the Inspector-General, who had greater authority than previously. Theoretically each member of the police was accountable first and foremost to the Inspector-General, whereas in England and Wales the constable was entrusted with the law, to which he was personally accountable and on the basis of which he was expected to make personal decisions. In Ireland the 1822 act stated that 'all Constables and Sub Constables shall attend and obey the Chief Constables in their respective Counties, Baronies, Cities and Towns', and . . . 'any Warrant, Order or Command of any Magistrate' should be 'show[n] or deliver[ed] to his chief constable for instructions'.[22]

Graham Ellison and Jim Smyth have argued that the primary function of the Irish Constabulary became one of repression of rather than co-operation with the Irish Catholic community, citing the 1917 Irish Convention Sub-Committee on Defence and the Police which noted that the Irish police lacked public co-operation in the maintenance of law and order, owing to its primary allegiance to the State.[23]

This situation continued in the wake of the 1920 Government of Ireland Act, which entrusted the Northern Ireland Government with limited security powers. In 1922, the Northern Ireland Government secured the passage into law of the Civil Authority (Special Powers) Act. The key point of this Act was that it transferred many peace preservation powers from the judiciary to the executive. The Minister of Home Affairs was given wider discretionary powers to preserve order, and could delegate powers to *any* officer of the newly formed Royal Ulster Constabulary (RUC).[24] The objective of preserving British interests up until the establishment of the Northern Ireland Government in 1920 was replaced by the aim of defending Unionist power.

The Royal Irish Constabulary

From 1822 to 1922, the policing of Ireland was undertaken by the Royal Irish Constabulary (RIC), which at some stages numbered some 10,000 men.[25] However, the extent to which the RIC retained its quasi-military outlook has been disputed by W. J. Lowe and E. L. Malcolm. They considered that by the twentieth century, the RIC was 'very much a Civil Police force, reflecting very accurately in its composition the socio-economic structure of Irish society and in its operations the needs of small, relatively law-abiding rural communities'. Lowe and Malcolm have explained that 'an important corrective' to the RIC's paramilitary role was provided by the variegated duties assigned to it by the Irish administration.[26] Yet, colonial-style police forces were required to carry out a wide range of duties as a way of measuring the pulse of the local community and gathering intelligence. Throughout this period, the RIC built up a reputation as the 'eyes and ears' of Dublin Castle. Intelligence-gathering remained a fundamental part of its work[27] and served to influence the creation of Police Special Branches in many British colonies.

While attempts were made to transform the Irish police into more of a civil force by the early part of the twentieth century, its military function in the suppression of public disorder continued. The Irish policeman came to carry fewer arms on duty. On a two-man patrol, one man typically carried a rifle and the other the sword bayonet. Truncheons were supplied to many RIC members and became the usual weapon for town and village duty. By the early twentieth century, RIC men 'maintained familiarity' with guns with once-a-year target practice. 'The military character of the Force is passing away' noted a Select Committee study in 1914. 'The men do not, as a rule, carry arms except for drill and for ceremonial occasions.'[28] By the First World War there were doubts expressed as to the effectiveness of the RIC in the event of a German invasion.[29]

Yet the RIC maintained its military organisation and ethos. The solid-frame cartridge 0.442 centre-fire revolver, manufactured by Philip Webley and adopted by the RIC in 1868, was one of the most copied firearms of the nineteenth century worldwide, and the RIC handgun was used throughout the British Empire.[30] Emphasis continued to be placed on drill, marching and military formations: 'We make them soldiers as far as we can', noted the Irish Inspector-General.[31] Despite the apparent *domestication* of the RIC, the police served as the Government's front-line force during both the Land War and the War of Independence (1919–21). It was the RIC rather than the military who bore the brunt of the fighting,[32] assisted by the infamous auxiliary corps the Black and Tans in their uphill struggle against the IRA. After the creation of the Irish Free State, many former members of the RIC took their policing experiences not only to the Palestine Gendarmerie but to the police forces of the Empire.

Spreading the Irish model

The Irish case is a logical starting point when considering the development of colonial policing.[33] The standards first set out in the Constabulary Code of Regulations of 1837, were drilled into the recruits at the central depot at Phoenix Park in Dublin several years later. Training was run on military lines with an emphasis on drill and use of weaponry.[34] Thomas Fennell, who served in the RIC in the late nineteenth century, explained that 'the Depot differed nothing from a military barracks . . . recruits were drilled as soldiers for six months or more, until proficient in the use of arms and military movement. The Force, therefore, became an important adjunct to the military, as an army of occupation in the country.' Even following their initial

Table 1.1   Colonial policemen trained at the RIC depot from 1907 to 1912[a]

Africa		Far East		Caribbean		Other		All
Northern Nigeria	26	Federated Malayan States	1	Jamaica	4	Malta	2	
Southern Nigeria	21			Trinidad	6	Fiji	1	
Gold Coast	12			Straits Settlements	1	British Guiana	5	
The Gambia	2							
Sierra Leone	3							
East Africa	15							
Uganda	11							
Somaliland	1							
Totals	91		1		11		8	111

Note:
[a] From 1912 to July 1915, a further forty-nine officers were trained in RIC policing practice: RUC Archives, Police Service of Northern Ireland (PSNI), Belfast.

training, 'the men continued throughout their service to practise drill and the use of arms. An abridged edition of the Army drill book was found at every police station and an annual target practice took place in every district. The Day or Orderly room in every station differed nothing from a squad room in a military barracks.'[35] These practices were on a par with those of the colonial constabularies during the twentieth century.

There were direct Irish influences in the paramilitary functions, training and nomenclature of the colonial forces spreading throughout the Empire. In the later decades of the nineteenth century, many colonial administrators insisted that their police forces were trained by the RIC. For example, in 1895, the Acting-Governor of Nigeria, W. C. Denton, stipulated that the Lagos police should receive training at Phoenix Park.[36] In 1907, the Colonial Office decided that all police officers of commissioned rank serving in the colonies would undergo training at the RIC depot. Evidence regarding the numbers of officers who did so is patchy, though it seems that relatively few officers visited Phoenix Park: from 1907 to 1912, it seems, there were 111, as shown in table 1.1.

The training available to RIC cadets comprised extensive musketry training, including the use of rifle and bayonet, military and physical drill, and equitation. It was even possible to study tropical hygiene. British criminal law, the law of evidence, police duties and police accounts were taught in a manner similar to that of British police forces.

Table 1.2 Overseas officers trained at RUC depot, 1924–32

Africa		Far East		Caribbean		Other		All
Bechuanaland	1	Hong Kong	1	Jamaica	1	British Guiana	3	
Egypt	2	Malaya	2	Trinidad	2	Colombia	1	
Gambia	1	Siam	4			Fiji	3	
Gold Coast	3	India	1			India	2	
Kenya	7					Leeward Islands	2	
Mauritius	1					Palestine	9	
Nigeria	36					Yugoslavia	1	
Northern Rhodesia	14							
Sierra Leone	1							
Somaliland	1							
Tanganyika	10							
Totals	77		8		3		21	109

Source: RUC Archives, 'Overseas Officers trained at RUC Depot, 1924–32', PRONI CAB 9G/56.

So Ireland provided training as and when required, and the RIC provided an important source of experienced professionals, both from the rank and file and the officer corps, for colonial and metropolitan police forces alike. Numerous former officers and members of the RIC became colonial policemen. Moreover, many Irish-trained members of the Indian police made their way to other colonial constabularies throughout the Empire, bringing with them their Irish influences. Between 1860 and 1922, a total of 325 RIC constables, sergeants and head constables joined colonial constabularies; a further 24 RIC officers went overseas between 1869 and 1922.[37] The style and policing culture of the RIC was, in part, handed down to its successor force, the RUC – the RIC disbanded in Northern Ireland in May 1922 and was succeeded by the RUC the following month.[38]

Following the establishment of the Irish Free State, the RUC provided a four-month training course at its depot at Newtownards for gazetted colonial police officers up until 1932, when the training programme was transferred to Hendon Police College. Table 1.2[39] gives a breakdown of the numbers of these officers and a handful of outsiders trained at the Irish depot between 1924, when RUC training commenced and March 1932, when it ceased.

Once again the numbers of officers receiving 'courses of instruction' was comparatively small. There is some evidence to suggest that the 4–6-month training course on offer was simply too lengthy to allow senior ranking officers to take leave of their posts. Courses for the non-gazetted ranks were also made available. Government records show that 86 gazetted and non-commissioned officers and 18 constables attended these courses between 1925 and 1932,[40] leaving unaccounted for 5 officers who attended courses in 1924. A 2-month course was provided for non-commissioned officers and a 6-month course for European police constables with no prior police experience. Each course was customised to meet the individual requirements of colonial governments.[41] Instruction offered to the small number of European police constables in Kenya, for example, appears to have been better attended than many other courses, possibly due to Kenya's higher number of recruits.

In 1926, provision was made to accept the full establishment strength of forty constables for training at Newtownards. The six-month course provided instruction in 'physical training, jiu jitsu, first aid and ambulance work, musketry, drill, police duties, detective training, footprint identification, criminal law, law of evidence and methods of making reports and taking statements', for which the total cost stood at just over £10, excluding living and salary expenditure.[42] A circular despatch issued by the Colonial Office in 1929 attempted to address the question of the flagging numbers of trainees. The possibility that 'the training of Colonial Police will be finally lost to Northern Ireland' was seized on by Charles Wickham, the RUC's Inspector-General. His concern was that training at Newtownards would close, bringing a loss of revenue of approximately £730, 'of which £30 goes to the Police Instructor and of the balance, one-third goes to the Depot Recreation Funds and two-thirds to the Constabulary vote'. More importantly, it also covered the rent.[43]

Despite concerns of a potential closure of the Newtownards Depot in July 1931, the Colonial Office was anxious that training should continue in Northern Ireland.[44] In the event, the Depot was kept open until January 1932 when training was transferred to Britain. By 1949, four training courses were available for colonial policemen: a course at Hendon for non-gazetted officers who had been selected for promotion to gazetted rank, a 6-month course at Ryton-on-Dunsmore for officers with 5–12 years' police service, a 3-month course at Ryton for senior officers, and specialised courses for CID officers held at a number of centres.[45]

'One of the most vital jobs in the British Empire': the growth of the Palestine Police

The Palestine Police Ordinance in 1921 stated that the 'general organisation of the Police Force appears to be similar to that of the Royal Irish Constabulary, in that control is centralised'. The ordinance then remarked on a number of similarities between the Palestine Gendarmerie and the RIC.[46] These included structure of the officer corps and ranks, training and importantly, the political situation within which each force operated. The disbandment of the RIC provided a rich recruitment ground for the Palestine Gendarmerie.

In the year preceding the disbandment of the RIC, E. M. Clayton and C. A. Walsh, both Assistant Inspector-Generals, were concerned that their men should find alternative police postings in the future and they conducted a great deal of correspondence with English and colonial constabularies regarding vacancies that had arisen.[47] Proposals were also made to recruit members of the RIC into the Irish Guards with whom the force had a long-standing connection.[48] Throughout this period, Clayton and Walsh made discreet attempts to secure recruitment into the Palestine Gendarmerie of 'a limited number of young District Inspectors and Constables – unmarried and under thirty years of age, of superior education and first class records. Head Constables and Sergeants up to thirty-five years of age would also be considered.' Recruitment details were circulated to all county inspectors on a confidential basis, 'except in Northern Ireland'.[49]

On standing down,[50] on 31 August 1922, the members of the old RIC were given various options. They could continue service in the Guarda Síochana in the new Irish Free State, or within the RUC in the North, established on 1 June 1922 (the Guarda Síochana absorbed a total of 180 former members of the RIC and the RUC 986).[51] Alternatively, they could be honourably discharged. If they chose the latter course, there was one further option: they could enlist in the newly created British Section of the Palestine Gendarmerie. Recruitment for the new unit was opened in London as well as Dublin, and some 700 men came forward. Brigadier General Angus MacNeill was placed in charge of taking the newly-formed corps to Palestine, following initial training at Fort Tregantle in Britain. McNeill had been authorised to recruit 49 officers and 701 other ranks. His second-in-command was Major G. Foley, who had joined the RIC in 1911 and had been responsible largely for training in County Mayo.[52]

By March 1922, the British Section of the Palestine Gendarmerie was made up almost exclusively of former regular and auxiliary RIC members.[53] Of these, 29 had been regular RIC officers and 10 auxiliary RIC officers. The figures for all ranks, up until May 1922, are given in the table 1.3.[54] The official documents do not specify the country of origin of those listed but it can be assumed that the regular RIC were predominantly Irish and that a high proportion of the auxiliary division were British. This would also be the case for the former army and navy servicemen.[55]

Table 1.3 Nominal roll of all ranks of the British Section of the Palestine Gendarmerie to the end of May 1922[a]

	Regular	Auxiliary	Armed forces
RIC	546	118	
Army			24
Navy			2
London Police	1		
Resigned	13	6	1
Dismissed	3		1
Deserted	3		
Deceased		1	

Note:
[a] *Source*: Nominal Roll of all Ranks of the British Section of the Palestine Gendarmerie to end May 1922, NA HO 351/66.

From 1922 until its disbandment in 1926, the British Section of the Palestine Gendarmerie was employed increasingly in policing as well as in duties of a military nature. The strength of the police increased dramatically by 1922 with 2,540 police for a population of 752,048, a ratio of 1:250.[56] Moreover, many of the military aspects of RIC training[57] were taken to Palestine by ex-RIC officer Jim Munro, who became the first Commandant of the British Police Training School, serving from 1926 until 1946. Munro was aided by Head Constable Wilkinson, a former-RIC sergeant. 'Wilkie's punishing drill and musketry training stayed with the Gendarmerie (renamed the Palestine Police in March 1926].[58] The Training School, then at the Russian Compound in Jerusalem, was overseen by Inspector Patrick 'Patsy' John Hackett. 'Patsy' had served in the Irish Guards and in the RIC, and 'believed fervently in the lessons learned on the parade ground and saw the wisdom in keeping to the rules whether it be the rule of law or the regulations of service'.[59]

With the advent of the Palestine Police in 1926, regular army units decreased, with the only land forces remaining being three sections of the Royal Air Force armoured-car division.[60] Of the two Gendarmeries, a proportion was absorbed into the Palestine Police, while the Palestinian Section formed the nucleus of the Trans-Jordan Frontier Force. Colonial Office figures from 1926 show that of the 151 former RIC men (of all ranks) who remained in the Gendarmerie at its disbandment, a mere 23 had requested a transfer to the Palestine Police; a further 3 officers had been accepted for transfer into the newly formed Trans-Jordan Frontier Force.[61] Although no precise figures are available, many former RIC men who transferred out of the Gendarmerie joined other colonial constabularies or returned to Northern Ireland and joined the RUC.

As for the number of officers who transferred to the Palestine Police via the Gendarmerie, the picture is not clear. A document relating to RIC pensioners and referring to compensation allowances for the period March–May 1926 stated that 2 former RIC officers, Major J. Munro and Captain R. L. Worsley, had joined the Palestine Police in March 1926 and referred to a further 33 former RIC men of all ranks and 3 inspectors who had joined the Palestine Police during that period.[62] Once again, there is a discrepancy in the numbers of former RIC men recorded. It is probable that the second set of figures is the more accurate, for by 1939 twenty-five former RIC policemen were still serving in Palestine.[63] The Irish imprint on the policing of Palestine continued, albeit to a lesser extent.[64] Despite tentative attempts at reform throughout its history, the Palestine Police retained its military character and developed colonial-style training. These influences and the development of paramilitary policing duties were carried throughout the Empire. Its importance cannot be underestimated both in terms of the numbers of officers trained in both paramilitary and counter-insurgency styles of policing and of their later postings throughout the Empire.

As the situation worsened in Palestine throughout the 1940s, so the Colonial Office increased its recruitment campaign, demanding 'men' rather than 'boys' aged 18–28, and offering a post within the Palestine Police in lieu of national service.[65] Crown agents set a target of 875 recruits to be sent to Palestine before the end of 1946.[66] The need to bring the force up to strength[67] led to recruitment from among former members of the armed forces, the home police forces and civilians. Indeed, in 1946, approximately 1,000 national servicemen opted to join the Palestine Police in lieu of military service. The size of the force had increased dramatically since 1926 when the British Section of the Palestine Gendarmerie, comprising some 212 British officers, was joined to the Palestine Section. It reached its peak in the spring of 1947, when the regular Palestine Police stood at 8,923, of whom 5,758 were British.[68]

When the new recruits reached the training school at Mount Scopus, 'the glamour of serving in a crack force' required weekly training in weaponry and target practice, necessitating accuracy at 100, 200 and 500 yards. Many, during the 1930s, were issued with cross rifles, suggesting that they were crack shots. The training of officers was undertaken by experts in this field: in his memoir, Harold Dibbens noted that in 1945 'Major Grant-Taylor, an expert in the use of the Tommy Gun and revolver was directing a small arms training course for the Palestine

1 Recruiting poster for the Palestine Police, *c.* 1944

Police. As a marksman, he was outstanding. He was partial to pink gin, especially at 1100 hours, and I have seen him swallow three if not four doubles and then from a distance of twelve feet knock the pips out of playing cards.'[69] Each officer was required to use a revolver, rifle and Lewis gun. Policemen were further issued with army Bren guns and Thompson submachine guns.[70] Overall, the Palestine administration considered it preferable to have former soldiers or those with military leanings within the upper echelons of the police. This ran counter to the wishes of the Colonial Office.

Indeed, the selection of a suitable candidate for the post of Inspector-General in 1945 caused a conflict of interest between the Palestine High Commission and the Colonial Office, the latter being rather keener to recruit a candidate of colonial police experience.[71] However, suitable 'police' candidates were in short supply and a compromise

2   Foot drill at Mount Scopus, *c.* 1932

from both parties was needed. From the short ('second best of the "soldiers"') list emerged Colonel Nicol Gray, a former Royal Marines' officer, who had served with distinction during the war.[72] He was the first non-policeman to lead the Palestine Police, yet his influence on the force was sufficiently deep to have remained with its former members after disbandment.

Spreading the colonial model throughout the Empire: Indian influences?

Irish influences not only shaped the Palestine Police but travelled further east to India and Ceylon. The Indian Police was the first and largest colonial police force to be shaped by the RIC.[73] Subsequently it had a formative influence on the Ceylon Police, the first force to be placed under the jurisdiction of the Colonial Office. Both the Indian and the Ceylon Police provided officers for colonial police forces up until their disbandment in 1947. The 'Irish model' was transported to India and Ceylon as it was throughout the 'old' Empire. Yet the number of officers who took their policing traditions to other colonial constabularies is limited when compared to the numbers of Palestine Police officers.

When the British East India Company (BEIC) annexed the Indian province of Sind in 1843, Sir Charles Napier turned to the Irish police for inspiration.[74] Napier may have been familiar with the Metropolitan Police, but it did not suit his policing requirements at that time, for they depended on a semi-military force that could relieve the army of its public order duties. His idea was based on the police being entirely separate from the military and the previous system of 'Collectors'.[75] Napier created a new force, the Sind police, and a contingent of Sikhs with its own officers, along the lines of the RIC. In each district, the police were separated into three parts: mounted, rural and city.[76] The difference between this new police force in Sind, and those of other provinces, was that there the police came under the control of the most senior member of police rather than a government administrator. This force of some 2,400 men was well armed, trained and supervised by English officers.[77] An Irish officer from the Sind Police came out from India to Hong Kong with the Sikh recruits and took up the post of Deputy Superintendent.[78] So successful was the Sind Police that it became the base on which other models of policing were developed throughout India.

A few examples can be cited here. In the Punjab, after its annexation in 1849, the BEIC set up a police force that drew on the Sind Police experience but evolved somewhat differently. It was divided into two branches: 'the military preventive police' under the direct control of the Chief Commissioner; and the 'Civil Police' who came under the district magistrates. The Civil Police was concerned with crime detection and prevention, while the military police took care of escort, guard and public order duties through the use of former soldiers.[79]

The Madras police was also based on the RIC's experience. Although early provincial police chiefs like Lord Harris had been attracted to the idea of law enforcement through an unarmed constabulary based on the Metropolitan Police model, the Madras Government perceived this style of system to be inadequate when it came to policing a colony.[80] While Harris described the police of Sind and Punjab as too military, a section of the Madras Police was armed. Every constable was expected to spend some time in the reserves undergoing a period of intensive arms training and 'stricter discipline'. With the advent of the Madras Police Act in 1859, a compromise of a 'police partly military and partly civil' was retained.[81] Describing the new police in Benghal, G. O. Trevelyan, who served in the Indian Police, wrote:

> The new police has been constructed on the Irish model . . . The Inspectors and Superintendents are taken for the most part from among regimental officers, and it is said that the tendency of the new force is become too decidedly military. The detective element is certainly rather weak at present.[82]

Overall, the Indian Police became organised on a provincial basis, with each district operating the administrative and executive units. Responsibility for the maintenance of law and order rested with the nine provincial governments. The Inspector-General, the Police

Commissioners and the district magistrates received orders directly from the Home Office of each province.[83] The Indian Police was, in a similar manner to other colonial constabularies, directly accountable to government. However, the question of whether a particular police force should be essentially military or civilian in nature was repeatedly raised.

The range of duties of the Indian Police bore no resemblance to the British Police and was essentially *colonial* in nature: they covered every aspect of Indian village life, including 'the state of crops, the irrigation of fields, the condition of roads and paths, private feuds . . . and all the thousand and one important, trifling, pathetic or humorous details which make up the existence of an Indian rural community'.[84] Moreover the armed policeman was perceived as 'simply a para-military soldier in a policeman's uniform. His justification was that he cost less than a military soldier.' Thus the colonial elements of policing – defence of the colony – far outweighed the civil side – the prevention and detection of crime, for 'the effect of the increase in the armed police was that the strength of the Civil Police was never adequate for [those] duties'.[85]

Following the passing of the Government of India Act in 1858, important Indian legal codes were enacted: the Code of Civil Procedure, the Indian Penal Code and the Code of Criminal Procedure. Importantly, at this time, the 1860 Indian Police Commission emphasised the need for 'good police' whose duties should lean towards the civil rather than the military, should be divorced from judicial functions with accountability to each provincial government.[86] It seemed that the Commission was attempting to move towards a more metropolitan style of policing.

Essentially there was little structural reform in terms of police administration and while civil policing may have been recommended by the Commission, circumstances dictated otherwise, and a semi-military force remained in operation:

> The Military arm should confine itself *absolutely* to the occupation of the country, for its proper function of preventing invasion, and supporting the Civil Power *only* in event of rebellion or extended insurrection. The Military arm should be relieved from all non-military duties; and the peace and order of the country should be preserved, on every occasion of tumult and apprehended disturbance, by the Civil power, and not by a Military force.[87]

The Police Act of 1861 came as a result of the 1860 Police Commission and founded the *modern* Indian Police Service, organised on a provincial basis under the leadership of an Inspector-General.[88] In theory, however, the senior officers above the rank of Deputy Superintendent were said to be part of the *imperial* Police Service, while all ranks below belonged to the different provincial police forces.[89] The subsequent (1902) Police Commission found that 'there can be no doubt that the police force throughout the country is in a most unsatisfactory condition, that abuses are common everywhere, that this involves great injury to the people and discredit to the Government, and that radical reforms are urgently necessary'.[90] While the idea of an English Civil Police had theoretical appeal, the reality for the administration lay in the need to maintain control. In operational terms it appeared that the Indian Police Service gravitated towards a colonial style of policing. Yet certain key differences with *colonial* police forces emerged as the Indian Police was reformed. The most important change within police organisation was the rate of Indianisation within the officer corps.

The 1858 proclamation had re-affirmed a promise made in 1833 that British subjects of whatever race or creed should be freely admitted to public service. Implementation of this policy was slow because, in many cases, European officers considered the entry of an Indian as a threat to their own positions.[91] Colonial police forces were typically divided racially into a two-tiered system. Between the 1880s and the 1920s, the organisation of the Indian Police moved from a two- to a three-tiered system: at the top, Europeans comprised the intermediate and senior ranks at the bottom, the constables were drawn from the local population. However, the middle tier that emerged comprised a new class of Indians, who were educationally and socially superior to the lower ranks. They were assisted by a series of commissions encouraging this organisational structure and promoting Indianisation.

The 1912 Royal Commission considered the employment of Indians to be within the gazetted ranks of the 'Indian Police Service'. Proposals were made to allow direct-entry recruitment for Indians who had been educated in Britain. By 1918, as the political conditions in India were changing, a 'Report on Indian Constitutional Reforms', considered the importance of accelerating these reforms within all branches of the Indian Civil Service. Progress was rapid, and by 1946 over thirty per cent of all senior police ranks were occupied by Indians.[92] However, only two Indians reached the rank of Deputy Inspector-General before independence: K. P. Janardhan Rao in 1944 and T. G. Sanjivi Pillai in 1946. The six positions of DIG and other key positions were held almost exclusively by Europeans.[93]

These early moves to Indianise the police certainly benefited both India and Pakistan at independence. The situation was very different in many other colonies, where inadequate preparations were made prior to the transfer of power to promote local officers. As a result, the newly elected Government asked senior-ranking European officers to stay on.

Overall no specific *Indian* model emerged, as police forces varied slightly from province to province.[94] Typically the police station staff, from circle inspector downwards, were referred to as the Civil Police and were unarmed. Sub-inspectors and inspectors were provided with .45-bore revolvers. Head constables and constables were typically unarmed, but carried a truncheon, or *laithi* (a 6-foot bamboo quarter-staff). Armed policemen, based in what was known as the Reserve Police Lines, provided support to the Civil Police and were used to guard and escort prisoners.[95] In addition, the system of *village* police was retained in many provinces.[96] This was mirrored, particularly in British colonial Africa, by the *native* or *tribal* police who provided the regular colonial constabularies with support in rural areas.

The Ceylon experiment

Ceylon, the territory closest, geographically, to India was unsurprisingly influenced by the police reforms taking place at this time.[97] Yet the moves to model the Ceylon Police – first established in 1834 – on Irish lines met with considerable resistance. In essence, the Ceylon Police was perceived by its European officers as quintessentially English. The 1864 Police Commission noted:

> [W]e cannot concede that the Irish Constabulary is at all an analogous Force to our Ceylon Police, and we would here beg leave to express our opinion, that it would have been more conducive to the efficiency of our Force . . . if the English Metropolitan Police had been preferred as a model to work from, instead of a Force, however, admirable in its own country, so unsuited to our requirements as would appear to be the Irish Constabulary.[98]

Indeed, before 1866 the Ceylon Police was influenced in its development by the Metropolitan Police as well as the RIC. In 1840, John Colepeper, a former sergeant of 'P' Division of the Met, was despatched to Ceylon. His reforms included refashioning the police uniform along Metropolitan Police lines. His short stay was followed by the appointment of Thomas Thompson in 1845 and William Macartney in 1848, both ex-RIC. Among his many reforms, Thompson changed the uniform from the blue serge to RIC green. However, as with the Indian Police, a Police Commission in 1864 underlined the need for reform, noting that policemen should be unarmed.[99] This was not to be, for in 1866 both Thompson's and Macartney's reforms were consolidated by a former officer of the Indian Police, George Campbell.[100] Campbell brought many additional features of the RIC to the Ceylon Police, including the adoption of the Irish and Indian title of inspector-general rather than chief constable. The Ceylon Police continued in its military mould in terms of training and outlook, and with much of its work taken up with guard, escort and patrol duties.[101] These were essentially military in nature and allowed for the decrease in the number of troops stationed on the island. Once again, defence of the colony, as opposed to the prevention and detection of crime, became paramount.

There have been conflicting views regarding the development and reorganisation of the Ceylon Police and the extent to which it was modelled on the RIC in subsequent years. The arrival of Campbell began some forty years of mixing colonial and English styles of policing.[102] In 1879, Campbell described the force as 'a Civil Police with a semi-military training. It is armed with Snider Rifles and Swords and drilled; but the men carry only batons when on duty other than Treasury, or Convict or Gaol Guard'.[103] As many of the duties required the carrying of weapons, the police could be more accurately described as a colonial constabulary. Yet subsequent Ceylon Police Chiefs attempted to move away from this model of policing, in line with Jeffries's paradigm of the third phase of colonial policing. Cyril Chapman Longden tried, when he became Inspector-General in 1905, to alter the status quo. Longden was particularly keen that officers were trained with the City of London Police rather than the RIC courses recognised by the Colonial Office, which he perceived as 'too elementary'. Police reforms had been encouraged at that time by Sir Henry Blake, then Governor. These focused particularly on relieving government agents of any police responsibilities and encouraging the recruitment of European officers from England: 'Their appointment marks an epoch in the history of the Ceylon Police and brings us in line with the Indian and Colonial Police Forces in the East.'[104] Several attempts were made at this time to recruit directly from the home police forces to encourage change. Since the Metropolitan Police was not prepared to release officers, the police forces of Sheffield, Westmoreland Cumberland and Leicestershire were seen as the only possible recruitment areas. In 1910, 2 Sub-Inspectors and 28 sergeants were recruited and sent to Columbo. The majority returned to Britain within a short space of time, complaining of insufficient pay, poor living accommodation and having to undertake the work of a police constable.[105]

Longden's work was carried on by his successor, Sir Herbert Dowbiggin, Inspector-General from 1913 to 1937, the 'Grand Old Man of the Colonial Police Service'.[106] Dowbiggin attempted to remodel the Ceylon Police as an unarmed civilian body. While firearms and weapons were available in the stations, policemen patrolled with only a truncheon or stick. Greater emphasis was placed on the prevention and detection of crime, with a Criminal Investigation Department

(CID) created in 1915. In terms of training police officers on more civilian lines, a new training school was established in 1925, the curriculum placing greater emphasis on academic work as opposed to drill and the use of firearms.

Yet the extent to which the Ceylon Police was really transformed from a 'colonial' style into a British constabulary is questionable. Dowbiggin's 1937 Report on the Ceylon Police, Jeffries claimed, dampened down the earlier RIC influences with an insistence on a civil rather than a militarised style of policing. This was in stark contrast to his comments on reorganising the Ceylon Police to provide a base on which to build the Colonial Police Service.[107] The Colonial Police Service provided a loose structure for the burgeoning police forces of the Empire but retained their semi-military traditions until after the Second World War and the disbandment of the Ceylon Police. Overall, Jeffries's view may be somewhat misleading. G. H. R. Halland became Inspector-General of the Ceylon Police in 1943. In a report written in 1944, he concluded that the force had 'many of the obvious characteristics of a military body', despite earlier attempts at reform.[108] Halland's recommendations to ensure a less militaristic force were rejected and he resigned in protest.[109]

In short, it appeared that the Ceylon Police retained an essentially colonial character of policing, which was subsequently passed on by some former members who rose to the very highest ranks of the Colonial Police Service.[110] Yet, ultimately, the Ceylon Police was too small a force to have any very extensive influence in the post-war era.

Notes

1   Quoted in W. K. Hancock, *Argument of Empire* (Harmondsworth: Penguin, 1943), p. 2.
2   Taken from an interview with Derek Franklin (Kenya Police, Bahrain State Police, Lesotho Police, Botswana Police, Deputy Head Special Branch, Sen. Sup., rtd, 1953–81), March 2001.
3   Brogden, 'The Emergence of the Police – the Colonial Dimension', pp. 4–14.
4   Brogden, 'The Emergence of the Police – the Colonial Dimension', p. 9.
5   For a detailed discussion that offers a critique of both the orthodox and revisionist viewpoints see Clive Emsley, *The English Police: A Political and Social History*, 2nd edition (London: Longman, 1996); Philip Rawlings, *Policing: A Short History* (Cullompton: Willan Publishing, 2002).
6   Rawlings, *Policing*, p. 1.
7   See for example: Robert D. Storch, ' " The Plague of Blue Locusts": Police Reform and Popular Resistance in Northern England 1840–57', *International Review of Social History*, 20 (1975), and 'The Policeman as Domestic Missionary: Urban Discipline and Popular Culture in Northern England 1850–1880', *Journal of Social History*, 9 (1976); Stanley H. Palmer, *Police and Protest in England and Ireland 1780–1850* (Cambridge: CUP, 1988).
8   Charles Reith, *British Police and the Democratic Ideal* (London: OUP, 1943), pp. 3–4.
9   Emsley, *English Police*, pp. 24–32.

10   Henry Goulburn, Home Secretary, in voicing his support of the Irish Police Bill, 1822, quoted in Reith, *British Police*, p. 35.
11   C. Steedman, *Policing the Victorian Community* (London: Routledge, 1984), pp. 21–24.
12   Emsley, *English Police*, pp. 54–55.
13   Other terms used included 'the blue army', 'the Blue Devils' and 'the household troops', despite a non-military style uniform having been designed for the police: Rawlings, *Policing*, pp. 120–121.
14   While the 'new' police were criticised for their military-style approach in policing riots, some 85,000 people volunteered as special constables to police the Chartist meeting on Kennington Common in April 1848. Support for the new police had thus materialised within the middle classes: Rawlings, *Policing*, p. 162.
15   Rawlings, *Policing*, p. 144.
16   Emsley, *English Police*, pp. 43–44, pp. 248–250.
17   Reith, *British Police*, p. 186.
18   Reith, *British Police*, p. 202.
19   David Fitzpatrick, 'Ireland and the Empire', in Andrew Porter (ed.), *The Oxford History of the British Empire: The Nineteenth Century* (Oxford: Oxford University Press, 1999), pp. 494–497.
20   Irish Statute 54 Geo. III, c. 13 (1814), quoted in John J. Tobias, 'The British Colonial Police', in Philip J. Stead (ed.), *Pioneers in Policing* (Montclair, NJ: Patterson Smith, 1977), p. 244.
21   Irish Statute 6 & 7 Will. IV, c. 13 (1836), quoted in Tobias, 'British Colonial Police', p. 246.
22   Irish Statute 3 Geo. IV, c. 103 (1822), quoted in Tobias, 'British Colonial Police', p. 247.
23   Graham Ellison & Jim Smyth, *The Crowned Harp: Policing Northern Ireland* (Dublin: Pluto Press, 2000), p. 16.
24   D. George Boyce, ' "Normal Policing": Public Order in Northern Ireland since Partition', *Eire–Ireland*, 1 (1979), pp. 35–39.
25   Thomas Fennell, *The Royal Irish Constabulary: A History and Personal Memoir* (Dublin: University College Press, 2003), p. 14. In contrast the Dublin Metropolitan Police, some 1,500 strong, confined its policing to an 8-mile radius around Dublin Castle.
26   W. J. Lowe & E. L. Malcolm, 'The Domestication of the Royal Irish Constabulary, 1836–1922', *Journal of Irish Economic and Social History*, 19 (1992), pp. 27–48.
27   Charles Townshend, *The British Campaign in Ireland 1919–1921* (Oxford: OUP, 1974), p. 41.
28   Stanley Palmer, *Police and Protest in England and Ireland 1780–1850* (Cambridge: CUP, 1988), p. 532, taken from ' "Assimilate": Opinion of Inspector Gen. Duncan McGregor', which was shared by London Commissioner Mayne in 'Report of the Commission to Inquire into the State of the Constabulary' (1866). The opinion of the 1914 Select Committee is quoted in Conor Brady, *Guardians of the Peace* (Dublin: Gill & Macmillan, 1974), p. 15.
29   'Defence of Ireland 1914–15', NA CO 904/174/2.
30   Palmer, *Police and Protest*, pp. 762–763.
31   Palmer, *Police and Protest*, p. 533, taken from Inspector-Gen. Duncan McGregor, 1853, quoted in Gregory Fulham, 'James Shaw Kennedy and the Reformation of the Irish Constabulary, 1836–38', *Eire–Ireland*, 16:2 (summer 1981), p. 100.
32   Palmer, *Police and Protest*, p. 534. During the fight for independence, the IRA specifically targeted the Constabulary, with 176 RIC officers killed in 1920 alone.
33   The influence of the RIC on the Palestine Police is given in Charles Smith, 'Communal Conflict and Insurrection in Palestine, 1936–48', in D. M. Anderson & D. Killingray (eds), *Policing and Decolonisation: Politics, Nationalism and the Police, 1917–65* (Manchester: MUP, 1992); Clark, 'The Colonial Police and Anti-Terrorism: Bengal 1930–36, Palestine 1927–47 and Cyprus 1955–59', DPhil (Oxford University, 1978). For the RIC and their links with colonial police forces see:

Richard Hawkins, 'The "Irish Model" and the Empire: A Case for Reassessment', in Anderson & Killingray (eds), *Policing the Empire: Government, Authority and Control* (Manchester: MUP, 1991); Kent Fedorowich, 'The Problems of Disbandment: The Royal Irish Constabulary and Imperial Migration, 1919–29', *Irish Historical Studies*, 30:117 (May 1996).

34 Chris Ryder, *The RUC: A Force Under Fire, 1922–2000*, 4th Edition (London: Arrow, 2000), pp. 13–20.

35 Fennell, *The Royal Irish Constabulary*, pp. 8, 39.

36 Tekena N. Tamuno, *Police in Modern Nigeria* (Ibadan: IUP, 1970), p. 30. His predecessor, Sir Gilbert Carter, had, in 1890, expressed a preference for the training courses offered by the Met but was overruled. p. 26.

37 Although outside the scope of this book, it should be noted that some RIC officers were appointed to senior positions within British police forces. Three former RIC officers, Sir Leonard Dunning, Sir William Knott-Bower and Sir Hugh Turnbull, were appointed in succession to the post of commissioner of the City of London Police. A further 14 former RIC officers were posted to the position of chief constable or assistant chief constable throughout Britain during the first 2 decades of the twentieth century.

37 Jim Herlihy, *The RIC: A Short History and Genealogical Guide with a Select List of Medal Awards* (Dublin: Four Courts, 1997), pp. 84–87; RUC Archives, PSNI, Belfast.

38 Between 1919 and December 1923, a total of 1,436 ex-RIC personnel emigrated overseas: Fedorowich, 'Problems of Disbandment', p. 105.

39 RUC Archives, 'Overseas Officers trained at RUC. Depot, 1924–32', PRONI CAB/9G/56.

40 'Colonial Police Forces trained by RUC', PRONI CAB/9G/56.

41 'Course Instruction for Colonial Police Officers', Circular Despatch, August 1929, PRONI CAB/9G/56.

42 W. O. Bottomley, Colonial Office to Under-Secretary of State, Home Office, 8 July 1926, PRONI CAB/9G/56.

43 Wickham to Secretary, Home Office, 22 May 1931, PRONI CAB/9G/56.

44 'Note on Position with regard to Newtownards Depot', NI Secretariat, August 1931, PRONI CAB/9G/56.

45 C. Jeffries, 'The Colonial Police Service', *Police College Magazine* (September, 1951), pp. 77–78.

46 Palestine Police Ordinance dated 1921, NA HO 45/24727.

47 RIC Correspondence 1921–1922, NA CO 904/178.

48 Colonel R. McCalmont, Commander Irish Guards, to C. A. Walsh, RIC, 6 Dec. 1921, NA CO 904/178/135.

49 Circular issued by C. A. Walsh, 25 Jan. 1922, NA CO 904/178/186.

50 Note that the formal standing-down occurred months after disbandment had commenced.

51 Herlihy, *The RIC*, p. 109.

52 Edward Horne, *A Job Well Done: A History of the Palestine Police Force 1920–48* (Tiptree: Anchor Press, 1982), pp. 76–77.

53 An earlier reference to the figure of three-quarters was quoted in Charles Smith, 'Communal Conflict and Insurrection in Palestine, 1936–48', in Anderson & Killingray (eds), *Policing and Decolonisation* (1992), p. 63. Joshua Caspi noted that the British Section was made up of 38 officers and 724 NCOs/constables, though there was no reference given to support this figure: Caspi, 'Policing the Holy Land 1918–1957: The Transition from a Colonial to a National Model of Policing and Changing Conceptions of Police Accountability', PhD (City University, 1991), p. 68.

54 Taken from the Nominal Roll of all Ranks of the British Section of the Palestine Gendarmerie to end May 1922: NA HO 351/66.

55 The figures given by the War Office are somewhat different. The War Office claimed that by mid-1922, the Gendarmerie comprised 63 officers and 1,247 other ranks, of which 44 officers and 700 other ranks came from Ireland. According to the Home Office figures shown above, 684 former regular and auxiliary RIC of all

ranks joined the Gendarmerie alongside 41 officers. This discrepancy was possibly an oversight on the part of the War Office, for the Home Office breakdown of figures is more detailed: Memo, 'Gendarmerie or a Semi-Military Force for Palestine', Jan.–Feb. 1939, NA WO 106/5720.

56 'Report on the Palestine Administration, 1922–28'. Horne, Family Papers.

57 Up until 1931, former servicemen only were recruited into the Palestine Police. This enabled a shorter period – two weeks – of foot and arms drill. With the recruitment of 'civilians', this training was increased to three months. Jack Binsley, 'Autobiography, 1910–1984, Book 3, 1930–1948 (Palestine)', unpublished, pp. 192–193, Binsley Family Papers.

58 Horne, *Job Well Done*, p. 79.

59 Obituary, Patrick John Hackett, Palestine Police Old Comrades' Association, *News Letter*, 101, December 1975, p. 47.

60 Memorandum entitled 'Gendarmerie or a Semi-Military Force for Palestine', Jan.–Feb. 1939, para. 2, NA WO 106/5720.

61 Taken from RIC Pensions Records dated 9 July 1926, NA CO 733/128/9.

62 'List RIC Pension struck off strength on 31 March1926', NA CO 733/128/9/53–54.

63 C. M. Martin Jones, CO, to F. G. Salter, Treasury, 30 March 1939, NA T 164/180/9.

64 Former RIC rose to the senior ranks of the Palestine Police as well as other colonial police forces. They included Michael O'Rorke, who finished his career as Commissioner of the Kenya Police; John Rymer-Jones, who was Inspector-General of the Palestine Police, 1943–46; T. V. Finlay, Commissioner of the Nigeria Police, 1946–55; and John Mullin, Commissioner of the Zanzibar Police, 1955–58, and Nyasaland Police, 1958–63.

65 M. Trafford-Smith, CO, to Messrs Mather & Crowther, 22 Nov. 1946, NA CO 537/1699.

66 MacMichael to Cunningham, Outward Telegram 75015/59/46, 1 Dec. 1946, NA CO 537/1699/11. Approval from the Treasury was sought for an additional £450,000 to ensure recruitment: NA CO 537/1699/16.

67 By January 1946, police strength stood at 8,923, of which 5,779 were British and 3,144 were Palestinian. Of this figure there were 158 British officers and 18 Palestinian officers, 168 British Inspectors and 108 Palestinian Inspectors: Jeffries, *Colonial Police*, p. 158.

68 Taken from an interview with Edward Horne (Palestine Police and the Met, Act. Insp., rtd, 1941–74), May 2001.

69 Harold J. Dibbens, *Dibbens' Diaries, 1925–1972* (Chichester: St Richard's Press, 1989), p. 42.

70 Horne (interview), May 2001.

71 Mr Bennett of the Indian Police was 'strongly' recommended by the Colonial Office. Also recommended were Sir Douglas Gordon, retiring Inspector-General of the Bengal Police, and Mr R. E. A. Ray, Commissioner of the Calcutta Police: NA CO 733/451/45. At a later date, Sir David Petrie was put forward as a candidate (Petrie had accompanied Tegart on his mission to Palestine): Sir G. Gater to Sir David Monteath, 25 Sept. 1945, NA CO 733/451/131. Sir Charles Wickham also recommended the appointment of a 'highly qualified police officer of considerable standing': NA CO 2269/51.

72 Recommendation made by Major-General R. H. Campbell for the appointment of Gray as Inspector-General of the Palestine Police, 1945: NA CO 733/451/1/63.

73 For an orthodox/'colonialist' viewpoint see: J.C. Curry, *The Indian Police* (London: Faber & Faber, 1932); Percival Griffiths, *To Guard My People: The History of the Indian Police* (London: Ernest Benn, 1971). For a revisionist viewpoint see: Anandswarup Gupta, *The Police in British India, 1861–1947* (Dehli: Concept, 1979); David. H. Bayley, *The Police and Political Developments in India* (Princeton, New Jersey: Princeton University Press, 1969); David Arnold, 'Power and the Demise of British Rule in India, 1930–47', in Anderson & Killingray (eds), *Policing and Decolonisation*, pp. 42–61; see also David Arnold, *Police Power and Colonial Rule Madras 1859–1947* (Delhi: OUP, 1986).

74 Sir Hugh Rose, Commander-in-Chief of the Indian Army in October 1861, who had served in Ireland, stated: 'No system of police has ever worked better for the suppression of political agitation, or agrarian disorder, than the Irish Constabulary': quoted in Arnold, *Police Power and Colonial Rule*, pp. 26–27.

75 Curry, *Indian Police*, p. 31, Griffiths, *Indian Police*, p. 69.

76 Considered the elite, the mounted police's duties were partly protective – to provide guard and patrol duties – and partly to gather intelligence. The rural police essentially provided guard and escort duties. The city police were split in two: the *nujjeebs*, who acted as watchmen and guards, and trackers, who could also be dispatched into rural areas. All the police within the province came under the command of European officers responsible to the Chief Commissioner. Under him were a European Lieutenant of Police and an Adjutant who were also army officers: Griffiths, *Indian Police*, p. 69.

77 British expatriate police officers were often referred to as 'Europeans', particularly in the twentieth century. They were mainly British or Irish, although a small number of Americans, Australians, New Zealanders and South Africans joined colonial police forces.

78 M. S. Gaylord & H. Traver, 'Colonial Policing and the Demise of British Rule in Hong Kong', *International Journal of the Sociology of Law*, 23 (1995), pp. 26.

79 Griffiths, *Indian Police*, p. 75.

80 The question of whether the police could successfully use the English law of evidence and criminal procedure in India was often raised. At the time of writing, in 1932, Curry believed that this was not the case, Curry, *Indian Police*, p. 343.

81 Secretary of State for India to Governor Madras, 16 July 1860, quoted in Arnold, *Police Power and Colonial Rule*, pp. 27–28.

82 Trevelyan, *The Competition-Wallah* (1864), p. 113, quoted in Gupta, *Police in British India*, p. 23.

83 Curry, *Indian Police*, p. 340.

84 Curry, *Indian Police*, p. 43.

85 Gupta, *Police in British India*, p. xii.

86 Griffiths, *Indian Police*, p. 88.

87 Report of the Indian Police Commission, 1860, para. 1, quoted in Griffiths, *Indian Police*, p. 89.

88 Jeffries, *Colonial Police*, p. 32.

89 Curry, *Indian Police*, p. 53.

90 Quoted in Gupta, *Police in British India*, p. x.

91 Gupta, *Police in British India*, p. 26.

92 Griffiths, *Indian Police*, pp. 189–191. The 1944 Indian Statutory Commission recorded that 100 per cent of the officer class was European in 1900. In 1920, this had dropped to 95.6 and by 1927 to 86.6 per cent. By 1943 the figure stood at 62.1 per cent: Arnold, *Police Power and Colonial Rule*, p. 86.

93 Arnold, *Police Power and Colonial Rule*, pp. 88–89.

94 Arnold, *Police Power and Colonial Rule*, p. 5.

95 At this time there were no more than 600 officers throughout India, of whom approximately 300 were European: Bill Chaning Pearce, *Indian Copper: Adventures of an Indian Policeman* (Sussex: Book Guild, 1990), pp. 11–14.

96 Griffiths, *Indian Police*, p. 103. Gupta has described these village police as 'a creation of the British Government' *Police in British India*, p. 31.

97 There is little written about the Ceylon Police. See G. K. Pippet, *A History of the Ceylon Police*, Vol. 1: *1795–1870* (Colombo: Times of Ceylon, 1938); & A. C. Dep, *A History of the Ceylon Police*, Vol. 2: *1866–1913* (Colombo: The Times of Ceylon, 1969).

98 Dep, *Ceylon Police*, p. 1.

99 Dep, *Ceylon Police*, pp. 1–4.

100 George Campbell had earlier served in Ireland: Jeffries, *Colonial Police*, pp. 29–30, 36; H. L. Dowbiggin, 'The Ceylon Police and its Development', *Police Journal*, 1 (1928), pp. 203–217.

101 Jeffries, *Colonial Police*, p. 32.
102 Tobias, 'British Colonial Police', p. 253.
103 Campbell, Administration Report (1879), quoted in Dep, *Ceylon Police*, p. 126.
104 Government 'Agent' to Colonial Secretary, 1906, quoted in Dep, *Ceylon Police*, pp. 411, 413.
105 Dep, *Ceylon Police*, pp. 463–464.
106 Jeffries, 'Colonial Police Service', p. 76. Dowbiggin was the first Inspector-General of the Ceylon Police to have risen up through its ranks. Before his appointment, inspector-generals were typically appointed from the Indian Police. His obituary noted that his 'influence extended over the whole British colonial empire and beyond . . . his counsel was frequently sought by the Colonial Office': Dowbiggin, Obituary, *The Times*, 26 May, 1966.
107 Jeffries, *Colonial Police*, pp. 36–39.
108 Halland, 'Proposals of the IG of Police, Ceylon for the Reorganisation of the Ceylon Police Force', Sessional Paper, no. 4, 1944, p. 1: NA CO 57/273.
109 Halland to A. Mahadeira, Minister Home Affairs, 13 March, 1944, NA CO 54/789/14.
110 Examples include: Roy Spicer, who joined the Ceylon Police in 1909 and became Commissioner of the Kenya Police in 1918 and Inspector-General of the Palestine Police in July 1931; Kerr Bovell and Adrian Davies, who became Commissioners of the Nigeria Police in the 1950s; Neil Hadow, who became Commissioner of the Gambia and Uganda Police during the same period.

CHAPTER TWO

Transferring policing models: Irish and English influences in Canada

The previous chapter explored the notion of a *colonial* model of policing. This developed over a time-frame similar to that of the *English* model, with significant cross-fertilisation occurring between the two. Throughout the nineteenth century, alternative police systems emerged in colonies where policing the indigenous population to protect European settlers became the initial priority. Any formal period of colonisation was characterised by violence and upheaval. The police played a crucial role in enforcing the power of the colonial state during periods of rapid social change. In British North America, South Africa, Australia and New Zealand elements of colonial policing were appropriated in British settlement colonies and adapted to individual constabularies.

The focus of this chapter is on the policing of Canada where *English* and *Irish* styles of policing intermingled, in particular after 1867 when Canada became a nation in its own right with the passage of the British North America Act. Among its provisions, the Act gave exclusive jurisdiction in certain areas to the central government and in others to the provinces. It assigned the responsibility for the enactment of criminal law to the central Government, although the responsibility for enforcement was placed on the provinces. Laws, therefore, were either central, for example in the areas of customs and immigration, or provincial, typically the criminal code. The provinces were assigned certain authority over and responsibilities to their cities and towns, which included policing. The vastness of the country and it geographical diversity meant that the historical development of the police was complex in the extreme.[1] Settlers pushing into the prairie and provinces of British Columbia required a mounted, rural-style, constabulary quite distinct from the quasi-civilian police forces that sprung from the impact of urban–industrial growth in centres like Quebec city or Toronto.

Policing in nineteenth-century Canada[2] was shaped by early French influences and thereafter by a mixture of Irish and English traditions. Across North America in the late nineteenth century and the early part of the twentieth century, the nature of policing changed from 'an informal even casual, bureaucracy to a formal self-governed, militaristic organisation'.[3] While modern police systems were initiated earlier and with greater rapidity in Lower Canada than in other parts of British North America, a backward glance shows that early police systems were in place in the French settlements of Quebec city and Montreal. The first police constable probably appeared on the streets of Quebec City in about 1651 and was responsible for the security of its citizens and keeping a watch for fires.[4] Yet *real* police work began only in 1673 with the drafting of formal police regulations. The creation of a police force, claimed its founder the Count de Frontenac, would allow Quebec City to 'become worthy of the title which it will surely one day enjoy, that of the capital of a very large empire'.[5] This of course became the role of the British, who, by the mid-eighteenth century, allowed certain influences to remain in the modern police systems established in the 1830s. These are still identifiable today in the policing of Quebec Province.[6]

The overhaul of mid-nineteenth century state machinery in Canada included the police. Strengthening the executive was key to providing responsible government in each province. By the same token this would give the new governments control over their own internal affairs. The police had essentially become part of the 'reconstruction in the Canadas' after the 1837–38 uprisings. The enhancement of state power required the police to 'intimidate and pacify a defiant populace'. Governments guarded against the use of the military other than for incidents of 'full-scale insurrection'.[7] In this manner, many of the colonial styles of policing were highly suited to the provincial heartlands of Canada.

In urban areas, the administration as a whole hankered after a 'nonpolitical Peel-style' police. Quebec became the first city in Canada to boast a police force which was, then extended to Montreal. The organisation and practice was borrowed from the Metropolitan Police. 'Uniformed constables, abandoning the sentry-boxes of the nightwatch, walked their beats, arresting criminals, reporting fires, supervising traffic, and getting to know all the neighbourhood residents.' The police of Toronto and Saint John were of a similar ilk. Toronto supposedly had five police constables in operation when it became an incorporated city in 1834. This small group grew into a larger police force during subsequent decades, organised purely on English lines.[8] While Peelite principles were favoured, they were not always copied: some police forces – Toronto for example – were armed with pistols.[9]

In some cases the creation of a rural constabulary came after that of the urban police. In Lower Canada, the rural police began patrolling the farming areas of Montreal District only in 1839, more than a year later than the urban police had come into existence, suggesting that rural police were deemed to be less useful than the military. Indeed the Government used troops from Montreal and Quebec city during the 1837–38 disturbances rather than creating a quasi-gendarmerie. It was forced into setting up its rural police only when it found the Quebec City garrison too depleted of manpower to be relied on in the event of further public unrest. In a manner similar to the RIC, the rural police of Lower Canada 'was designed to permit the central government to bypass traditional local institutions and assert direct control over agrarian communities'.[10] The rural police increasingly became a complement to rather than a substitute for the military. In this manner their function could be likened to the role of the colonial police as the first line of defence.

Canada gradually developed a three-tiered system of policing. City and town police forces became responsible for general law enforcement within the boundaries of their municipalities. Rural areas, beyond the towns, became a provincial responsibility and led to the development of provincial police forces. Areas for which the dominion Government assumed control came under a national police force. In 1868, the Dominion Police Force was created; and although given jurisdiction for the whole of Canada, in practice its functions were confined to the eastern regions. The Dominion Police, replacing the defunct Western Frontier Constabulary in 1868, was given the task of gathering intelligence on 'the existence of any plot, conspiracy or organization whereby peace would be endangered, the queen Majesty insulted, or her proclamation of neutrality infringed'.[11] This force carried out its national duties on an ever-increasing scale until it was absorbed by the Royal Canadian Mounted Police (RCMP), the successor to the North West Mounted Police (NWMP).

Today, the RCMP is responsible for the enforcement of federal statutes in all 10 provinces and in the 3 territories. Provincial police forces exist in Ontario, Quebec and Newfoundland and provide policing for rural areas as well as a few urban communities. In other provinces, policing is the domain of the RCMP under a contract undertaken between the province and the federal Government. Although every province at some stage in its history had its own provincial police force, Canada also boasts autonomous local police forces, 'special' police forces, e.g. the National Harbour Board Police, and 'private police forces' such as those serving the national railways and security services.[12]

Drawing on the RIC: urban policing

Immigration from Britain to Canada took place throughout the nineteenth century. Some of those immigrants joined Canada's new police forces, having previously served in Irish or English police forces, and their descendants continued a similar trend, reflected in the relatively high proportion of high-ranking officers of English or Irish ancestry. A number also made their way south to the United States, as land suitable for agricultural colonisation quickly disappeared in parts of Lower Canada.[13] Thus RIC personnel and their practices influenced the embryonic provincial and municipal Canadian constabularies.

Irish influences certainly appeared in the cities of Lower Canada in the late 1830s. Faced with unrest, the British administration took over the control of policing within the largest cities with the creation of a mounted police and a system of stipendiary magistrates who were sent out to control problem rural areas. While parallels with Irish policing became obvious to members of the military and the administration, some officials, notably Sir John Colborne, favoured a strong civil police. (His military and civil secretary was William Rowan, the brother of the Commissioner of the Met.[14])

Prior to 1841, the Montreal and Quebec City constabularies included many Irish within their ranks. In February 1839, A Division of the Montreal Police comprised of 31 Canadians and 24 Irishmen, and B Division had 61 officers of whom one-third were Irish. Of the Quebec City force in March 1840, four-fifths of the men were Irish, commanded by an Irishmen, R. H. Russell.[15] The main role of the Quebec City and Montreal forces in the early stages was the protection of government buildings. In addition to their protection duties, these small police forces undertook law enforcement with duties ranging from tackling counterfeiting and 'white slave trafficking', to maintaining the National Fingerprint Bureau and operating the Parolled Prisoners Branch.[16] Until 1843, both Quebec City and Montreal were policed by forces that resembled, from an administrative perspective, the Dublin Metropolitan Police (DMP) or the RIC. Sub-constables were housed in barracks to prevent fraternisation with the local community.

After 1848, policing became the responsibility of the elected politicians who controlled the Legislative Assembly rather than of appointed officials. Garrison officers essentially wanted to distance themselves from carrying out public order duties; British colonial policy similarly favoured Civil Police for the protection of property and maintenance of order within urban areas. However, following riots in Montreal in 1853, a government inquiry recommended reforms which included the creation of a constabulary. This was proposed along lines similar to the

RIC's. The 1854 commission on the militia recommended a larger provincial force than the 415-strong force previously proposed. Justification for this was provided by the successes of the RIC and the English county police.[17]

Other urban constabularies drew on Irish experiences, particularly in the light of the population they were policing. The first professional police force in Canada, the Toronto Police, appropriated Metropolitan Police practices as well as drawing on the experiences of former members of the RIC. Toronto itself was a city that remained predominantly British and Protestant. In 1851 out of a total population of 30,775, those who were of English, Scottish or Irish origin numbered 28,000. With the increase in Irish Catholics to 25 per cent of the population by the 1850s, the city faced increasing tensions between the different Irish groups as the number of immigrants swelled.[18] It was hardly surprising that by the late 1850s the police had recruited a number of former RIC men whose experiences were useful when dealing with civil disorder provoked by their own countrymen. By comparison, the force developed certain practices and traditions similar to those of the Metropolitan Police. In this way, the legitimacy of the police became 'closely tied to the ideals of impartiality, adherence to legality and military standards of discipline'.[19] Patronage in appointments and promotions as well as political activities among the police were strictly prohibited.

In a similar manner, the Vancouver Police had by the late nineteenth century copied the uniform and regulations of the Metropolitan Police. Its Constables' Manual stipulated that 'they must see every part of their beat in a given time, walking at the rate of two-and-a-half English miles an hour'. In 1908, an English-style helmet was introduced. At the same time it was felt necessary for police officers to carry firearms, even if they were carried 'under their tunics' rather than being exposed 'on the belt'. By this stage, however, greater emphasis was placed on the Metropolitan Police model. W. J. Bingham became Chief Commissioner in 1929, having served with the Metropolitan Police for twenty-five years. He was responsible for reorganising the Vancouver Police, making considerable use of his police experiences with the Metropolitan Police. As a result he formally partitioned the force into a uniformed and a CID section. Thereafter, two Chief Commissioners were appointed with direct links to English policing: Donald McKay took over in 1939, having served in the Glasgow Police, and Walter Mullagan, the son of an Inspector in the Liverpool Police, in 1946.[20]

From the 1830s, the emphasis on controlling public disturbances shifted from urban centres like Quebec city and Montreal to rural areas. Thus, the rural constabulary proposed in 1838 by William Coffin, assistant civil secretary to the Governor, carried Irish rather than English overtones. Coffin wanted to equip the police with cutlasses and pistols, and advised that 'in the insurgent or suspected sections it should assume a military, in the more tranquil sections a civil character'. The rural constabulary that had evolved by 1839 was headed up by Coffin. Working with stipendiary magistrates in the Montreal region, its main role became the collecting of political intelligence. Coffin appeared to have followed similar guidelines laid down for the RIC. He suggested that officers be predominantly Protestant, with the lower ranks French Catholic.[21] This rural constabulary was disbanded in the early 1840s owing to financial constraints and an improving political climate.

'We enforce British law, Sir!' Provincial policing

Prior to joining the confederation, the colonies of British Columbia and Newfoundland, policing drew on the Irish experience. The police force of St John, New Brunswick, also had direct links with the RIC, being formed in 1871 along RIC lines.[22] Its establishment came about with the departure of the garrison that had been stationed in the city of St John which had assisted with the maintenance of law and order. The scanty records that survive suggest that some organised policing took between 1729 and 1811 which involved constables patrolling the streets and undertaking investigative duties. It was not until 1849 that the St John Police was officially established to tackle ongoing 'conflict' between Catholics and Protestants.[23] Initially the force was placed under the supervision of the police magistrate, although some seven years later they were brought under the auspices of a Chief of Police appointed by the Governor in Council.

Leadership of these police forces came partly from Irishmen: 4 out of 5 of the St John Police's first Superintendents had served in the RIC. This began in 1853 when Timothy Mitchell was appointed. He served until 1871 when he was replaced by an ex-RIC Head Constable and Town Inspector of Belfast, Thomas Foley, whose brief was to reorganise the police to ensure that officers 'kept order rather than fight petty crime' Irish-style. He remained in situ until his death in 1873. An officer from the RIC was sought once more, with Paul Carty, a Catholic, who had previously served as a constable, being recommended. He remained at the helm until 1885, at which time the strength of the constabulary had risen to 125 members. Under Carty, new out-stations were set up and constables accompanied stipendiary magistrates to tackle crime in areas that had previously not been policed. In 1895, another Irishman, John R. McCowen took over, having served as a policeman in Canada since 1871. By the late nineteenth century, the St John Policemen were more *Irish* than the personnel of the police forces of other provinces in

their manner of organisation, uniform and housing. However, a fundamental difference in their policing practices had emerged: they were not
armed. This was due to the provinces more peaceful character compared
with the wilds of the North-West Territories.

Indeed between 1890 and 1908, more arrests were carried out for
drunkenness than for any other offence. The use of the 'vile liquid' and
the prominence of public drunkenness elicited periodic denunciations
from the police, although little change occurred.[24] It appeared that
throughout Canada the focus of urban policing was on the regulation of
working-class lifestyles and morality. Contemporary thought linked
drunkenness and immorality with crime, and the majority of arrests
during the nineteenth century stemmed from public order offences,
notably drunkenness, disorderly conduct and vagrancy. In Toronto, for
example, from 1859 to 1900, this comprised 51 per cent of all arrests
compared to 24 per cent for offences against persons and property.[25]

English-style policing, though, slowly crept into the practices of the
St John Police by the latter part of the nineteenth century, despite the
earlier influx of Irish-trained officers. A public safety board, reporting
to the Common Council, was created to which the police force was
accountable, theoretically underpinning notions of impartiality. By
1890, a new Chief of Police, William Walker Clark, was preaching that
policemen should always be reminded of their 'grave responsibilities as
servants of the public, not of class or faction'.[26] Clark was deeply interested in the workings of the Metropolitan Police, changing the St John
uniform to resemble that of the London Police and insisting that his
men carried a truncheon and remained unarmed. During periods of
public unrest – the royal visit in 1901 for example – the police were
assisted by the militia regiments.[27]

In British Columbia the use of an Irish model of policing initially
dominated. So when in the 1850s the colonial authorities in British
Columbia, faced with threats from the United States, intensified by the
discovery of gold, requested police support, the Colonial Secretary sent
an officer of the RIC to establish a similar force to maintain order. Sub-
Inspector Chartres Brew, British Columbia's first Chief Inspector of
Police, arrived in Victoria in 1858. Brew, who had joined the RIC as a
cadet in 1840, was invited to 'organize the British Columbia Colonial
Police to carry out the general policing of the district, taking special
care that drinking and gambling are as much as possible put down'.
Brew's initial idea was to create a police system along similar lines to
the RIC's. This would involve the recruitment of 100 men, who would
undergo 4 months training in preparation for the second season's gold
rush. Brew had wanted a nucleus of some sixty officers recruited
directly from the RIC for the fledgling British Columbia Constabulary

(BCC). He had counted on the support of Douglas, but soon realised that the Governor was more interested in setting up a system of tax collection than a police force. Although the new colony required an improved tax collection system as well as law enforcement, the funds were apparently not available to secure the recruitment of former RIC officers. Douglas claimed that the colony needed to secure more revenue.[28] Extraneous duties undertaken by officers of colonial police forces did sometimes involve the supervision of tax collection, as was the case in territories of British colonial Africa, where native police worked alongside the regular police to ensure that taxes were collected. Brew preferred to keep the two functions separate, but was often forced by lack of manpower to use 'his most reliable constables' to collect the gold tax, to the resentment of the mining community. During this early period, Brew was often sent relatively prosperous recruits from Britain, and these men sometimes demanded 'a more respectable position than that of constable'. They had no interest in joining British police forces. 'Young gentlemen' like Thomas Elwyn, John Hayes and William Cox sought adventure in the British Empire and were often sent by their families. This created a sense of elitism within the BCC, reminiscent of the officer corps within the RIC.

The BCC became a provincial force when the colony formally joined Canada on 20 July 1871. John Howe Sullivan, veteran of the RIC, was to become their second Superintendent, appointed on a temporary basis. From this period, the responsibility for law enforcement was divided into provincial and Dominion areas, although the police continued to enforce almost all the statutes and ordinances over the coming years. The BCC was dealing with a huge unchartered territory that was sparsely inhabited by aboriginal peoples, fur-traders and American bootleggers. The policing of aboriginal peoples gradually increased as settlers encroached upon their land. In a similar manner to the later colonial police officers, British Columbia constables learned to speak the local language, Chinook, and attempted communication, however limited.[29] Policing this wilderness between Canada and British Columbia[30] would become the domain of the NWMP in 1873.

The North-West Territories: extending the frontiers

In 1869 a military-style constabulary was felt to be the most appropriate way of securing control of the north-west, a vast swathe of territories that had been under the jurisdiction of the Hudson Bay Company since 1660. Thomas Blackiston, who accompanied a British expedition to the north-west led by Captain John Palliser in 1859, described the area as one of 'general lawlessness'.[31] He recommended that a 'military police somewhat on the system of the Irish Constabulary' be established to control an area dotted with 'outlaw' trading posts from which 'whiskey was poured to the Indians in exchange for buffalo, furs and horses'. Plans to adopt a *national*-style police force were put forward by Sir John A. Macdonald, the first Canadian Prime Ministry, who believed that a military presence of sorts was of particular value to discourage any incursions by the US and thus safeguard Canada's political union. Macdonald stated:

> I have no doubt, come what will, there must be a military body, or at all events a body with military discipline at Fort Garry. It seems to me that the best Force would be Mounted Riflemen, trained partly as Cavalry, but also instructed in rifle exercise. They should also be instructed as certain of the Line are, in the use of artillery. This body should not be expressly military but should be styled Police, and have the military bearings of the Irish Constabulary.[32]

Providing effective and cheap law enforcement was Macdonald's aim. The police would pave the way for European settlement by forcing the aboriginal peoples to live on the reserves. Macdonald's original plan was altered to draw on the British experiences of policing India as well as Ireland[33] although neither Macdonald nor his colleagues considered how the earlier rural police, in Quebec, had been established along Irish lines.[34]

Thus in May 1873, an Act which allowed for the establishment of a mounted police force in the North-West Territories was passed under Dominion Statute 56 'for the purpose of carrying out the criminal and other laws of the Dominion'.[35] By August, 153 of the 300 authorised establishment had been recruited and despatched to winter over at Fort Garry. The police were mounted, armed and organised along the lines of a cavalry regiment, equipped with field artillery in the event that they were required to act in a purely military capacity. They were also provided with a Maxim gun on the Chilkoot Pass.[36] A red tunic, similar to the British Army's, was adopted which the authorities considered would be a greater symbolic deterrent than the RIC's rifle-green and more in keeping with their semi-military role.[37] In a manner similar to many colonial territories, this new force was granted sweeping legal powers, operating as police officers and magistrates.

The NWMP was initially responsible for law enforcement in the central plains and later, in the Yukon and North-West Territories. As the mounted police marched into western Canada in 1874 wearing their scarlet coats and armed with lances and carbines, they looked and behaved like cavalry troops prepared to maintain order within the unstable frontier areas.[38] Their first priority was to establish and maintain friendly relations with the aboriginal peoples to pave the way for treaty negotiations over land. Once the treaties had been signed and reservations allotted, the aboriginal peoples could theoretically be settled, and converted to an agricultural rather than nomadic way of life. This phase completed, settlement of Europeans could occur, allowing the NWMP to act as police rather than soldiers towards the settler population. The interlinking of these two processes of coercion and consent confirmed Jeffries's theory of colonial policing. During the implementation of these phases the mounted police were advised to avoid the use of firearms except as a last resort.

A. L. Haydon, who served in the NWMP from 1873 to 1910, was critical of this point of view, for 'in the event of serious disturbance a Police Force, acting alone and unsupported by a disciplined military body, would probably be overpowered in a Province of mixed races, where every man is armed', although he did concede that the use of military force in aid of the civil power was the preferred course of action within the North-West Territories. 'The presence of a certain force' remained sufficient 'to prevent bloodshed and preserve peace' until 1885, when the police used force.[39] Yet the North-West Territories faced greater threats from outside than from within during the late nineteenth century. After the Native American victory over General Custer and the 7th Cavalry at the Little Big Horn in 1876, Sitting Bull brought 3,000 followers across the border to the area surrounding Fort Walsh in the Cypress Hills. This kept the mounted police fully occupied for several years to come.

From that time on, the expansion of the NWMP depended on the gradual opening up of the country. Making their symbolic 'long march' across the west in 1874 the mounted police undertook 'developmental tasks' colonial-style, restricting aboriginal peoples' movements to the reserves, upholding law and order on new settlements and importantly, maintaining Canadian sovereignty.[40] In the Yukon, for example, gold was discovered in 1894, prompting the despatch of Inspector Charles Constantine to investigate. He reported back to headquarters that American miners were invading the area, prompting the use of the NWMP to reassert Canadian sovereignty. This led to the creation of B and H Divisions, stationed in the Yukon, bringing the NWMP to the fringes of the Arctic region. During the latter part of the nineteenth century, the police adopted an additional role as *explorers* rather more than policemen, carrying out epic patrols throughout the western and eastern Arctic regions.[41] Their northerly expansion provided the basis for Canada's sovereignty over the Yukon and the North-West Territories as the frontiers were gradually extended.[42]

Aside from its *developmental* role, the NWMP maintained a 'symbolic sovereignty' by 'explaining and enforcing laws, mining codes drawn up in Ottawa, customs regulations, gambling and liquor laws; and later still they were the first agents of the modern welfare system'.[43] In effect, this additional role justified their continued use between 1900 and 1914,[44] and they became essentially 'agents of external control' making their role akin to that of the colonial police. In essence the NWMP was more intimately linked to government than to the community it was purported to serve. Like the colonial police and the RIC, the force was officered by an elite who had attended the Royal Military College in Kingston.[45]

Overall, there were real links between the RIC and the NWMP in terms of the export of officers, the organisation and role of the force. The internal structure of the NWMP reflected its quasi-political nature. The headquarters and recruit training centre were located at Regina. Liaison with the Government in Ottawa took place through a 'comptroller', a civilian, who 'was the voice of the government to the police'.[46] The first Commissioner George Arthur French served from1873 to 1876, following brief service in Ireland. He was less than impressed with the calibre of early recruits compared to RIC men whom he saw as having an inflexibly military outlook. French urged some changes. The study and use of RIC manuals was encouraged. R. Burton Deane, who joined the NWMP in 1883, noted that he 'studied' the Constables' Manual 'to inform himself as occasion might require'.[47]

Despite the links with Ireland the NWMP was forced to recruit heavily from the army during the early years. This pattern of recruitment and the continued use of military titles led to questions as to the force's precise nature. In 1901, the Commissioner A. Bowen Perry wrote to Fred White, the Comptroller, asking for clarification as to whether the NWMP was an 'auxiliary corps' as under the NWMP section 10 'we are liable for military service'.[48] Overall, police officers were treated more like soldiers, being on duty for twenty-four hours a day, required to 'turn their hands to whatever tasks, however prosaic or bizarre, that the government should lay before them'. The Comptroller took up the issue with the Ministry of Militia and Defence who described the NWMP as 'a Colonial Auxiliary Force'.[49] The force was 'on the same footing as the Permanent Force of the Active Militia'.[50] In the eyes of the Canadian Government, the NWMP was perceived more as an armed militia than a police force, which pointed to its colonial-style tendencies. Besides, this had been amply reflected in the type of training undertaken by recruits in previous decades.

Indeed, the third Commissioner, the Canadian-born A. G. Irvine, had visited the RIC prior to his appointment in 1880. Irvine inspected constabulary operations and was so impressed by Phoenix Park that he subsequently founded the NWMP depot and training base at Regina. Foot

[46]

and arms drill drew heavily on the methods employed by the RIC. Recruits undertook regular target practice and were required to shoot at 200, 500, 600 and 800 yards. Differences between NWMP and RIC training lay essentially within the equestrian sphere. In the NWMP this formed the core element of a six month training course. In 1881, Irvine noted that 'a man who cannot ride is useless for service in the force: worse than useless, in fact, a mere incumberance [sic]'.[51] RIC training, on the other hand, centred on foot and arms drill. At Regina, 'the question of horsemanship is of the greatest importance, as so much of his time will be spent in the saddle'. This emphasis on equestrian skills was noted in Irvine's official orders outlining training:

> The efficient training of a recruit requires twelve months. He must be drilled, set up, taught to ride (cavalry fashion), to shoot with a carbine and revolver, acquire a knowledge of his duties and powers as a Police officer, be instructed in simple veterinary knowledge, understand how a horse should be taken care of, and become an efficient prairie man, by which is implied a smattering of cooking, and the ability to find his way about and to look after the comfort of himself and his horse.[52]

There was no equivalent emphasis on horsemanship in the RIC. In Ireland there were no mounted squads undertaking routine target practice at a 'full gallop'. Yet senior figures in the NWMP, as well as officials in government circles, took a keen interest in RIC and military-style training. This interest heightened following serious public unrest in Saskatchewan in 1885. Described by the police as an 'open rebellion' against the Government, the force's inability to restore law and order quickly necessitated the use of the army in aid of the civil power. Irvine later reported that the 'withdrawal of every available man and horse for duty in the north left large districts in the south with very inadequate police protection . . . consequently there was an increase in crime'. Herchmer would report that a radical overhaul of the police patrol system resulted in a complete line of outposts being set up between the Manitoba frontier boundary and the Rocky Mountains. Following a toughening in attitude towards the aboriginal peoples, and the use of scouts to patrol and gather intelligence, the NWMP gradually gained the upper hand.[53] Using police officers regularly to patrol remote regions and creating police outposts became a feature of colonial policing. In Ireland after 1921, the Ulster Special Constabulary was used to patrol Northern Ireland's partition line to prevent border incursions. They manned small posts dotted along the boundary line which became the focal point for attacks during the IRA border campaign of the late 1950s.

The reorganisation that occurred within the NWMP at this time was underpinned by RIC-inspired training. Officers visited the RIC, and in turn, ex-RIC men offered their services to the Canadian Government. In June 1897, W. H. Vallency wrote to the Lieutenant-Governor in Regina regarding his instruction of the NWMP in 'the organization, discipline and performance of the Royal Irish Constabulary'. Vallency had 'ample practical experience' of how the RIC had operated during 'the troublesome times of Ireland' and he felt its methods to be 'particularly adapted to the police of the North West Territory'. If the NWMP could learn from the ways in which the RIC had dealt with the 'wild disloyal Irish', its men would 'certainly be able to act against the Indians or any other people, either as a police force or as a Military body'. Vallency stressed how keen he was to offer 'any information or assistance in my power of thought necessary in introducing such a system into the N.W. Police force in future'. He remained convinced that had 'the police system of Ireland' been fully integrated into the training and structure of the NWMP, 'the late rebellion would not have gone so far'.[54]

Vallency's involvement with the NWMP coincided with Bowen Perry's visit to Britain in the summer of 1897. He was at that time the Commander of E Division, although clearly being groomed for the position of commissioner at a later stage. On his arrival at Salisbury Plains, he first visited the Cavalry Brigade Camp where he 'observed' the Dragoon Guards and the Scots Greys. 'I was afforded every facility for seeing the interior economy of the different Regiments', he wrote to Commissioner Lawrence Herchmer, and was able to

> inspect the saddlery and equipment, and to examine the horses. The treatment of sore backs, and the shoeing received my attention . . . I attended all parades and saw the advantages of a thorough uniform system of instruction. The work was very varied and consisted of reconnaissances, patrols, outpost duties, and Brigade and Division drill.[55]

From the surviving reports of this visit, it appears that Bowen Perry was importing British cavalry practices into the NWMP. In other areas, he turned to the RIC. He wrote to his Commissioner stressing that he had taken 'every opportunity to learn what I could', before proceeding to Phoenix Park. There he wanted to learn about

> the interior economy of the Depot, and the system of instruction carried on. All recruits join at the Depot, so that I had an excellent opportunity of seeing the class of men who compose this celebrated Corps. I went into the financial methods and was supplied with a complete set of returns and forms in that department. Sir Andrew Reid, Inspector-General, was kind enough to supply me with copies of the General and Finance Codes. He was also good enough to explain how discipline [was] maintained and punishment inflicted, both among officers and men; and generally posted me on the organization of the Force.

[48]

Having completed his fact-finding mission at Phoenix Park, Bowen Perry then visited Belfast and Londonderry to conduct further observations and meet with senior RIC officers, including a Mr Siddal, in charge of Belfast CID, for Bowen Perry was particularly interested in the RIC's 'semi-political' and crime work.[56] His interest in the RIC continued throughout his career in the NWMP and he made regular requests for updates on aspects of reform and reorganisation that took place in the former.[57] His correspondence with Dublin Castle covered numerous issues, including enquiries as to the whereabouts of former members of the RIC who had emigrated to Canada.[58] Indeed, Bowen Perry encouraged RIC traditions wherever possible and was interested in the widest possible range of duties and responsibilities.

Certainly the NWMP was involved in a colourful array of duties in a similar vein to the RIC and to any other colonial force. Romantic as it appeared at first glance to police the prairies in 'their scarlet tunics, brown Stetson hats and mounted on glossy, well groomed horses', the reality was somewhat different. The NWMP trooper was required to sign up for a minimum of five years, was poorly paid and subjected to 'severe discipline'. Moreover, he required extensive knowledge of a range of provincial ordinances that covered criminal codes, dominion laws concerned with Indian Acts, Customs Acts, Fisheries Acts, Railway and the Dominion Lands Acts passed by Ottawa. Patrols within the northerly regions to monitor gold- and copper-mining had their 'rough sides'. Special Constable Ford wrote in his diary of how the police gathered geological and meteorological data for different government departments which 'in addition to endurance, resourcefulness, and other qualities essential to Police work, [he] must possess keen powers of observation, and be well trained in more than one branch of science'.[59]

Officers were involved in all aspects of administration outside law enforcement; the 'all-purpose government bureaucrat', policing vast areas with all the responsibilities that entailed as reflected in the tasks of G Division in 1924:

Non-commissioned Officers and Constables on detachment [acted] as Postmaster, Veterinary Inspectors, Immigration Officers, Customs Officers, Collectors of Royalties, etc. The Officer commanding Whitehorse and the District [acted] as Sub-mining Recorder, Crown Timber and Land Agent, Deputy Sheriff. The Officer Commanding Division [acted] as Immigration Inspector and Fisheries Inspector for the Yukon territory, Registrar of Vital Statistics and Chief Registrar of Weights and Measures. All members of the force [were] Game Wardens ex-officio. Besides enforcing Federal and Yukon statutes and ordinances, [they enforced] the city by-laws, [collected] Royalties on gold exported, [issued] permits for the export of furs and [issued] licences to big game hunters. Under the direction of the administration, estates of persons dying from accidental, sudden or violent death, and those of insane persons in outlaying points, [were] looked after by [them].[60]

Thus in this northern part of the second-largest country in the world, the NWMP enforced the law and like colonial policemen undertook a multitude of extraneous duties. These notions of colonial policing were reinforced by subsequent commissioners. Herchmer, who took over from Irvine in 1886, had served with the British Army in both India and Ireland. He served until 1900, illustrating that a military or colonial policing background was highly desirable. This was also reflected in a survey of the nationalities of serving 'gazetted' officers in May 1894: of the 50, 38 were Canadians, while of the remaining 12 officers 6 had been born in Britain, 5 in India and one in Jamaica. Each of these officers had either military or colonial policing experience. The myth of Britishness, in its broadest sense, became part of the NWMP's culture at this time. Indeed 'few police officers would have been offended at being mistaken for a member of the English gentry'.[61] There was a distinction made between Canadians and non Canadians. In the year that this survey was conducted, 3 of the 11 Superintendents and 7 of the 31 Inspectors were British, although, for some, the recruitment of police officers from outside of Canada was considered offensive. In 1888, on hearing that a recruiting agent had been sent to London to find officers for the Winnipeg force, the Ottawa *Free Press* complained:

> One could imagine that Captain Grahame could find plenty of recruits in Canada without importing English dudes. If we are to have 'Canada for the Canadians' why send to England for troopers when Canadians can be obtained? The recruiting of the mounted police force with strangers who have no sympathy with Canada, who know nothing of the country and who imagine that all their follies and vices should be condoned because 'they are English don't cher know . . .'.[62]

Yet recruiting outsiders allowed for the colonial notion of 'policing by strangers', according to which sympathy with the community policed was not an essential feature. The percentage of British-born recruits continued to rise until 1890 when, with the onset of the Boer War, it reached a high point of 50 per cent. The majority of these recruits had emigrated to Canada and then joined the police primarily in the rank-and-file and non-commissioned ranks.[63] The final Commissioner, the Canadian-born A. Bowen-Perry, oversaw the force's transformation into the RCMP.[64] With its creation, the NWMP merged with the smaller Dominion Police that had existed since 1868. As *the* Canadian mounted police, its headquarters were relocated from provincial Regina to Ottawa.

Officers recruited from the United Kingdom to the RCMP continued to be a source of influence despite its name change. In 1914, Prime Minister Robert Borden noted with considerable pride that 79 per cent of the 'mounties' had originated in the United Kingdom. Of a total of 617 officers, this amounted to 490 men who were either first- or second-generation *British*. The remainder comprised 76 Canadians, 24 from 'other British possessions', 10 from the US and a further 17 from 'foreign countries'. The previous year, ninety-eight recruits had been English, most of them former Guards and cavalry officers. Stephen Hewitt calculated that within the Alberta and Saskatchewan mounted-police divisions during the interwar period, 25 per cent were English, 3 per cent Irish and 3 per cent Scottish and Welsh. Of these a small number had previously served in the Metropolitan Police, the Middlesborough Constabulary, the Glasgow Police and the British Army.[65] This suggests that there had been clear Irish influences on the NWMP during its formative years, in terms of the leadership of the force and the training and instruction that followed the RIC pattern. Thereafter, the force was more heavily influenced by *English* officers. Yet a far higher number had seen military service, suggesting that they replaced the earlier Irish semi-military traditions with those of the British Army, though a sense of Irishness remained in the policing traditions of the RCMP, which was described as a 'genteel foreign legion'.[66]

Prior to confederation each area developed its own policing ventures. Broadly speaking, this revolved around the use of a loosely connected group of constables as watchmen and peace-keepers. Thereafter, legislation allowed for the formal development of policing institutions that reflected the territory and the origins of its settlers. This stemmed essentially from two traditions; the English–metropolitan and the Irish–colonial. In urban areas, police forces were able to assume an English mantle once the community was regarded as sufficiently settled. Initially, the rural constabularies – municipal, provincial and mounted – drew heavily on the experience of policing Ireland. Mounted rural constabularies, particularly the NWMP and its successor the RCMP, came closest to being the Canadian equivalent of a colonial police force.

Notes

1   C. H. Talbot, C. H. S. Jayewardene & T. J. Juliani, 'Policing in Canada: A Developmental Perspective', *Canadian Police College Journal*, 8:3 (1984), p. 219.
2   The interest in Canadian policing has grown although the primary interest remains centered on the history of the NWMP and the RCMP. See Lorne & Caroline Brown, *An Unauthorized History of the RCMP* (Toronto: James Lorimer, 1978); William R. Morrison, *Showing the Flag: The Mounted Police and Canadian Sovereignty in the North 1894–1925* (Vancouver: University of British Columbia Press, 1985); Rod C. Macleod, *The NWMP and Law Enforcement 1873–1905* (Toronto: University of

Toronto Press, 1976); Rod C, Macleod, *The North West Mounted Police 1873–1919* (Ottawa: Canadian Historical Association, 1978); Rod C. Macleod & David Schneiderman, *Police Powers in Canada: The Evolution and Practice of Authority* (Toronto: Toronto University Press, 1994); William & Nora Kelly, *Policing in Canada* (Toronto: Macmillan, 1976); Keith Walden, *Visions of Order: The Canadian Mounties in Symbol and Myth* (Toronto: Butterworth, 1982); Carl Betke, 'Pioneers and Police on the Canadian Prairies, 1885–1914', *Journal of the Canadian Historical Association* (1980); William R. Morrison, 'Imposing the British Way: The Canadian Mounted Police and the Klondike Gold Rush', in Anderson & Killingray, *Policing the Empire*; Harwood Steele, *Policing the Acrtic: The Story of the Conquest of the Artic by the RCMP* (Toronto: Ryerson Press, 1936); and *To Effect an Arrest: Adventures of the RCMP* (Toronto: Ryerson Press, 1947); Donald Klancher, *The North West Mounted Police and the North West Rebellion* (Kamloops, CV: Goss Publishers, 1999); Donald Klancher & Roger F. Phillips, *Arms and Accoutrements of the Mounted Police, 1973–1973* (Bloomfield, ON: Museum Restoration Service, 1982); Ronald Atkin, *Maintain the Right: The Early History of the NWMP, 1873–1900* (New York: John Day, 1873); Hugh A. Dempsey (ed.), *Mounted Policemen* (Calgary: Glenbow–Alberta Institute; Edmonton: Hurtig Publishers, 1973).

There is limited material on other Canadian police forces. See for example: Lynne Stonier-Newman, *Policing a Pioneer Province: The British Columbia Provincial Police 1858–1950* (Madeira Park, BC: Harbour Publishing, 1991); Helen Boritch, 'Conflict, Compromise and Administrative Convenience: The Police Organization in Nineteenth-Century Toronto', *Canadian Journal of Law and Society*, 3 (1988); Gerald F. Wallace, William Higgins & Peter McGahen, *The Saint John Police Story: The Clark Years 1890–1914* (Fredericton, NB: New Ireland Press, 1991).

For general overviews of the policing of Canada see: C. K. Talbot, C. H. S. Jayewardene & T. J. Juliani, 'Policing in Canada: A Developmental Perspective', *Canadian Police College Journal*, 8:3 (1984), and *Canada's Constables: The Historical Development of Policing in Canada* (Ottawa: Crimecare Inc., 1985); Jeffrey Ian Ross, 'The Historical Treatment of Urban Policing in Canada: A Review of the Literature', *Urban History Review*, 24:1 (October, 1995).

For police autobiographies and memoirs see for example: A. L. Haydon, *The Riders of the Plains: A Record of the Royal North West Mounted Police of Canada, 1873–1910* (Edmonton: Hurtig Publishers, 1912); R. Burton Deane, *Mounted Police Life in Canada: A Record of Thirty-One Years' Service* (Toronto: Cassell & Co., 1916); Roderick G. Macbeath, *Policing the Plains: Being the Real-Life Record of the Famous RNWMP* (London: Hodder & Stoughton, 1921); Rowland Walker, *The Blue Ridge Patrol: A Story of the RNWMP of Canada* (Toronto: Musson, 1920); Samuel B. Steele, *Forty Years in Canada: Reminiscences of the Great North-West with Some Account of His Service in South Africa* (Toronto: Musson, 1915).

3 Eric H. Monkkoven, *Police in Urban America, 1860–1920* (New York: CUP, 1981), p. 31.
4 Talbot, Jayewardene & Juliani, *Canada's Constables*, pp. 14–15.
5 Quoted in Talbot, Jayewardene & Juliani, 'Policing in Canada', p. 260.
6 R. I. Mawby, *Comparative Policing Issues: The British and American System in International Perspective* (London: Unwin Hyman, 1990), p. 73.
7 Phillip A. Buckner, *The Transition to Responsible Government: British Policy in British North America 1815–1850* (Westport, CT: Greenwood Press, 1985), p. 335.
8 Allan Greer & Ian Radforth, 'Birth of the Police in Canada', in Greer & Radforth (eds), *Colonial Leviathan: State Formation in Mid-Nineteenth-Century Canada* (Toronto: University of Toronto Press, 1992), pp. 21–22; H. S. Cooper, 'The Evolution of Canadian Police', in W. T. McGrath & M. P. Mitchell (eds), *The Police Function in Canada* (Toronto: Methuen, 1981), p. 39.
9 Greer & Radforth (eds), *Colonial Leviathan*, p. 11, 19–21.
10 Greer & Radforth (eds), *Colonial Leviathan*, pp. 29–32.
11 Quoted in Talbot, Jayewardene & Juliani, 'Policing in Canada', pp. 220–221.
12 Ross, 'The Historical Treatment of Urban Policing in Canada', pp. 36–41.

13 Greer & Radforth (eds), *Colonial Leviathan*, p. 5.
14 Greg Marquis, 'The "Irish Model" and Nineteenth-Century Canadian Policing', *Journal of Imperial and Commonwealth History*, 25:2 (May, 1997), pp. 194–195.
15 T. Murdoch to D. Daly (not dated, 1840), National Archives of Canada (NAC) File 1, RG4 B14.
16 Talbot, Jayewardene & Juliani, *Canada's Constables*, p. 48.
17 Marquis, 'The "Irish Model" and Nineteenth-Century Canadian Policing', p. 199.
18 D. C. Masters, *The Rise of Toronto 1850–1890* (Toronto: Toronto University Press, 1947), p. 21.
19 Helen Boritch, 'Conflict, Compromise and Administrative Convenience: The Police Organization in Nineteenth-Century Toronto', *Canadian Journal of Law and Society*, 3 (1988), p. 148.
20 Joe Swan, *A Century of Service: The Vancouver Police, 1886–1986* (Vancouver: Vancouver Police Historical Society, 1986), pp. 18–29, 57, 69, 71. See also: Swan, *The Police Murders: True Stories from the Vancouver Police Archives* (Vancouver: West Ender Books, 1987).
21 Instructions for the direction and governance of the officers and men of the Police Establishment, District of Montreal, 26 Dec. 1838, quoted in Marquis, 'The "Irish Model" and Nineteenth-Century Canadian Policing', p. 196.
22 Cooper, 'Evolution of Canadian Police', p. 40.
23 Gerald F. Wallace, William Higgins & Peter McGahen, *The Saint John Police Story: The Clark Years 1890–1914* (Fredericton, NB: New Ireland Press, 1991), pp. 10–11.
24 Total number of arrests and those for 'drunkenness', Saint John, 1890–1908, quoted in Wallace, Higgins & McGahen, *Saint John Police*, p. 30.
25 Boritch, 'Police Organization in Nineteenth-Century Toronto', p. 161.
26 *Saint John Daily Sun*, 24 May 1890, quoted in Wallace, Higgins & McGahen, *Saint John Police*, p. 15.
27 Wallace, Higgins & McGahen, *Saint John Police*, pp. 16, 39.
28 Sir Edward Lytton, Colonial Secretary, to James Douglas, Governor, 11 Nov. 1858, PABC GR 1372 B-1326, quoted in Stonier-Newman, *Policing a Pioneer Province*, pp. 10, 11–13.
29 Stonier-Newman, *Policing a Pioneer Province*, pp. 29–31.
30 The RCMP assumed all policing responsibilities within British Columbia on 15 August 1950.
31 Charles K. Talbot, *The Thin Blue Line: An Historical Perspective of Policing in Canada* (Ottawa: Crimecare Inc., 1983), p. 8.
32 Macdonald to Cameron, 21 December 1869, Macdonald Papers, Vol. 516, quoted in Macleod, *NWMP and Law Enforcement*, p. 8.
33 Macleod, *NWMP and Law Enforcement*, p. 8.
34 S. W. Horrall, 'Sir John A. Macdonald and the Mounted Police Force for the Northwest Territories', *Canadian Historical Review*, 53 (June, 1972); Jeff Keshan, 'Cloak and Dagger: Canada West's Secret Police, 1864–67', *Ontario History*, 79 (Dec. 1987).
35 Haydon, *Riders of the Plains*, p. 19.
36 Morrison, *Showing the Flag*, p. 3.
37 Macleod, *North West Mounted Police*, pp. 4–5.
38 Emsley, *English Police*, p. 254.
39 Haydon, *Rider of the Plains*, pp. 15–16.
40 Morrison, *Showing the Flag*, p. 2.
41 In 1918, Inspector F. H. French led a patrol on an epic 4,000-mile trek to search for the murderers of the explorers Radford and Street. The search lasted for four years. The extent of their journey took the NWMP into unchartered territory, with only the Arctic islands to bring under police jurisdiction during the 1920s.
42 Morrison, *Showing the Flag*, p. 1.
43 Morrison, *Showing the Flag*, p. 2.
44 Macleod, *North West Mounted Police*, pp. 16–17.
45 Morrison, *Showing the Flag*, p. 6.

46 Morrison, *Showing the Flag*, p. 2.
47 Deane, *Mounted Police Life*, p. 4.
48 Perry to White, 29 April 1910, 'Colonial Auxiliary Forces', NAC RG 18 A-1 225 88–02.
49 L. J. Pinault, Deputy Minister of Militia and Defence, to White, 20 July 1901, NAC RG 18 A-1 225 88–02.
50 Maj.-Gen. R.H. O'Grady-Haly, GOC Canadian Milita, to Pinault, 28 Jan. 1902, NAC RG 18 A-1 225 88–02.
51 Irvine quoted in Talbot, *Thin Blue Line*, p. 14.
52 Quoted in Haydon, *Riders of the Plains*, pp. 327–329.
53 Irvine, 1886; Herchmer, 1887, 1888, 1889: correspondence quoted in Talbot, *Thin Blue Line*, pp. 12–13.
54 Vallency to Gov., 18 June 1897, 'Instruction in Discipline and Organization as in RIC', NAC RG18 B-1 1082 471–1887.
55 Bown Perry to Herchmer, 13 Nov. 1897, 'Perry Attachment to Cavalry and visit to RIC', NAC RG18 A-1 141 622–97.
56 Bowen Perry to Herchmer, 13 Nov. 1897, NAC RG18 A-1 141 622–97.
57 'Report of Committee of Inquiry into RIC', Nov. 1902, NAC RG 18 A-1 236 490–02.
58 N. Chamberlain, RIC, to Bowen Perry, Enquiry re. Myles Campbell, 16 Aug. 1902, 'Campbell, Myles, a pensioner of Royal Irish Constabulary, Information requested', 1902', NAC RG 18 A-1 248 1–4–03.
59 Ford quoted in Haydon, *Riders of the Plains*, p. 322.
60 RCMP, G Division, 1924, quoted in Talbot, *Thin Blue Line*, p. 19.
61 Macleod, *NWMP and Law Enforcement*, p. 74.
62 Ottawa Free Press quoted in Macleod, *NWMP and Law Enforcement*, p. 75.
63 French-Canadian representation with the NWMP was also perceived as problematical, and it engendered debate: Macleod, *NWMP and Law Enforcement*, pp. 78–82.
64 Marquis, 'The "Irish Model" and Nineteenth-Century Canadian Policing', pp. 208–209.
65 Stephen Roy Hewitt, ' "Old Myths Die Hard" ': The Transformation of the Mounted Police in Alberta and Saskatchewan 1914–1939', unpublished PhD thesis (University of Saskatchewan, 1997), pp. 63, 71, 72.
66 Marquis, 'The "Irish Model" and Nineteenth-Century Canadian Policing', p. 210.

CHAPTER THREE

'Too little, too late': post-war reforms within the Colonial Police Service

By 1945, Britain was in decline as a world and imperial power. The colonies found themselves on a conveyor-belt transporting them, albeit at varying speed, towards political independence. Decolonisation did not, however, follow a grand plan drawn up by the government departments of Whitehall. While the transfer of power after 1945 necessitated a rationale of sorts to justify British policy and satisfy both domestic and American concerns,[1] circumstances dictated that decolonisation was essentially reactive. The Colonial Office sought to sustain day-to-day control in colonial territories rather than implement any long-term plan or phased devolution of power.[2]

The 1948 public disturbances in Accra marked a watershed in colonial policy, ushering in the long period of decolonisation. Commanding the Gold Coast Police during the rioting, Colin Imray was faced with

> a vast milling crowd of very excited shouting men, filling the road and even now starting to envelop our flanks. Two thoughts dominated: 'They must not pass' and 'Minimum force'. Many were in fact waving sticks, cudgels, and anything else that came to hand . . . baton charges were clearly out of the question. Again I shouted, but this time it was 'Disperse or I fire'. More and more stones and yells of derision. Desperately I tore the rifle and bandolier from the nearest man, stuffed six rounds into the magazine, levelled on the man with the horn – now very close – and fired. He went down in a heap.[3]

The rioting that occurred that day had disastrous consequences for Imray and through a chain of circumstances, brought renewed attempts to reform the Colonial Police Service. The riots were preceded by a trade boycott – sparked by the disastrous cocoa swollen-shoot episode – that ended on 28 February. By that time, the police were faced with large hostile crowds in the centre of Accra, wanting to march to Government House to present Governor Creasy with a petition of grievances. The Commissioner Richard Ballantine sanctioned the march, which went ahead only to result, some days later, in the police opening fire at the Christiansborg crossroads. In terms of the colonial police, the Gold Coast riots prompted a government enquiry, which untimely led to the despatch of Arthur Young of the City of London Police to enact reforms. On a much broader level, 1948 marked the start of the Colonial Office's attempts at bringing standardisation to the Colonial Police Service, through reform, with the appointment of its first official Colonial Police Advisor (CPA), William Johnson.

Standardisation was perceived as useful considering the number and spread of forces throughout the Empire. In 1948, there were 43 separate police forces[4] in the Colonial Police Service, with a total regular establishment of 1,160 gazetted officers[5] and 56,912 other ranks. These police forces ranged in size from the Falkland Islands' force, with a total of 8 (all ranks), to Malaya, with a total of 15,854[6] (excluding auxiliaries[7]) By contrast, there were 176 police forces in England and Wales in 1945. The need for standardisation of the English forces resulted in a number of amalgamations. By the time of the Royal Commission, the number had dropped to 124 and was further reduced to 46 by the end of the 1960s. Despite the changes occurring in the British police, Robert Reiner has described the 1950s as 'a golden age' in which policing by consent was well-achieved. The police became 'an aspect of being British',[8] an institution that enjoyed 'the sacred aura . . . of being, like the Queen, above party politics'.[9] It was partly this aspect of Britishness, along with notions of civil policing – and the image of the community-friendly bobby – that the Colonial Office wanted to export to the police forces of the Empire. This, however, required a uniform approach to colonial policing.

Up until this period there had been little consideration given to a concerted central policy from Whitehall regarding police organisation and its role within the colonial state. Suddenly the Colonial Office was preoccupied with global security, with the onset of the cold war. Consideration was given to the likelihood of civil disturbances throughout the colonies and the manner in which they would be dealt with by the local security forces.[10] Colonial Secretary Arthur Creech-Jones wrote in a 1949 report of 'social and political developments of the Colonies . . . and the signs of deliberate attempts to provoke unrest in some colonial territories as part of the "cold war" [which] made it necessary to reconsider the position of the colonial police service'.[11] The Colonial Office's objectives were two-fold: to reform the colonial police to ensure that they could provide adequate security as the cold war unfolded; and to ensure that notions of *Britishness* were inculcated to leave an acceptable face of imperialism at independence.

Unifying the colonial police: 'an impracticability except in name'?

The Colonial Police Service came into existence on 1 October 1936. At the same time discussion was underway at committee level to find ways of divorcing the police from the prison service within the colonies.[12] Unifying the police forces of the Empire was the first real attempt at implementing any degree of standardisation. The whole process came about as a result of the 1930 findings of the Warren Fisher Committee. This brought three principal consequences: the possibility of tracking the career paths of colonial officials; better career prospects through inter-colony promotion and raising the overall profile of the colonial service, which would enhance potential recruitment. In short, unification was about improving the 'efficiency and prospects of serving officers' and bringing prestige to the Colonial Police Service as a whole.[13] Up until this period, senior British officers had been appointed to serve on commissions of inquiry and appointment boards in relation to colonial affairs. This had been a Home Office measure designed to tighten the colonial police apparatus. Yet, overall, this had made little difference and each constabulary remained molded within its own traditions and practices. Moves to unify these colonial police forces in the mid-1930s raised issues relating specifically to police practices.

Unifying the colonial police implied standardisation and this brought many issues to the fore. For example: which officers should be part of this new service? Should selection be confined to commissioned (or gazetted) officers or should constables in the British Section of the Palestine Police, and the non-commissioned officers in both the Kenya and Malay forces be included?[14] How would that decision then affect officer training programmes that had previously taken place at Newtownards?[15] In relation to the methods of recruitment and the initial training of selected candidates there were felt to be disadvantages to including commissioned ranks, the inspectorate and European constables within similar training programmes. The Colonial Office's R. D. Furse noted: 'you will attract better raw material if you recruit straight to the commissioned posts than through the ranks', adding that Spicer's success in recruiting first-class constables for the Palestine Police was to be attributed to the 'wholly abnormal state of the employment market during the last few years'.[16]

Standardisation would affect the ranking systems, which varied throughout the colonies. Colonial Office officials debated the use of the title 'inspector-general', which was disliked 'because the Head of a Police Force is not an Inspector at all: he is an Executive officer'. Moreover, the term 'inspector' was more suited to non-commissioned ranks. It was suggested that while the title was traditional and there-fore, could 'cause offence' to a police force if removed, it should be retained only in the 'larger' colonies. Preferences were for a chief com-missioner or, in the case of 'smaller' colonies, simply a commissioner of police. Titles with military connotations, for example 'comman-dant', should be removed.[17]

This led to an enquiry into the professional standing of the police. A study in 1952 of the 'current Precedence Table' for Commissioners of Police throughout the Empire revealed widespread disparity. (These tables of precedence were important in that they revealed the hierar-chical structure of the colonial administration. In terms of policing, this indicated the standing of a commissioner of police in relation to other senior-ranking colonial officials.) For example, in the Gold Coast, the commissioner of police was placed at the top of the administrative structure, preceding 'officers class II'. In Hong Kong, the commissioner was on a par with members of the Government's Legislative Council. In Kenya, the commissioner's post was ranked below that of 'Post Master General and above [the] Provincial Commissioners (outside their own Province)'; while in Mauritius, it was 'between Director of Agriculture and General Manager Railways'; and in Zanzibar, it came 'after Director of Public Works and before Port Officer'. In some colonies, like British Honduras, the commissioner's status relative to other administrative heads was 'at the Governor's discretion'.

Precedence tables raised important issues in relation to the colonial police. First, the actual position of a police commissioner was linked to the relative importance of the police within the overall machinery of colonial administration. Second, the lack of standardisation, and in some cases a failure to register, firmly placed the police outside the structure of the colonial administration's 'heaven born'. Indeed a place on the colonial regulations table of precedence would 'raise the status of [a] Police Force and thus its morale and efficiency'. Attempts to stan-dardise the position of police commissioners had already been raised as an issue in 1946 by Sir Alan Burns. However, up until the appointment of an official police advisor in 1948 and the outcome of the first colo-nial police commissioners' conference in 1951 no change had occurred. By 1952, the position of many police commissioner vis-à-vis heads of other colonial government departments was 'sinking lower and lower by reason of the policy which excluded them from membership of the Legislative Council while many heads of department are ex-officio members of the legislative bodies'. Only in Fiji and Nyasaland were police commissioners members of the legislative council.[18]

This issue raised some debate between supporters of the colonial police, the CPA and officials like Jeffries, and colonial office mandarins.

On the one hand the colonial police was described as an 'essential pillar of democracy'. This necessitated a high-profile position 'immediately below the Puisne Judges and the President of the Legislative Council and immediately above members of the Legislative Council'.[19] For the Colonial Office, a 'democratic society should avoid over much publicity of police duties'. Their recommendation was that 'as they have so often done so well on so many occasions, "grin and bear it" '.[20] Despite the issue being raised at subsequent police commissioners' conferences, standardisation to the precedence tables and, by extension, the position of police commissioners within the colonial hierarchy did not occur. Once again this revealed the ambiguous nature of colonial office policy in relation to the colonial police. Any plan to bring change through standardisation to the overall structure was swept away by the practicalities of policing the end of the Empire. In this instance, the very nature of the democratic ideal which the Colonial Office sought to impose would be eroded by the presence of *undemocratic* policemen. Policing and the process of self-government did not sit comfortably with the Colonial Office mindset. Having its own personal CPA might change this viewpoint.

'An advising head' for all colonial police forces

The unification of all colonial constabularies (bar Malta's) was recognised as a necessary step forward by the early 1930s. At the same time, some senior colonial officials and policemen, like Roy Spicer, the infamous Palestine Police Chief, advocated the idea of a CPA. The Colonial Office was urged to select a candidate who 'can advise on disputed matters and sum up the weaknesses and strength [*sic*] of the multi-fold Forces'. This 'Advising Inspector-General of Police' would 'live at home' and thus be at the Colonial Office's beck and call to advise on appointments, promotions, technical matters, and to undertake annual inspections and oversee colonial police conferences.[21]

Spicer was no doubt ahead of his time over this question of a CPA, along with such other champions of the cause, like Jeffries, although he warned that the colonies would need to make a financial contribution in order for this to occur. Spicer preferred to side-step financial questions, concentrating on whether the appointment would be for a 'co-ordinating head', i.e. an official inspector-general of colonial constabularies, or, 'an advising head', i.e. advising on the unification of the colonial police. Possible candidates included the former Ceylon Police Chief Dowbiggin, 'an obvious square peg for the much needed square hole'. Although due to retire early in 1937, it was thought he might be persuaded to stay on for a further three years:[22] he was, after all, 'young for his years and exceptionally energetic'.[23] Dowbiggin, however, had other irons in the fire. By 1934 he was considering the post of 'a kind of Inspector of Borstal Institutions', and one of the two posts of inspector of constabulary. As a career policeman his preference lay with the latter although he privately admitted that 'he would feel morally bound to regard the C.O. as having a prior claim'.[24]

Dowbiggin had an excellent police pedigree and could be described as the first *unofficial*, roving, CPA. While Commissioner of the Ceylon Police in 1926, he was asked by the Colonial Office to inspect the Cyprus Military Police. In a lengthy and detailed report, Dowbiggin laid the foundations for the export of *Britishness* to colonial police forces. His famous comment, 'The notebook is to the Policeman what his rifle is to the soldier', reflected his deep-seated belief that the police should essentially carry out duties of a civil nature.[25] He adapted this principle, with some success, during his leadership of the Ceylon Police.

Dowbiggin was aware that the essentially military nature of the Cyprus Police was 'on account of the fact that there is no Defence Force on the Island'. However, the 'strictly "police" side of their duties' was hampered by a variegated set of responsibilities which Dowbiggin believed were simply not appropriate to the police. Dowbiggin recommended that European officers receive training in Britain and preferably that gazetted officers be recruited from Britain: 'A police force, however military their [sic] functions may be, is none the less essentially a police force, and the worst of military officers is that they usually confine themselves to questions of drill and discipline . . .'.[26] The foundations were thus in place for the regular use of an ' "expert advisor" on colonial police forces' who was prepared to bring about gradual change to their military nature. Dowbiggin's visit to Cyprus had demonstrated 'the value of periodical inspections of colonial police forces by trained police officers as opposed to those carried out by military officers purely from the standpoint of home defence, as in the West Indian colonies'. Similar routine inspections were recommended throughout the empire which would 'do much to raise the standard of the local Police qua Police'.[27]

The question of whether an *official* police advisor should be appointed was occasionally raised between 1932 and 1934. It was felt that the matter needed to be settled prior to unification as 'the advice of the Inspector-General would be of the greatest value in regard to this important question of preliminary training. [However], the question of finance is likely to be the deciding factor in terms of a potential appointment'.[28] Indeed throughout this period the issue of the cost of an advisor outweighed all others. Opinions differed on whether this advisor's salary should be paid by the Colonial Office vote or, whether it should be 'moderate' and supplemented by 'fees fixed ad hoc from the Governments of any Colonies which might visit'.[29]

Issues surrounding cost threw up a new set of arguments centred on whether there was a real necessity for a CPA. Those officials who were not in favour suggested using senior police officers from the home forces to offer *ad hoc* assistance. It was felt that an advisor would be unable to liaise sufficiently with the Colonial Office if he spent lengthy periods overseas. Besides, was it really possible for one police officer to 'adequately perform these duties' when his own personal experience could be limited to one specific colony? Furthermore 'a retired officer very soon gets out of touch with current developments'.[30] This raised a further disagreement among senior colonial officials, who argued that the 'larger' police forces, including Kenya, Uganda, Nigeria and the Gold Coast, simply did not need inspecting let alone reforming. It was not the role of the Colonial Office 'to shove Inspectors and inspections down the throat of the Governor', and the arrival of a police advisor could be misconstrued as 'a slur on their capacity'.[31] Ultimately each colonial police force was unique:

> Police forces in Africa have to stand on their own feet and conditions vary considerably. Would an officer who knew nothing of Africa or African mentality prove really capable of advising on the position of an African Police Force? Palestine has got a peculiar Force of its own which could be inspected by almost anybody. Cyprus has also got a small and peculiar Force. But the large Forces in the African Colonies have each to be treated in their own way.[32]

Such objections ensured that the proposal of an official police advisor was quietly dropped. Yet Dowbiggin went on a grand tour in 1935, apparently on his way home from Ceylon on leave. Visiting the police forces of Southeast Asia as well as 12 cities in the US, 2 in Canada, 2 in Japan, and ending with a visit to the Metropolitan Police, his subsequent mammoth report left few in doubt that he was acting in an unofficial capacity for the Colonial Office.[33] Up until his retirement, he kept up a stream of correspondence with the heads of many forces, advising on an array of policing issues. This culminated in a final whirlwind tour in 1937 with visits to the police forces of Zanzibar, Kenya, Sudan, Mozambique, northern and Southern Rhodesia, Australia, New Zealand Canada and Honolulu.[34] Having set a precedent for grandiose tours, the first official Colonial Office appointee, William Johnson, stepped into the limelight a decade later.

Yet the adage 'famous last words . . .' never rang truer. William Johnson, stood accused by senior colonial policemen of the problem that Furse had earlier outlined: attempting to provide adequate knowledge of each and every police force inspected. Certainly Dowbiggin's voluminous reports provided plenty of detailed information, but they lacked a grasp of local matters and the foresight to predict the direction of the police. There was the distinct impression from those pages that the future Colonial Police Service would be little more than a 'name', a necessary appendage following the unification of the Colonial Administrative Service.

Bringing colonial police forces into line: the impact of William Johnson

Bringing reform to the Colonial Police Service during the post-war era, prompted by the onset of colonial conflict, was simply a matter of too little, too late. Most police forces badly needed modernising by this period, due chiefly to the pressures and financial consequences of the Second World War. Police forces of smaller territories like Basutoland Bechuanaland Eritrea and British Somaliland were reminiscent of nineteenth-century establishments.

The best way of dealing with this situation was to ensure that police forces were standardised through the appropriate reforms. The means to resolve it came on 1 November 1948 with the appointment of William Johnson, a former Inspector of Constabularies, as the very first official Colonial Police Advisor. Johnson was to report directly to the Colonial Office on all matters regarding the Colonial Police Service, assisted by his second-in-command, Sir George Abbiss.[35] Johnson's primary task was to provide an ongoing review of the 'organisation, methods, administration, discipline and technical efficiency of all Colonial Police Forces'.[36] He was also to advise colonial governments and their commissioners of police on methods of improving and modernising their police forces,and to brief the Colonial Secretary and colonial governments on all aspects of intelligence gathering and information dissemination, as well as liaising with British police authorities. These duties required a tour of the Empire to visit every police force. Johnson's appointment – he had been Chief Constable of the Birmingham Police – caused consternation among senior colonial policemen.[37] The selection of a member of a home police force rather than of a colonial force clearly indicated that the Colonial Office wished to introduce British policing standards within the colonial police. It also assumed, wrongly those senior officers believed, that the practice of policing the colonies could be similar to British policing methods.[38]

Johnson's visits to forces throughout the colonies[39] culminated in a report submitted to the Colonial Secretary on 28 December 1949.

Johnson's main conclusion was that the level of administrative and operational efficiency varied considerably from one territory to another, but 'regarded as a whole it leaves much to be desired'. Overall he was highly critical of the colonial police, perceiving the organisation, methods and equipment used to be 'completely out of date' when compared to the home forces'. The contents and consequences of Johnson's report were something of a mixed bag. From a positive viewpoint, Johnson's comments on the need to modernise colonial police forces brought pressure on the Colonial Office to initiate long-overdue reforms. From a negative perspective, Johnson failed to grasp the complexity of colonial police practice, with its deeply embedded military tradition. This could not be easily changed to a more civil style of policing in view of the turmoil erupting at that time in many colonies.

Johnson voiced many other criticisms, noting, for example, the bias towards Europeans in the recruitment of the intermediate and senior ranks, and their lack of training to deal adequately with future modernisation. The crux of the matter – reform to ensure the efficiency and welfare of the police – obviously depended on the amount of financial support that a colonial government was prepared to offer. The colonial welfare and development schemes in previous years had not considered the social aspects of a police force and the need to create a police *service* rather than a police force.[40]

Yet these very opinions, expressed throughout Johnson's report, reflected the duality of Colonial Office thinking vis-à-vis the colonial police at this time. On the one hand, reform was considered necessary to modernise the colonial police along British lines; but, on the other hand, it was felt that a civil rather than a militarised system of policing could jeopardise a colony's internal security. In hindsight it could be argued that the speed of decolonisation precluded the necessary process of reform. Johnson's view that colonial police forces should modify their outlook in line with that of a civil police force rather than a military 'spit-and-polish'-style organisation simply was not suited to the security needs of that particular time.[41]

While reactions to Johnson's report caused some division within the Colonial Office, his first tour provoked real dismay among many senior colonial police officers. There were numerous examples. Johnson had written of how replacement uniforms were badly needed, particularly for new recruits. He had, however, failed to take on board the comments of senior colonial policemen that repeated requests to the crown agents to supply boots and uniforms to many parts of British colonial Africa had gone unanswered. Depleted crown agent funds, delayed deliveries and ill-fitting boots, when and if they arrived, would not provide a quick solution to the issues Johnson had raised.[42] The problem of police equipment was not limited to uniforms and boots, for the Second World War had deprived the police in many colonies of transport and communications systems, and these had not been replaced. John Coles, who served in the Gold Coast Police during the disturbances of 1948, explained how troop-carrying vehicles, signals equipment, riot equipment (batons, steel helmets, tear gas, wicker shields) and armoured-car units had to be urgently brought into the colony in the wake of the Accra riots.[43] He further noted that 'had the equipment we subsequently received not been available, we still could not have coped with the scale and intensity of the disorder that occurred'.[44] Police accommodation was also a sore point with many senior officers. Local constables had made their feelings known during Johnson's visit to the Gold Coast. A fatigue party had refused to limewash the building prior to his arrival, stating that the colonial police advisor should see the dilapidated buildings for himself. On his arrival, some 100 policemen marched to protest at the poor state of their pay and uniforms; and when ordered to parade, they did so in their oldest uniforms.[45]

However the greatest concern of senior colonial policemen were Johnson's recommendations that a British civil system of policing be introduced and the military *colonial* style dampened down. It was pointed out that the police comprised essentially a colony's first line of defence, if only because the presence of the armed forces in most colonies was minimal. Johnson considered regular arms and foot drill to be excessive; yet, the colonial police, unlike the home police forces, were expected to undertake regular ceremonial duties that necessitated arms and foot drill.[46]

Johnson was, therefore, the means by which the Colonial Office would create a uniform system of policing in the colonies. Following his individual country reports, the structure and operational side to each constabulary could be standardised. This could take the route, for example, of systematic training and drill procedures.[47] Yet how could standard policies realistically be applied to forty-three police forces, each of which was unique – from type of territory policed right down to the style of uniform worn? Regardless of this point, the Colonial Secretary was urged to use all his powers of persuasion in his dealings with colonial governments to establish some measure of standardisation.[48] And in fairness to colonial governments, many of them accepted that there was need for modernisation and change, particularly in view of the worsening situations in Palestine, Malaya and the Gold Coast in 1948. Lord Winster, Governor of Cyprus at that time, remarked: 'It is difficult for colonies, especially those not grouped regionally to maintain contact with and obtain information on any tactics or techniques from other colonies. It occurs to me that experience gained in Palestine,

Gold Coast and Malaya could most usefully be organised and the results together with any reports circulated to all Colonial Police Forces . . .'.[49] Similar views were aired in other territories. Training was perceived as a key area as colonial policemen could be taught to apply similar policies and procedures. With this in mind, the Colonial Office recommended an increase in the numbers of colonial police undergoing training at the Police College at Ryton. This would be partially enabled through an allocation of £1.5 million under the Colonial Development and Welfare Act of 1945,[50] though in reality additional training was not taken up by many colonial police forces. By 1950, most forces were below their established strength, and because often faced with an escalation of events, were unable to spare officers for training.

Commissioners of police conferences

The Colonial Office persisted in its attempts to standardise the policies of the colonial police. A measure introduced shortly after Johnson's report was the Conference for the Colonial Commissioners of Police. The first conference was held in March 1951 with delegates from Aden, the Bahamas, Cyprus, the Gold Coast, the Gambia, Hong Kong, Jamaica, Kenya, Malaya, Mauritius, North Borneo, Sarawak, Sierra Leone, the Somaliland Protectorate, Tanganyika, Trinidad and the Sudan.[51] The Colonial Office announced that the main objective of the conference was to 'discuss the functions and responsibilities of police forces in the colonies in relation to normal police work, 'cold war' conditions, and in the event of a major war.' The onset of the cold war had increased both the importance and the responsibilities of colonial police forces. They were faced 'not only with the menace of ordinary crime – including inter-tribal feuds in certain areas – but with the task of extirpating or at least keeping under supervision and control the internal canker of Communist-inspired subversion and treachery'.[52]

The conference was addressed by General Brownjohn, Vice Chief of the Imperial General Staff, Percy Sillitoe, Director of the Security Service, MI5, and his subordinate Dick White, who looked at anti-communist propaganda and police organisation, and Johnson. Advice on police matters – on the influence of the RIC on the Colonial Police Service and the need for Home Guard forces – was also provided by senior ranking members of the Colonial Office.[53] Delegates were provided with Henry Gurney's 'Despatch 5' and the Colonial Office's 'Lessons of Malaya' pamphlet dated July 1950. Colonel Gray discussed Malaya and the lessons that could be learnt from 'that situation'. There seems to have been a consensus that, although events arising in Malaya were 'abnormal', they could occur elsewhere.[54]

Neil Hadow, who, as Commissioner of the Gambia Police, was present at the first conference, felt that its real purpose was to build up a 'team spirit' among the commissioners during a period of uncertainty and conflict. Groundwork was being laid to ensure a common imperial police response to insurgency.[55] Individual commissioners were asked to give papers in an attempt to find areas of common ground between the forces and to allow for some 'measuring up of one another'. Matters discussed included recruitment, promotion and the transfer of members of the colonial police, as well as sensitive issues surrounding colonial security and defence. Despite Johnson's earlier recommendations and the aspirations of some senior members of the Colonial Office, the conference concluded that colonial police had to be trained and organised in a *military* fashion rather than in the manner of a *civilian* police service.[56] Recommended reforms included the 'downsizing' of the traditionally Europe-based officer corps and the bringing up through the ranks of locally recruited policemen. Attention also focused on the key issues of police accountability and independence.

Colonial police accountability

A fundamental difference between colonial and British policing lay in the structure of accountability. As one official at the Home Office commented: 'Under the British police system day-to-day administration and day-to-day operational work is a matter for the force itself and the Chief Constable: it is not a matter for a Minister or for an elected body . . . Such traditions do not exist to the same extent in Colonial police forces, which have been in the past, to a large degree, agents of the Government and subject to governmental interference in the enforcement of the law.'[57] The desire to create a British-style Civil Police force pointed to the need for a lessening of control by government.

Brigadier Piers Dunn, previously Commandant of the Police College at Ryton, wrote in 1952 that the British police system was the best in the world and should be transplanted throughout the Empire. '[We] are therefore seeking in the colonies a means to turn a semi-armed State police into a locally controlled, non-State, unarmed police.'[58] Dunn concluded: 'it is essential that police forces should not be administered by, or under the control of, any department of the Central Government. The relationship between the Government in power and the police – a constitutional issue – is a fundamental one if any freedom within the law is to survive in the democracies.' Working parties were established throughout the 1950s to look at ways of decentralising the chain of command and addressing this fundamental question of accountability.

There was no simple remedy. Colonial police forces were caught in a cleft stick. One of their principal duties was the internal defence of the colony, and this required a tight link between the colonial government and the police commissioner. And yet by 1956 the Home Office had entered the fray and was challenging the Colonial Office regarding the very nature of the colonial police and its accountability to government. This brought the dual role of the police into question. The Home Office maintained that, 'the important point is that without an independent and impartial police force which is respected by the community and which can rely on the citizens for information and help no democratic system can work efficiently. *The police ought not to be used as soldiers or soldiers as police.'*[59]

It was at this time that Home Secretary Gwilym Lloyd-George wrote to the Colonial Secretary, Alan Lennox-Boyd, specifically outlining his office's desire to see British-style policing in place following independence in Cyprus. He raised concerns that touched on this question of accountability. Lloyd-George explained that 'a law enforcement agency which is efficient and impartial is so fundamental to the existence of a free and democratic society that I ought to raise the question with you'.[60] The future of policing within the colonies would, he claimed, benefit from the experience of the Home Office:

> I would not contend that the police system in this country is by any means perfect. It works as well as it does . . . [due] in some measure to our special circumstances and the lessons of the virtue of compromise and tolerance which we have learned over the centuries. Under our law, the police are not subject to political interference in the enforcement of the law . . . [The police] have no monopoly of law enforcement . . . [T]his is partly because of the balance of powers in our system and partly because the climate of public opinion is such that it would be easy to mobilise it against any attempted misuse of those powers.

He concluded that 'we should put something in the Constitution which would safeguard the police from direct interference by Ministers in the enforcement of the law. I notice that it has been envisaged in the Federation of Malaya.'

Lennox-Boyd responded with gratitude for the 'heroic efforts' of the Home Office to assist the Colonial Office in matters of police policy. He added:

> Like you, we consider that a police and security system which serves the law and not any political party is the object. In particular, we have sought to insulate the administration and the police from political influence by promulgating the idea of putting them under the management of independent statutory Police Service Commissions, composed of persons outside politics, and having a quasi-judicial type of status. The idea has

[67]

on the whole been welcomed by the Colonial politicians to whom it has been put, whose natural relish for the idea of having a police force under their direct control is tempered by the consciousness that it might at times be under the direct control of their political opponents![61]

Yet implicit in Lennox-Boyd's remarks was the idea that such reforms were sometimes difficult to implement in the conditions prevailing in certain colonies.

A British use of force

The question of the use of force in dealing with civil disturbances was important in that it reflected the nature of Colonial Office thinking during this period, particularly over the question of a civil versus a military-style organisation. The response of the colonies was typical – an acceptance, in theory, of the importance of reform through standardisation, but in practice doing little to change police procedures.

In 1948, as plans were under way to appoint a police advisor to the colonies, Creech-Jones sent a circular letter to each colonial government, discussing potential methods of dealing with civil disturbances. He explained that from the Colonial Office's perspective the police should employ only minimal force and that firearms should be resorted to only in extreme circumstances. Creech-Jones recommended greater use of tear-smoke and noted that while many police forces possessed tear-smoke equipment, a lack of training courses had precluded its widespread use.[62]

This provoked a flurry of responses from the colonies. Several governors pointed out that armed force was, in theory, 'employed only as a preventative measure and never as a punitive measure'.[63] However, Colonial Office *theory* was not commensurate with prevailing police *practice* . John Fforde, Commissioner of the Northern Rhodesia Police (NRP), pointed out that armed force had been more readily used in practice, for example during the civil disturbances on the Copperbelt in 1935 and 1940. He suggested that the importance attached to the training of both European and African police in dealing with civil disturbances left them well equipped to make the necessary judgements on the ground.[64] The Governor of Trinidad, Sir John Shaw, who was shortly to join MI5 as the head of its colonial branch, took this one step further and endorsed the view that the use of force must 'always be left to the unfettered judgement of the man on the spot'. Furthermore, 'at the ultimate court of inquiry it is easy to say that the decision was taken too soon, or it may be too late . . . There is certain to be political misrepresentation and the exploitation of extreme political views afterwards . . . however volatile crowds can quickly become criminally dangerous.'[65]

Overall, many senior colonial policemen were doubtful of the efficacy of tear smoke in controlling civil disturbances. Fforde commented
that its use had not been properly assessed and that 'it would be unwise
to gamble upon [its] efficacy as a deterrent to violence'. He added that
the African environment, with its 'open spaces and warm still air', did
not lend itself to the use of tear-smoke.[66] Comments of a similar nature
were made by many other police forces.[67]

The following year, Creech-Jones, in response to Johnson's earlier
reports on the colonial police, appeared to have changed course, no doubt
in taking into account the flare up of serious public disorder in many
colonies. Despite Johnson's earlier criticisms that the colonial police
were more closely related to a military organisation than to a civilian
police force, Creech-Jones found that they were 'capable of rendering
loyal and efficient service as a gendarmerie . . . shown by the fact that in
recent years (e.g. Trinidad, 1949, Nigeria and Gold Coast, 1949 and 1950),
they have been able to deal frankly with fairly considerable civil disturbances without the necessity of calling in the military'. He conceded that
if the police could act on 'modern lines with the first task as in this
country', their second task could be 'to train and act in their traditional
role as a gendarmerie'.[68] Once again this pointed to a dichotomy in the
thinking of the Colonial Office at that time: the Colonial Police Service
was expected to modernise on British lines and embrace the concept of
civil policing; on the other hand its officers would still be expected to
operate in a military capacity as a colony's first line of defence.

Yet the use of force did increase during this period as public order situations worsened. 'There were minor disturbances in most of the big
towns yesterday', wrote the Deputy Commissioner of the Cyprus
Police to the Commissioner in 1955, 'and Police and Military between
then coped effectively. In Larnaca, demonstrations were very quickly
dispersed by baton parties and I am glad to report that a few heads were
broken . . . In Nicosia the Mobile Reserve, which has been champing at
the bit for some times, was allowed to put one platoon into actions and
they performed their function very well indeed. One bomb was thrown,
but a Turkish Constable removed the fuse before the bomb could
explode.'[69] Indeed the Cyprus Police alongside other colonial police
forces tested newer methods of riot control ranging from tear-smoke
and sickening gases to riot batons, shields and rubber bullets.

In Cyprus, for example, proposals were made for the use of a 'dye
sprayer'. What was required was 'a mobile and easily manoeuvrable
sprayer that will have an effective range equal to or preferable greater
than that of stones or other missiles coming from the mob'. This dye-
sprayer had a range of up to 50 yards with a jet duration of 3 minutes.[70]
Riot shields, of varying weights and sizes, were extensively tested in

[69]

Cyprus during this period. Cane shields were found to be unsuitable; expanded metal shields of close mesh developed by the army were also discounted owing to their weight. It was decided to adopt the light metal shield, weighing approximately four pounds. This shield was initially used by the Mobile Reserve and then used within all riot units. The advantage of this particular shield was

> that instead of having to pass one's arm through a loop, there is just a leather covered and padded metal hook which goes over the forearm near the elbow and the shield can therefore be picked up or discarded very rapidly. Moreover, there is no danger of a Constable's arm becoming immobilized in the event of the shield being seized.

Devised by Fairburn, the colonial police 'expert' on riot drill and practice, use of this type of shield was adopted by many colonies throughout this period.[71]

As late as 1968, Eric St Johnston, Inspector of Constabularies, on a visit to Northern Ireland noted that the RUC riot squad was similarly equipped. Each officer, he wrote, 'was equipped with a long baton and a light aluminium shield which has a lattice top through which the holder can look. The arm grip of the shield was of a safety type so that, if twisted, would come away and not break the officer's arm.' He urged the Home Office to consider use of 'colonial style' riot equipment within the home forces.[72]

The replacement of European officers

Consideration of the use of force throughout the colonies was but one example of the problems faced by the Colonial Office during this period when it came to standardising colonial police procedures and policies. Another issue raised concerned the replacement of Europeans by local officers, an inevitable consequence of the moves towards self-government. This posed yet more quandaries. Nigeria was one of the better examples of early attempts to *Africanise* its force. W. R. Shirley noted in 1947 that there were ten Nigerian assistant superintendents.[73] The first Nigerian had been promoted to that rank in 1941; and by 1949 a further thirteen were promoted.[74] From 1948, Nigerians were increasingly sent to Britain on gazetted officer training courses or to specialist attachments in Britain to enhance their prospects for promotion. Philip Milton, George Willis and Colin Limb, who served in the Nigeria Police during this period, noted the presence in their early training of 'a Nigerian 3 pip officer, George Amman'.[75] Indeed by 1955, a Nigerian, A. Agbabiaka, held the rank of Senior Superintendent. By 1964, police strength stood at 16,815, including 534 gazetted officers, of whom only

94 were European, 44 of them on short-term contracts; the remaining 50 career officers retired shortly afterwards.[76]

Within other African territories, localisation followed a similar, if slower, pattern. For example, the recruitment of Africans had been suggested by Arthur Young in 1951 in his report on the Gold Coast Police. Direct entry would require simply the necessary academic qualifications.[77] John Coles, who served in the Gold Coast Police, stated that Africanisation occurred by independence in 1957 as a result of ten years' planning. He noted that in 1948 there were 2 African gazetted officers and 120 Europeans, but that by 1960 the proportions were almost the reverse.[78] In Uganda, by 1951, of 139 gazetted officers, 69 were African and 14 were Asian sub-inspectors. Promotion of Africans and Asians continued within the police despite the Commissioner of Police being informed by the Colonial Office in 1957 that independence was fifteen years away.[79] Expatriate recruiting to general posts in the Uganda Police ended early in 1959. By mid-1960 most districts and many of the police stations were run by African officers. So at the end of 1960, 14 Africans and 8 Asians had been appointed to gazetted ranks, with a further 23 Africans and 11 Asians acting in the gazetted ranks for a period of 12 months on a trial basis. [80] In Nyasaland, Africanisation was very slow. Dr Banda encouraged European policemen to stay on after independence, which slowed down the numbers of Africans put forward for promotion. A number of Europeans stayed in the Malawi Police until the early 1970s.[81] This was a common feature within African colonies. A dearth of middle-ranking African officers led to European officers being asked to stay on. The lack of earlier forward planning by the Colonial Office had meant the policy of localisation came too late, resulting in a shortage of local officers in many territories. The Colonial Office had, however, outlined the means by which indigenous policemen could join the gazetted ranks. The most relevant was through an extension of training facilities, which the Colonial Office had been keen to promote at Hendon and at Mill Reece. Additionally it was proposed that 'promising' sergeants and inspectors be seconded to the home force for 1–2 years to learn British styles of policing. The training of instructors, to be sent out to the colonies, was also suggested.[82] Between 1951 and 1952, 196 officers visited the UK for training, of whom 26 came from the colonies.[83]

At the East African governors' conference in 1961, discussion took place regarding the steady increases in the number of Africans appointed to gazetted ranks in Uganda and Tanganyika. (Four Africans in the Tanganyika Police had reached the rank of superintendent by this stage.) This had not been the case in Kenya or Zanzibar and was a source of concern.[84] In Northern Rhodesia, localisation also came at a later stage, from 1958 onwards, caused by the creation of the Central African Federation, which had delayed the process. Indeed by 1963 there were only a handful of African Assistant Superintendents in charge of local police stations. This led to 'crash courses' in administration, law and police duties, and the rapid promotion of senior African officers.[85] A few of the smaller police forces encountered difficulties with Africanisation owing to a lack of suitable recruits. The Eritrea Police Force, on becoming an autonomous part of Ethiopia in September 1952, retained a British Commissioner, 4 British Superintendents and 12 of the former Italian staff for this reason. A similar situation occurred in British Somaliland with difficulties in recruiting even at the inspector level.[86]

Outside British colonial Africa, the policy of recruiting local officers directly into the officer ranks had been discussed prior to the Second World War. In Malaya, for example, by 1945, members of the Chinese population were being recruited directly into the officer ranks of the CID to deal with rising crime linked to the triads. This practice was promoted still further in the wake of the emergency with the need to control the Chinese squatter population.[87] Following General Sir Gerald Templer's arrival in Malaya in 1952, attempts were made to increase the 800 Chinese in the uniformed branch by 2,000. This included a number of officers and was part of the overall 'hearts and minds policy'.[88]

Loaning English policemen: Arthur Young at the Gold Coast, Malaya and Kenya

Preparing colonies for independence required localisation of the gazetted ranks coupled with the necessary police reforms. Other means by which the Colonial Office sought to export Britishness was through the loan of senior officers to head up colonial police forces on short-term contracts. Colonel Arthur Young was the first high-profile officer after 1945 to leave his City of London post on a short-term assignment overseas as Commissioner of Police. He was posted initially to the Gold Coast in 1951 and then moved on the following year to Malaya. Following that posting, in March 1954 he was sent to Kenya, where he resigned only nine months later following serious disagreements with the administration. Despite the furore over his time in Kenya, he established a precedent which was followed by the loan of Eric St Johnston, Chief Constable of the Lancashire Police in the 1960s.

These were by no means the first British officers to be dispatched to the colonies. Individual officers had been *loaned* on a discrete basis by the Metropolitan Police to colonial police forces on and off since the latter's establishment. In 1945 there were about thirty, mostly in West

Africa, 'all more or less on long term loans'.[89] In the mid-1940s, a Scotland Yard Superintendent was sent to report on the perceived weaknesses of the Jamaica and Barbados forces, and in the 1950s other officers took up training duties in Malaya and Kenya.[90] Young ended his overseas career with a posting to the RUC in 1970, from which he departed rather hastily, Kenya-style, barely a year later.

His earlier colonial missions were rather more successful. His first brief, in September 1951, was to report on the Gold Coast Police in the wake of the 1948 disturbances and the findings of the Watson Commission. He was accompanied by Chief Superintendent Wilson on loan from the Metropolitan Police. Young later noted that the Gold Coast was undoubtedly tipped to be 'the first of our colonial possessions to achieve self-rule'.[91] As such, efforts were to be made to dampen down the 'militaristic' nature of the police 'as it was evident that, in the hands of an African Government, it could too easily become a political weapon'. Besides, Young professed to be unused to 'the whole character of the use of force in crowd control'. He believed then, and indeed throughout his overseas sojourns, in 'more persuasive methods rather than physical ones to control the crowds . . . instead of whacking people over the head with your riot sticks it would be much better, and I think, more effective if you exercised tact and tolerance'. The extent to which this message was delivered was reflected in the parting gift he received from the Gold Coast Police, which consisted of two riot sticks, one labelled 'Tact' and the other 'Forbearance'.

Young's two-month tour of the Gold Coast culminated in a hefty report prepared for the Commissioner, Matthew Collens, and the Colonial Office. The most important points raised were largely comparable with the earlier comments made by Johnson on his previous tour. Young recommended, for example, the unification of the regular and the escort police, provisions for a police council to oversee the force's general workings and an overhaul of police administration to fall in line with the local administration it served.[92] More crucially, however, he noted the police lacked adequate intelligence, with a staff of only ten European Special Branch officers. This issue was to be repeatedly raised over subsequent years.

Young's life-long quest lay in securing equality of opportunity for *all* police officers, and he took an interest in the process of localisation. In 1949, following Johnson's visit, it had been recommended that recruitment should allow for the direct entry into the gazetted ranks of two-thirds Africans and one-third European. A lack of training facilities at senior level had prevented the implementation of that scheme by the time of Young's visit. Despite his general view that the police should be adequately prepared for independence with an upper tier of African rather than European officers, he concluded that direct entry should be applicable only to those Africans of 'exceptional' standard. However, officers joining the lower ranks should be 'provided with suitable training to encourage their promotion'. The key lay in promoting adequate training both locally and in Britain.[93] Young's policing philosophy stayed with him throughout his career, being put to the test the following year in Malaya.

As Commissioner of the Malayan Police, taking over from Nicol Gray who had been pushed out by the new High Commissioner, General Templer, his brief was to assist in the 'reorganisation' of the police, ostensibly with a heavy dose of *Britishness*. Young became involved in a public relations exercise to raise the profile of Templer's notion of 'winning the hearts and minds' of the Malayan public. This could be perceived as a public apology, an olive branch for the coercive measures used since the outset of the emergency. Young devised his partially successful 'Operation Service', which set out to instil a sense of service and courtesy to the community as practised in Britain. Crucially, Operation Service hoped to put across the message that 'as Government servants, we are the *Servants* of the public, not its masters [who must] 'always be kind, civil and understanding . . . the people who come to you to ask you to solve their problems need all the help and friendliness that you can give to them'.[94] Launched in December 1952, the principal objective was to improve relations between the Malay policemen and the general population. The Malayan policemen possibly entered into the spirit of Operation Service so willingly because of the view that their promotion prospects were directly linked to their performance.[95] Former Malayan Police Officer Jim Godsave commented that many Malayan policemen went 'overboard' in their attempts to befriend the local population. 'They would run after women in the streets who had dropped their hat and pick it up for them. Normal police work sometimes went out of the window.'[96]

Not long after his return from Malaya, there was a further need for Young's services. In March 1954, he was loaned to the Kenya Police. Once again, Young was faced with the prospect of reforming a police force faced with an ongoing emergency. During his nine months as Commissioner, Young was confronted with colonial concepts of policing emergencies which went against his own policing philosophy. He firmly believed in the doctrine of a police force operating independently of the executive and responsible directly to the law. The principle of serving the community rather than operating as a police force had been reflected in Young's 'hearts and minds' approach during his brief leadership of the Malayan Police. In Kenya his views met with considerable opposition, leading to his early resignation.

The real reason for Young's mission had been to oversee police reforms, emerging from the 1953 Kenya Police Commission and highlighted in a 1954 White Paper. While contemplating the means by which he could undertake these reforms, Young perceived a 'lack of a positive and decisive Government policy in police affairs', coupled with complete 'failure' to make good use of his services. His stay was blighted with 'anxiety at the continuance of [the] rule of fear rather than of impartial justice', which he felt would not change in the foreseeable future.[97] In private conversation with the Colonial Secretary in 1959, Young commented that 'of all the colonies that I know the Administration [in Kenya] has more power than anywhere else, and I think this wrong'.[98]

Young took up matters that had been raised in the Kenya Police Commission of 1953, drawing attention to the difference between the status of the police in Kenya and in Britain. Certainly the most controversial issue raised was that of 'a constable in common law' as practised in Britain. The home police service was not directly accountable to the Government and could, he felt, be described as an impartial organisation, exercising in its own right the function of preserving the peace and upholding the law. The report recommended that all members of the Kenya Police be given the 'status of constables either by common law or by virtue of any law in force in the colony'.[99] The Commissioner, Michael O'Rorke, opposed the notion of the police being accountable to the public on the grounds that it was too sophisticated for Kenya's political culture and unfeasible within the current climate. The police had, after all, 'unpleasant and unwelcome duties to perform, and are a branch of the security forces using armed strength'. In these circumstances, the necessary ingredients for giving the policeman the status of constable in common law did not exist.[100]

Both O'Rorke and the Kenya Government, which comprised a high proportion of settlers, felt that this status should be given only to those police with the rank of inspector and higher. (At this time there were singularly few Africans and Asians at this level.) Besides they believed that police officers were in the main drawn from a background which 'enabled them to be completely impartial'. This was not the view held by Young which he took up with O'Rorke and the Kenya Government. His main contention concerned the administration's perceived hold over the force, preventing impartial policing. The 1949 Kolloa affair had clearly illustrated to Young how the administration could interfere with policing and cause political problems as a result. At Kolloa, during an outbreak of civil unrest, the District Commissioner countermanded an Assistant Superintendent's order to fire, and two policemen were killed as a result.

Moreover, Young would appear to have been disliked by the majority of the European members of the Kenya force. Press reports at that time described how members of the colonial administration and the police were opposed to the proposals for 'constable status'. They considered that that the majority of Africans would regard constable status as meaning that the police were a law unto themselves.[101] By giving every African policeman constable status, their accountability to their officers would have changed, and they would have been entitled to apply law and order on a more personal basis rather than simply obeying a lawful (or possibly unlawful) command.

There were more sinister issues at stake of alleged police brutality to Mau Mau suspects. Young perceived that malpractice by members of the Kenya Police Reserve, the African Kikuyu Home Guard and Native Authority Police (NAP) had not received a full government enquiry. Justice had not been carried out, and as a result a 'rule of fear' or 'counter-terror' prevailed.[102] This was firmly rebuked by the Government which eventually disclosed that some cases of malpractice 'and even murder' were under police investigation against a 'background of Mau Mau terror and butchery'. In a letter dated 20 October 1955 to the Colonial Secretary, Governor Evelyn Baring noted that police discipline and relations between the administration and the CID had improved and that this would do much to iron out incidents of brutality.[103]

The struggle that ensued over this issue was linked to the crucial matter of police independence. The 1954 Report had suggested that the police have complete independence from government. The Government rejected this on the grounds that, particularly during an emergency situation, the administrative hierarchy had to retain the powers to control the police. Baring and a majority of his ministers were particularly insistent that the Kikuyu chiefs and headmens' authority would be weakened if the police acted without the approval of the administrative officers.[104] Baring considered that a weak police force allowed for a strong administration.[105] He clearly felt that the government would be hampered by a police force that was less accountable to the administration.

Young persisted in his attempts to establish a greater degree of independence within the Kenya Police. The matter caused political outcry both within the Kenya Government and at Westminster. Barbara Castle, in a written parliamentary question to Lennox-Boyd, challenged a Kenya Government White Paper on policing and took up Young's case. This White Paper had stated that administrative officers were entitled to give 'general directions concerning the preservation of peace and good order and that in all such matters the police force is subordinate to Government'.[106] The Colonial Secretary replied that while there had been 'no general right given to administrative officers to interfere in the work of the police', it had been accepted policy that that African tribal areas be administered, and thus policed, by the district administration and its tribal police.[107]

In the event, these issues led to Young's acrimonious resignation from the force. The episode raised further issues. In theory, the Kenya Police was part of a chain of command that stemmed down from the Governor. In practice, police departments like the Special Branch and its various units had operated independently and unsupervised, with sometimes reprehensible outcomes. Sir Richard Catling, who became Commissioner, commented later that while the force may have been subordinate to the Governor, he was opposed to 'detachments of the police being at the whim of provincial administrative officers . . . and that such general directions as the Governor might have reason to give the Police to public order I required to be given to me as Commissioner who would transmit them down to the police chain of command'.[108]

The Colonial Office engaged in lengthy correspondence, over several years, in an attempt to resolve the question of police independence. It was agreed that it would not be possible to apply the 'constable at law' policy in Kenya but that 'this [was] not the only road by which the goal of police independence can be approached. The crucial issue to be addressed was the question of police accountability to government, an issue that the White Paper had shown to lie with the Provincial and District Commissioners who represented the Governor within their area.'[109] While an emergency was ongoing in Kenya, it was accepted that 'administrative officers as the representatives of the government should have the right to give general directions to the police'. Once the emergency was over, however, it was considered that a different course should be taken. The example of Nigeria was given: there 'the rule of law and liberty of the subject can be safeguarded only by ensuring the complete operational independence of the police'. Thus, the Colonial Office conceded that the British doctrine of police independence should be the future goal of every colony prior to attaining self-government. This could occur only 'if in practice relations of mutual confidence exist between the services (i.e. the Police and the Administration)'.[110] They conceded that 'what is meant by the independence of the police in the colonial, and in particular the African, context' was very different from British doctrine.[111] It was even suggested that the status of the RUC be studied to shed greater light on this question of police independence, as clearly that force did not operate along British lines.[112] In the event, the Colonial Office made recommendations to introduce into the Kenyan legal framework the use of the term 'constable in common law', though the issue remained a subject of discussion up until independence. The desire to leave a legacy of Britishness in place underpinned Colonial Office policy throughout the era of decolonisation. In certain territories, notably the British Caribbean, attempts at reforming the police along English lines had been taking place since the 1930s.

Notes

1 John Darwin, 'British Decolonisation since 1945: A Pattern of a Puzzle?', *Journal of Imperial and Commonwealth History*, 12 (1984), pp. 186–190.
2 Philip Murphy, *Alan Lennox-Boyd: A Biography* (London: I. B. Tauris, 1999), pp. 102–105.
3 Colin Imray, *Policeman in Africa* (Lewes: Book Guild, 1997), pp. 124–126.
4 See Appendix 1 for a breakdown of the authorised regular colonial police establishment in 1948.
5 The term 'gazetted officer' was borrowed from India and stemmed from promotions and appointments to the higher ranks, which were published in the *London Gazette*. (This was also true of senior-ranking army officers.) Similar appointments in the lower ranks were announced by force order. For the Indian Police, these details were also published in the government *Gazette* of the province in which policemen served. In the main gazetted officers were expatriates, the rank and file and subordinate officers being recruited locally. There were exceptions to this rule: in Palestine, there was a large contingent of European constables and Hong Kong recruited European inspectors, a non-gazetted rank. Officially gazetting was 'confined to appointments made by, or by direction of, the King': T. E. Lloyd, CO, Minute, 14 June 1935, 'Gazetting and Press Arrangements for Colonial Service', National Archive (NA) CO 850/56/2.
6 The figures for Malaya reflected the expansion in the police force as a result of the emergency, 1948–60. In all colonies faced with emergency situations the police were strengthened.
7 The number of police per head of population varied from one territory to another. For example, in Uganda there was one police officer per 3,500 head of population; in Tanganyika, one per 2,000, in Kenya, one per 1,800. Colonies with large settler populations, as in the case of Kenya and Northern Rhodesia, had proportionately more policemen; in Southern Rhodesia there was one police officer per 769 head of population. See W. C. Johnson, Police Advisor to the Secretary of State for the Colonies, 'Report on the Colonial Police Service', 28 Dec. 1948, NA CO 537/5440/5.
8 Ben Pimlott, *The Queen: A Biography of Elizabeth II* (London: Harper Collins, 1997), p. 254.
9 Reiner, *Politics of the Police*, p. 74.
10 Colonial Office Notes, 'Likelihood of Disturbances in West and East Africa and Cyprus: and the Capacity of the Security Forces to Deal with Them', 1949, NA CO 537/4384.
11 Creech-Jones, 'Recent Developments in Colonial Police Forces (to December 1949)', CO ref. 14882/37/50, NA CO 537/5439.
12 'The Colonial Police Service, Special Regulations by the Secretary of State for the Colonies', NA CO 850/40/7; 'Colonial Prison Service Unification, 1936', CO 850/46/7.
13 Minute (unsigned), 'Question of Appointment of Inspector-General Police', NA CO 850/54/20.
14 Aside from the Palestine Police, European constables were phased out of the Colonial Police Service by the Second World War; thereafter, expatriates joined either as sub-inspectors or as gazetted officers.

15 A. B. Acheson, Minute, 13 March 1934, 'Unification of Colonial Police Service, 1934–36', NA CO 850/40/7.
16 Furse, Minute, 24 April 1934, 'Unification of Colonial Police Service, 1934–36', NA CO 850/40/7.
17 'Superscale Posts', NA CO 850/40/7.
18 W. A. Muller, Inspector-General Colonial Police, Minute, 25 Oct. 1952, NA CO 1017/34.
19 Muller, Minute, 25 Oct. 1952, NA CO 1017/34.
20 Q. R. Lomey to Blaxter, Minute, 16 Dec. 1952 and 9 March 1953, NA CO 1017/34.
21 Spicer to Major A. C. C. Parkinson, CO, Private and Confidential Correspondence, 24 Dec. 1932, NA CO 850/32/2.
22 Spicer, Minute, 24 Dec. 1932; Jeffries & S. J., Minute, 12 Jan. 1933, 'Colonial Police Service Unification', NA CO 850/32/2.
23 Furse, Minute, 15 Feb. 1933, NA CO 850/32/2.
24 Fiddler, Minute, 13 Aug. 1935, NA CO 850/54/20.
25 Dowbiggin, 'Inspection of Cyprus Military Police, 1926', NA CO 67/218/3/59.
26 A. Fiddian, CO Minutes, 18 Aug. 1926, NA CO 67/218/3.
27 Popham Lobb to Gov. Cyprus, despatch, 25 March 1927, NA CO 67/218/3.
28 A. B. Acheson, Minute, 9 Aug. 1933, 'Unification of Colonial Police Service, 1934–36', NA CO 850/40/7.
29 For example a Colonial Office salary of £500 plus a £50 per month inspection fee with expenses: 'Question of Appointment of Inspector-General Police', NA CO 850/54/20.
30 Minute (unsigned), 1934, 'Question of Appointment of Inspector-General Police', NA CO 850/54/20.
31 J. L.W. Flood, Minute, 14 May 1934, NA CO 850/54/20.
32 Minutes, 1934, signed Fiddian, Furse, Parkinson, Jeffries, Acheson, 'Question of Appointment of Inspector-General Police', NA CO 850/54/20.
33 Dowbiggin, 'Police Forces Visited 1935', Vol. 1, RHL MSS Ind. Oc. s. 288.
34 Dowbiggin, 'Sir Herbert L. Dowbiggin Tour 1937', RHL MSS Ind. Oc. s. 288.
35 W. C. Johnson, Police Advisor to the Secretary of State for the Colonies, 'Report on the Colonial Police Service', 28 Dec. 1949, NA CO 537/5440.
36 'Terms of Reference for the Police Advisor to the Secretary of State', 1948, NA CO 537/2770.
37 Taken from an interview with Ted Eates (Nigeria Police, Sierra Leone Police, Gambia Police, Royal Hong Kong Police, Com., rtd, 1946–69), July 2001.
38 Taken from an interview with Neil Hadow (Ceylon Police, Gambia Police, Mauritius Police, Uganda Police, Com., rtd, 1935–58), Jan. 2002.
39 In 1949, Johnson visited Cyprus, the Gambia, Sierra Leone, the Gold Coast, Nigeria, Hong Kong, Singapore, Malaya, north Borneo, Brunei and Sarawak.
40 Johnson, Police Advisor to the Secretary of State for the Colonies, 'Report on the Colonial Police Service', 28 Dec. 1948, NA CO 537/5440/5.
41 Johnson, Police Advisor to the Secretary of State for the Colonies, 'Report on the Colonial Police Service', 28 Dec. 1948, NA CO 537/5440/5.
42 Eates (interview), June 2001.
43 John Coles, aide memoir, RHL MSS Afr. s. 1784 Box I, f. 1.
44 Coles, RHL MSS Afr. s. 1784 Box I, f.1.
45 Clayton, Thin Blue Line, p. 20.
46 Eates (interview), July 2001.
47 Circular Despatch Distribution to Colonial Governments, D 61241–1,000 D/d 454 5/46, 12 May 1949, NA CO 537/6932/22.
48 Cabinet Minutes, 19 Dec. 1949, NA CO 537/5439.
49 Winster to Creech-Jones, Savingram no. 54, 16 Aug. 1948, NA CO 537/2712/17.
50 Colonial Office circular telegram to the colonies, 9 Jan. 1949, NA CO 537/5439/10.
51 'Members of the Conference of Police Commissioners, 1951', NA CO 537/6942.
52 Note to G. E. Curtis, CO, re. conference, ref. 14882/p/8, NA CO 537/6939.
53 'Opening Address by the Colonial Secretary', Draft, 19 March 1951, NA CO 537/6941.

54 'Record of the Conference of Colonial Commissioners of Police', 4 September 1951, NA CO 537/6941.
55 Hadow (interview), Jan. 2002.
56 'Report of the 1st Conference Colonial Commissioners', 1951, p. 7, NA CO 885/119.
57 Home Office (HO) Minute, signed I. A. N., 19 April 1956, NA HO 287/250.
58 P. W. D. Dunn, 'The Role of the Police in a Democratic State', *Journal of African Administration*, 4 (1952), p. 50.
59 HO Minute, signed I.A.N., 19 April 1956, NA HO 287/250.
60 Lloyd-George to Lennox-Boyd, 3 May 1956, NA HO 287/250.
61 Lennox-Boyd to Lloyd-George, 30 May 1956, NA HO 287/250.
62 Creech-Jones, 'Methods of Dealing with Civil Disturbances', secret circular despatch, 24 June, 1948, NA CO 537/2712/1.
63 Governor Nyasaland to Creech-Jones, Savingram, 3 Aug. 1948, ref. MIL. 17/5.11, NA CO 537/2712/5.
64 Fforde to N. Rhodesian Government, letter dated 16 July 1948, NA CO 537/2712/13a.
65 J. V. Shaw to Creech-Jones, Savingram, ref. D1051, 31 July 1948, NA CO 537/2712/6.
66 Fforde to N. Rhodesian Government, 16 July 1948, NA CO 537/2712/13a.
67 Examples included Uganda, where the conditions were not suitable for the use of tear-smoke, and Aden, 'as there is so often a high wind which disperses the smoke too rapidly': NA CO 537/2712/17–19.
68 Creech-Jones, 'Recent Developments in Colonial Police Forces (to December 1949)', CO Ref. 14882/37/50, NA CO 537/5439.
69 Biles to Robins, 24 Nov. 1955, John Biles, Family Papers.
70 'Notes on Dye Sprayer', Cyprus Police, 1955, John Biles, Family Papers.
71 The Royal Hong Kong Police used shields made of rattan, which was an easily available material but made the shields lighter than those manufactured from metal and more resilient material: Ivor Stourton, Deputy Inspector of Colonial Police, CO, to John Biles, Deputy Commissioner, Cyprus Police, 16 Feb. 1956, John Biles, Family Papers.
72 For example, use of the new CS grenade (T. 792) had been discussed following its testing in Singapore on 14 May 1960 in comparison with tear gas (CN). Testing at Lagos had also occurred on 28 May and was discussed: NA CO 1037/192.
73 W. R. Shirley, *A History of the Nigeria Police* (Lagos: Government Printer, 1948), p. 36. Nigeria was one of the first colonial police forces to promote women officers to gazetted rank, starting in 1961 (women had been introduced into the Nigeria Police in 1955): see Ann Turnbull, RHL MSS Afr. s. 1784, Box VII. Tanganyika introduced the first woman gazetted officer in 1957: Clayton, *Thin Blue Line*, p. 212.
74 James A MacDonald, RHL MSS Afr. s.1784, Box VII, f. 12.
75 Taken from interviews with: Philip Milton (Nigeria Police, ASP, rtd, 1955–66), July 2000; Colin Limb (Nigeria Police, Nyasaland Police, ACS, rtd, 1950–71), Aug. 2000; George Willis (Nigeria Police, Chief Sup., rtd, 1954–66), Sept. 2000.
76 John E. Hodge, RHL MSS Afr. s. 1784, Box VII.
77 Young, 'Report on the Gold Coast Police', 1951, NA CO 537/6960.
78 Coles, RHL MSS Afr. s. 1784, Box I, ff. 1–2.
79 Hadow (interview), Jan. 2002.
80 Acting Governor Uganda to Colonial Secretary, Telegram, 24. Dec. 1960, NA CO 822/2690.
81 Limb (interview), Aug. 2000.
82 R.R.C., HO to Pittam, CO, 22 July 1956, NA HO 287/250.
83 'Visits by Foreign Police Officers' (1952–52), HO 287/ 122. 'Non-colonies' are taken here to include Canada, RSA, USA and Israel, as well as obvious candidates like Germany, while ex- and semi-colonies include Libya, Eritrea, and Egypt.
84 Minutes, Meeting of the Police Service Commission, 11 July 1961, NA CO 822/2690.
85 Clayton, *The Thin Blue Line*, pp. 73–75.
86 Clayton, *The Thin Blue Line*, pp. 197–208.

87 Taken from an interview with Jim Godsave (Palestine Police, Malayan Police, Dep. Sup., rtd, 1946–60), July 2001.
88 Simon S. Smith, 'General Templer and Counter-Insurgency in Malaya: Hearts and Minds, Intelligence and Propaganda', *Intelligence and National Security*, 16:3 (autumn 2001), p. 68.
89 Memo, 21 Feb. 1945, NA MEPO 2/6093.
90 Young, address to 1960 ACPO Conference, *Police Review*, 3 June 1960, p. 42: NA MEPO 2/6093.
91 Young, 'The Gold Coast Police', May, 1967, RHL MSS Brit. Emp. s. 486, Box 1, f. 9.
92 Young, 'Gold Coast Police Report', Accra, 1952, RHL MSS Brit. Emp. s. 486, Box 1, f. 20.
93 Young, 'Gold Coast Police Report', Accra, 1952, RHL MSS Brit. Emp. s. 486, Box 1, f. 20.
94 Templer, 'A New Year Message from the High Commissioner to all Public Servants', 1 Jan. 1953, R. J. W. Craig, Family Papers.
95 Smith, 'General Templer', p. 68.
96 Godsave (interview), July 2001.
97 'Resignation of Colonel Young and Relations between the Administration and the Police', Minutes, 1959, NA CO 822/1293/4.
98 Colonial Secretary to Gorell Barnes, CO, Minute, 17 June 1959, NA CO 822/1293/3.
99 Kenya Police Commission, 1954, NA CO 1037/36.
100 'Resignation of Colonel Young and Relations between the Administration and the Police', Minutes, 1959, NA CO 822/1293/4.
101 *Kessing's Contemporary Archives*, 4–11 June, 1954, p. 14248.
102 Cases of brutality towards Mau Mau suspects occurred within regular police activities. Inspectors Copper and Bosh were prosecuted for maltreating a prisoner resulting in his death in 1957 'Cases of Ill-Treatment of Mau Mau Suspects by Inspectors of Police in Kenya, 1957–59': NA CO 822/1223.
103 'Resignation of Colonel Young and Relations between the Administration and the Police', Minutes, 1959, NA CO 822/1293/4.
104 Murphy, *Lennox-Boyd*, pp. 152–153.
105 Baring to Gorell Barnes, 4 Nov. 1954, NA CO 1037/2, quoted in Murphy, *Lennox-Boyd*, pp. 152.
106 Colonial Office, Reply, Statement to the House, 10 Jan. 1954, NA CO 1037/36.
107 Colonial Office, Reply, Statement to the House, 10 Jan. 1954, NA CO 1037/36.
108 Sir Richard Catling, RHL MSS s. Afr. 1784, Box 20, f. 18.
109 K. P. Witney, CO Minute, 21 Dec. 1956, NA CO 1037/36.
110 K. P. Witney, CO Minute, 21 Dec. 1956, NA CO 1037/36.
111 P. A. P. Robertson, CO Minute, 1 Jan. 1957, NA CO 1037/36.
112 W.A.G., CO Minute, 2 Jan. 1957, NA CO 1037/36.

CHAPTER FOUR

Policing the British Caribbean

In his capacity as a roaming police advisor, Arthur Mavrogordato inspected the St Lucia Police in 1948. An experienced colonial policeman, Mavrogordato had headed up the Palestine Police from 1923 until 1931. He was no stranger to the police forces of the Caribbean. He had paid an earlier visit to St Lucia in 1937 as an official police advisor in a mould similar to Dowbiggin's. At that time he had been critical of the force's overall efficiency. A decade later he reported that their efficacy had deteriorated still further. He explained this deterioration in terms of the post-war environment in which he observed changes in

> the political situation, labour conditions, trade union activities, education, cinemas, subversive movements . . . During the last few years the people of the West Indies have come into contact with a good many ex-soldiers who have returned from the war areas, imbued with half-baked subversive ideas which they air in and out of season. All these and other influences cannot have failed to infiltrate into the minds, not only of the public but of the men of the Police Force themselves.[1]

The colonial territories and islands of the Caribbean were often described by colonial policemen as 'backwaters' which constituted a retrograde step in terms of a career posting. Yet the Caribbean boasted some of the oldest police forces of the Empire which had been a testing ground for reform along British lines since the nineteenth century. The Bermuda Police was one of the earliest police systems, with mention of 'constables' appearing first in 1620. By 1624, Governor Woodhouse prescribed law and order duties which were summarised within an oath of allegiance. Constables should

> well and truly serve our Sovereigne Lord the King in the office of a constable. You shall see and cause his Master's peace to be well and truly kept and preserved according to your power. You shall arrest all such persons as in your sight shall go around offensively or shall commit or make any

riot, affray or breach of his Master's peace. You shall do your best endeavours upon complaint to you, made to apprehend all felons, Barrators, and riotous persons riotously assembled; and if any such offender shall make resistance with force, you shall levy hue and cry and shall persue them until they may be taken.[2]

Government policy towards the Caribbean constabularies related specifically to the longer term transformation from a semi military – colonial to an English – civil Police. However, in the first instance, policing through coercion was the norm. Jeffries noted, when commenting generally on the police forces of the Caribbean, that the abolition of slavery created the need for organised police forces 'due to a well-justified fear on the part of the governing class that the existence of this mass of unstable, excitable, ignorant and discontented people offered a serious threat to law and order'.[3] He was highlighting the first of his three laws of colonial policing: maintaining law and order through force. The transformation from a semi-military to a civilian model, in line with this theory, was attempted in the Caribbean well in advance of other territories, with the notable exception of Ceylon.

While reorganisation, and indeed modernisation, within the Caribbean was labelled 'civilianisation', police forces essentially remained within the same colonial mould. Policing the end of the Empire in the British Caribbean was as fraught with difficulties as it was in the rest of the Empire, although the disturbances that took place in the early part of the twentieth century were not as widespread as the Colonial Office had expected.[4] While the subsequent struggle for nationalism was less violent and prolonged than in certain African and Southeast Asian colonies, the police of the Caribbean still faced considerable difficulty in containing civil disorder. An earlier lack of funding to provide adequate modernisation within individual colonies typically resulted in *ineffectual* policing during periods of public disturbance and rioting. Although very early attempts had been made to reform a number of constabularies along the same lines as applied to the Ceylon Police, it was not until 1945 that some changes were in evidence. In line with official thinking toward the Colonial Police Service, exporting Britishness became a key objective during the 1950s and 1960s. In the case of British Honduras and Anguilla, it attained farcical proportions.

The problem in administering the Caribbean segment of the Empire was complicated by the historical legacy of colonisation. The area remained at the heart of competing European colonial rivalries during the early stages of formal colonisation. This impacted on the development of social, political and economic traditions.[5] In the early part of the twentieth century, those colonies under European or American control experienced a surge in nationalism, with the growth of the working class and development of the middle classes – 'island specific' in the case of Britain.[6] This prompted the appearance of labour movements and political parties pushing for constitutional reform and independence. Strikes and public disorder occurred in the immediate aftermath of the Great War and into the early 1920s in Trinidad, St Lucia, Jamaica, the Bahamas and British Honduras, triggered principally by wage disputes and dissatisfaction with working conditions. As trade union activity gained momentum in British Guiana, Jamaica and Trinidad, the Government failed to halt public violence through declaring strikes illegal. By the 1930s, as worsening economic conditions forced down the standard of living, protests had become all too commonplace. Strikes and disturbances became a regular feature of the inter-war years, the most serious being the labour rebellions of 1934–39, which affected the colonial economies within the region. (This began in British Honduras in February 1934, ending with rioting in September.) By July, a similar problem had occurred in Trinidad on several sugar estates, involving more than 15,000 workers. On the sugar estates on the west coast of British Guiana, disturbances broke out from September.[7]

During the inter-war years, public disturbances had become a regular feature in colonies like Jamaica. By the end of the Second World War, a government inquiry led by Lord Moyne – the West India Royal Commission – was asked to investigate the reasons for social unrest and the creation of the Bustamante Industrial Trade Union.[8] With a 'familiar blend of coercion and concession', British forces were used to restore order where the police had failed,[9] and the latter naturally came under scrutiny as a result. In 1945, the Metropolitan Police loaned Superintendent William Calver for a short-term mission to visit a number of Caribbean police forces and advise on their reform.

Once again this would be a case of too little, too late. The Second World War brought about an unravelling of Empire far more quickly than any would have believed. There was no exception in the British Caribbean, where the first glimmers of independence came with the extension of adult suffrage to women in British Guiana, Barbados and Bermuda in 1944, and the adoption of limited self-government in Jamaica and Trinidad in the same year. In contrast, the creation of the West Indies Federation (comprising Jamaica, Barbados, Trinidad, and the Windward and Leeward Islands) between 1958 and 1962 was perceived as a means of minimising the cost of Empire.[10] The British Government responded with a period of 'tutelary democracy' whereby the Westminster framework of government was put in place (or the Westminster parliamentary system was 'Caribbeanised') to facilitate the process of self-government, paving the way for independence.[11] Movements towards self-government naturally affected the police.

Exporting Britishness to the Caribbean

Attempts to reform the Caribbean constabularies had occurred sporadically since their inception. The long-established Bermuda force was subjected to frequent inspections during the nineteenth century, ostensibly to ensure that officers were carrying out the correct duties and to determine into which category they fell, military or policing. In 1835, for example, questions arose as to the manner in which the police handled public disturbances. Following the inspection, a police act stipulated specific actions to be undertaken by the 'Justices of the Peace' and constables during a riot. This required the JPs to place a 'white flag in their midst for a period of ten minutes'. If the rioters had not cleared within the ten minutes, they were arrested and liable to imprisonment not exceeding three months.[12] This no doubt presupposed that the justice of the peace was able, first, to place the white flag in the required spot, and secondly that the local population were well aware of its significance and consequences.

In 1903, under the provisions of the new Police Establishment Act, which authorised an increase in police establishment, officers were told that 'handcuffs had to be kept bright and clean, and in the event that they were found rusty they had to be cleaned, and the cost of doing so was deducted from the constable's salary'.[13] Meanwhile, attempts to instil a measure of Britishness involved the recruitment of members of the home forces to serve in the Bermuda Police. In August 1920, 18 recruits were selected from 500 applicants; of these, 11 had served in the Metropolitan Police.[14] By the Second World War, with the need for a rapid increase in the number of officers, the Colonial Office was forced to recruit local officers and forego earlier plans to second officers who had been trained in the home forces.[15]

Yet in terms of real attempts to export Britishness, the Jamaica Police was a better example. Set up in 1835, this force had an establishment of 40 gazetted officers and 1,889 all other ranks by 1952. Throughout its history, it was regarded as one of the 'finest' constabularies in the Caribbean area, although retaining a strong military character.[16] Reorganisation of the Jamaica force had occurred as early as 1867 in the hope that its military character would be diluted:

> The officers being called Inspectors and Sub-Inspectors, while in the other ranks the purely military designations of corporal, sergeant and sergeant-major [had been] adopted. The Inspector-General, Major J. H. Prenderville, was an ex-officer of the then recently disbanded 3rd West India Regiment;

and there was among the other officers a sprinkling of men from the same corps. [They] were armed with muzzle-loading rifles of the Snider patter.[17]

An early outcome of this reorganisation was a reduction in the overall size of the police with a view to improving its efficiency and reshaping its character. In 1866, the total strength of both regular and auxiliary police stood at almost 5,000. By 1880, this had been reduced to less than 1,760, including 1,000 part-time 'rural police', 'a disorderly set of men', who operated in a similar manner to the earlier watchmen in Britain.[18]

Through the latter part of the nineteenth century, repeated attempts were made to civilianise this police force in a similar vein to Trinidad's or British Guiana's. Yet by 1932, the organisation of the Jamaica Police had not changed since 1866. The use of military ranks and titles abounded and training continued along military lines, including frequent drills and use of weaponry. While some modernisation had occurred in terms of communications, transport, and crime detection and prevention, the force was still essentially an old-fashioned paramilitary outfit.

By 1944, an acute shortage of officers, following wartime transfers, had placed the police under 'great strain'. Operational efficacy was lacking and the training perceived to be entirely inadequate. To remedy the situation the Colonial Office selected Calver to inspect the Jamaica Police.[19] The loaning department, either the Colonial Office or the Foreign Office, negotiated an inclusive payment with the borrowing colony. In Calver's case, he cost the Jamaica Government the sum of £1,246 which took into account his salary, pension and allowances.[20] Calver arrived in Jamaica in May 1945 with an official brief to report to the Jamaica Government and the Colonial Officer on 'the administration, efficiency, discipline, work, strength and condition of employment'. He was to make recommendations that would lead to the eventual civilianisation of the police.

Calver's lengthy report compiled over several months provided an in-depth account of the structure of the police. When examining the training undertaken by recruits he recognised that its central ethos revolved around

> the Jamaica Constabulary Force] [being] partly a Military organisation and liable to be called out for Military service vide part II of Jamaica Constabulary Law. Much of the training, therefore, is upon Military lines such as drills, marchings, musketry etc . . . [This] is not wholly peculiar to Forces of partly military character. But drill and its beneficial effects are only one side of policing.[21]

This pinpointed Calver's perception of the colonial policing model. He saw that by enforcing military practices from the onset, a policeman could become moulded in one particular style. This Calver sought to avoid by urging that new 'officer blood' be brought into the training school, and into the Jamaica Police as a whole.[22] By the same token he recommended the scaling down of certain police units that had failed to come up to scratch. Within this group he included the 'Water Police', established in 1876 to patrol the harbour areas. Calver commented that rather than patrolling the waterways, these so-called 'water police' spent rather too much time in their office. Besides, 'the office was untidy . . . there were in a cupboard some 20 passport books relating directly to Chinese people who could not be accounted for . . . there were in the bottom of a cupboard forty electric torches, all unserviceable'.[23] In fact, from Calver's point of view, the Jamaica Police was distinctly 'average' and in need of 'refinement'.

Indeed his visit prompted the Jamaica Government to accept that some measure of reform had become inevitable. The Colonial Office approved the loan of members of the home forces to help with modernisation, particularly with the training and the development of the CID. Governor J. Huggins formally requested that three officers be urgently despatched, with the proviso that one of them have colonial policing experience.[24] This caused the Colonial Office to respond with some alarm as the definition of 'home' policeman was blurred and 'obscure'. Would Huggins be prepared to 'accept either a proper member of the Colonial Police Service or a Home policeman who had had sufficient Colonial experience'?[25] In the follow-up correspondence, a higher number of candidates serving in the colonial police was put forward, thus negating Calver's earlier advice to bring in solely 'British blood'. The officers available in the 'transfer market' included some colonial policing heavyweights: A. F. Giles, Assistant Inspector-General of the Palestine Police; Colonel Bacon, Inspector-General of the Ceylon Police; Colonel A. S. Mavrogordato, who had headed up the Palestine, Nigeria and Trinidad Police; M. S. McConnell, the retiring Deputy Inspector-General of the Palestine Police; J. Pennefather-Evans, retiring Commissioner of the Hong Kong Police; W. C. C. King, retiring Commissioner of the Nigeria Police; and Michael O'Rorke, Superintendent of the Palestine Police (who went on to lead the Kenya Police).[26] Finding potential candidates from the home forces was another story. Officers serving at Scotland Yard were asked to apply for the post of 'Assistant Executive Officer' in the Jamaica CID. Seven officers came forward, including Detective-Sergeant A. Martin and Major R. L. Hill. Six officers were rapidly considered 'unsuitable', with the post finally being offered to Hill, who had colonial police experience, having served as a Superintendent with the Gambia Police.

As it transpired, Calver became the only senior member of the home forces to be seconded to Jamaica. Following his Caribbean tour, he was despatched in 1946 to inspect the Northern Rhodesia Police, to assist with reform. On his return to London, he agreed to be seconded to Jamaica as Commissioner. He took up his post after an enquiry into the serious disturbances of 1948 and remained in situ until 1953. Shortly after his arrival, Calver became embroiled in serious allegations made by Wills Isaacs, a member of the House of Representatives, concerning the Jamaica Police. These included reports of a 'substantial deterioration' in the force's administration, which had dented 'not only the morale and discipline of the Force [but] the very root of the administration of justice'.[27] In particular, this 'scurrilous attack on the Commissioner of Police and other white police officers' had led to a lowering of morale and general disgruntlement among the police, with the Government fearing a backlash. A subsequent investigation into these allegations found them to be groundless, although it did appear that the need for reform, particularly of the conditions of pay and service of the rank and file, had reached a critical stage.[28] This became Calver's initial task, and he sought to undertake it while applying as many British policing principles as he was able to.

During Calver's leadership, the Jamaica Police received two inspections by the IGCP: Johnson first visited in 1950 and then Muller in 1953. Both were highly complimentary of the Commissioner's methods of implementing reform. Muller wrote in his report that Calver had 'inherited a legacy of bad organisation and bad discipline'. Through his ongoing restructuring he had 'succeeded in laying the foundations of a modern Civil Police Force on sound lines in better relation with the public it serves'. Calver's reforms stretched across the board, touching the Special Branch, the training school, transport, communications, women police officers, police buildings, welfare, and conditions of work and pay. Overall, he succeeded in increasing the police establishment by approximately 10 per cent, an improvement which included the secondment of two additional officers from the home forces by 1951.[29]

Calver put his own ideas regarding the 'bobby on the beat' into practice, with importance attaching to 'on-beat' rather than 'off-beat' policing to ensure regular contact with the general population. This resulted in the formation of special units known as the 'Flying Saucers' and 'Twenty-Two Squad' operating in the capital, Kingston. An 'Island Special Constabulary' was set up in 1950 along lines similar to those of the regular police, with a section attached to each police division. An additional legacy of Calver was the creation of two annual scholarships for 'promising sub-officers and men' to attend police training schools in Britain. The first awards were given to Sergeant-Major N. S. Houston and Detective Acting Corporal K. C. Mayne in 1947.[30]

Paradoxically, Calver came to believe that aspects of conventional colonial policing were essential to the successful policing of *any* colony. He commented to Muller during his visit that the rank and file required 'sufficient physical training and drill . . . [which contribute] so much to discipline and smartness, qualities which keep [the police officer] alert, give him self-respect and earn him the confidence of the Public'.[31] The style of colonial policing was directed not only at the local community but also at the locally recruited policemen. Training and subsequent policing along purely civil lines could result in a lessening of discipline, which would undermine the role of a comparatively small number of gazetted officers. Despite his earlier *British* training, Calver was persuaded that policing a colony required an approach different from that of policing London.

British Guiana

The British Guiana Police, too, was unable to take on the mantel of British policing during its lengthy history. The origins of this police force were reputedly older than Peel's 'new police'. It is alleged that provisions for 'police board' were made in 1812 in the towns of Georgetown and New Amsterdam, with armed officers, accountable to local magistrates, appearing some ten years later. An ordinance formally establishing the police came on 11 June 1839 under the leadership of William Crichton. From the onset, officers were given special powers to deal with suspected smuggling and boats to patrol the inland 'rivers creeks and canals' in search of 'sugar, rum, molasses, coffee', and the authority to search 'any sloop, schooner, drogher, punt or other colonial craft'.[32]

The idea that the British Guiana Police would function civilian-style was in line with the practice of many of the long-established Caribbean constabularies, epitomising Jeffries's beliefs. Yet, while the case of the British Guiana Police certainly illustrated an attempt at the theory, its own practice was somewhat different. From the onset, this remote constabulary was plagued by public unrest and rioting. Continuously under strength, the force was simply overpowered and resorted quickly to military techniques. After the 1856 riots and the death of one constable, the Colonial Government quickly concluded that 300 muskets and some 30,000 cartridges should be supplied to the police armoury. 'Under such a plan the Governor thinks that it would be practical to ensure the presence at various points of a body of trustworthy armed men, sufficient to arrest at once, and before the arrival of the Troops.'

In reality, the frequent disturbances that would occur throughout the nineteenth century on the sugar estates could not be controlled by civil-style policing. Besides, the administration had soon overridden earlier considerations of civil policing by pledging that a small number of armed officers should attend public demonstrations. Training for police recruits emphasised drill with arms organised along similar lines to RIC training at Phoenix Park.[33]

The force gradually expanded, recruiting more officers from outside Britain than from within. By 1883, of the 624 officers, only 178 were from Britain. Approximately 250 were recruited locally, with an additional 246 coming from Barbados. In addition, the Inspector-General reported that there were 3 Germans, 1 Dutch, 4 Swedish, 2 Norwegian, 1 American, 1 Madeiran, 21 African, 47 Indian, 2 Chinese, 4 Irish – 3 of them ex-RIC – and the remainder from a number of Caribbean islands.[34]

Indeed, by 1891, questions of civilianisation seemed to have been all but forgotten. The British Guiana Police was suddenly and radically overhauled, transformed into a semi-military force in the mould of the RIC. With the withdrawal of British troops from the colony, the police became in true colonial fashion the first line of defence. The need for an armed police continued because strikes and disturbances worsened as the century drew to a close. The 1894–95 disturbances among sugar workers were contained by an armed police response under the leadership of Captain De Rinzy who reported to his superiors that the 800-strong 'mob' at the Plantation Non Pareil had to be contained in the appropriate manner. The police had been forced to open fire, but

> no one fell after the first volley and we were again attacked with renewed energy; several were struck the second volley, but it appeared to have little effect as they continued to 'rush' us. My sword was knocked out of my hand with a blow from a stick and the coolie who struck me advanced at me with a cutlass at the end of stick. I fired at him with my revolver and at another coolie who was backing him up, but I am unable to say if I struck them or not.[35]

The military reputation of the British Guiana Police was even carried back to Britain. While performing in London at the 1897 Royal Tournament, a police cohort from British Guiana was commended for being 'a Semi-Military Police Force, second to none in Her Majesty's vast Colonial Empire in matters of discipline, Police work, and military training'. So ten years after this force had been officially recognised on a semi-military basis, Inspector-General Colonel McInniss remarked on how the reorganisation from 'purely Civil into a Semi-Military' was not without its problems in terms of how the force was perceived and in terms of its efficiency. By 1900, the annual police report was lamenting a rapid increase in crime, with 9,074 persons prosecuted and 5,723 convicted. That year, 'strikes throughout the Colony over wages, with assaults on overseers and drivers', intensified. The police contained every situation with the benefit of '800 Martini–Enfield .303 rifles and a Maxim gun of the same calibre . . . the police turned out in khaki'.[36] A mounted section was established in 1905 to help establish order during rioting.

Throughout the remainder of its colonial history, the British Guiana Police was to operate along increasingly military lines. Being geographically at the periphery of the Caribbean made it more difficult to request support in aid of the civil power if the need arose. Moreover, training of officers was restricted to the colony itself. Despite this, a number of inspection reports pointed to the 'excellent standard of training . . . with weapons in good order and well-maintained . . . [within] a very happy atmosphere'.[37] Indeed up until 1943, a former army officer was responsible for training recruits. When W. A. Orrett took over as Inspector-General during the Second World War he noted to the Governor in an early report that the police force was 'highly and efficiently trained as a Military unit, being equipped with up-to-date weapons such as Bren and Tommy Guns'. The police had been called out for military service in defence of the colony in September 1939, thus carrying out the role for which they were principally equipped. Other aspects of the force had suffered as a consequence, with little attention having been paid to the condition of some police stations.[38]

In the aftermath of the Second World War, British Guiana faced regular public disturbances and civil unrest, as did many of the islands of the British Caribbean. The creation of the new British Guiana Industrial Workers' Trade Union in April 1948 contributed to a widening of public discontent.[39] There were occasions when the heavy-handedness of the police in containing a situation brought widespread criticism from the general public. In 1948 the grievances of Enmore Plantation sugar workers toward the 'cut and load' system in operation led to a strike, which rapidly spread to neighbouring areas. Indeed, following prolonged rioting, which resulted in 5 deaths and 14 wounded, George Abbiss at the Colonial Office minuted:

> I am not too optimistic that the memory of the Enmore riots will die down quickly. Criticism of the police and East Indian political feeling will be mixed up and will remain a potential source of trouble. If the courts decide against the police the Governor will be faced with embarrassing demands to revise the attitude he has shown in endorsing the police.[40]

Essentially the police force was both inadequately prepared and lacking in the manpower to have contained the disturbances using *minimum* force. Any wish to civilianise the police was overshadowed by the practical realities of containing civil unrest. At Enmore, the police considered that they were being rapidly 'overpowered' by a 'crowd variously armed . . . with sticks, cutlasses, pieces of iron pipe, bricks, bottles and similar weapons'. In the event, officers James, de Groot, Nedd and Haniff felt the 'necessity to open fire', having been unable to repel the crowd through the use of tear smoke, which had never before been used in British Guiana. Besides, they were being repeatedly taunted, the crowd shouting: 'Dem can't shoot, and if dem shoot, dem can only shoot two ahwee, and the Governor got to come and read the riot act.'[41]

The police were blamed for having opened fire too quickly, allowing insufficient time to warn the crowd that injuries would be the likely outcome if they failed to withdraw. Even though the Commission of Enquiry 'leaned over backwards', asserting that the police were fully justified in opening fire, it concluded that the crowd should have 'retreated' when instructed by the police.[42] In effect, it took these disturbances to force through an increase in police strength, with 350 special constables enrolled alongside 1,033 regular police.[43]

By the time British Guiana's constitution had been suspended in 1953, the colony was governed by an interim administration composed of nominated members. Police officers were able to resume part of their normal civil duties with the reassuring presence of a detachment of the Argyll and Sutherland Highlanders. The military role of the police, however, was reinforced with the introduction of searches for firearms and explosives, and the control of public meetings through the issuing of permits. The police were equipped with the latest communications technology, which allowed for the setting up of a force control/operations room, additional police transport and later an independent communications branch.[44]

Modernisation continued the following year when the Metropolitan Police sent an officer to help reform the CID. At the same time Mick Edwards, who had returned from a tour of duty with the Cyprus Police, having started out with the Montgomeryshire Police, arrived to help restructure the training school. A Cardiff City Police Inspector, Llewelyn Evans, was also despatched under contract to head up the traffic unit for a short period.[45] This tradition of exporting officers from the home forces continued until independence and beyond. By the time British Guiana had advanced to virtual full self-government under a new constitution in 1961, its police force was continually challenged by public order disturbances. The rioting that erupted in Georgetown in February 1962, resulting in deaths and injuries, brought the police into the line of fire and necessitated the use of the army as back up. An enquiry found that while police officers had performed their 'difficult' task admirably, they were inadequately prepared. As a result, each riot squad had its own baton, tear-gas and rifle section.[46]

By 1962, the British Guiana Government considered that it was involved in a 'fiendishly complicated situation' in terms of filling police posts. The police force had always been under-strength, vacillating between a semi-military and a civilian organisation. As independence grew closer, so the need increased for a 'top-notch Security' organisation and 'the need to strengthen the law-enforcement side of the police'.

In March 1962, the Colonial Office had received a formal request for three senior policemen to fill vacancies. None were forthcoming. By June, the local administration pleaded for 'help' as 'circumstances here are so complex and there is need of help from someone with personal knowledge and a personal interest if we are to thread our way through successfully'. Five vacancies for senior positions still had not been filled, including the 3 posts of assistant commissioner in the CID, the administration and the Special Branch, and 2 senior superintendents. If the three posts of assistant commissioner were filled by local promotions, an additional three vacancies would arise for senior superintendents. Moreover, some officers were attending training courses in Britain, which further depleted the establishment: 'I need to keep the Police functioning *now*, despite vacancies and absences on leave', wrote Ralph Grey of the British Guiana administration.[47] The only post the Colonial Office was able to fill immediately was that of senior superintendent: it appointed Andrew McGill-Smith, a career colonial policeman who had served in the Nigeria Police.[48] Once again, reform had travelled full circle, with any attempts at civil-style policing reverting back to colonial policing.

Trinidad

The same had been true of the force of Trinidad, where repeated attempts were made to reform the police along civil lines. In January 1942, Major R. H. Onreat, an experienced colonial police officer, was given a Colonial Office brief to recommend 'reorganisation and training' of the police forces of Trinidad, Jamaica and British Honduras. On his arrival in Port of Spain, Onreat was informed that the police had been for some time in a phase of transition from 'a Semi-Military Force with definite military responsibilities into that of a Civil Police Force'. With the added complications of the police's wartime duties (the island had been turned into a busy US base), the police were 'in need of drastic pruning and reform'.[49]

The Trinidad Police followed the Caribbean blueprint, having been set up earlier than Peel's 'new police'. Formally established in 1823, the earlier Spanish institutions and titles were maintained for some time. The new constables retained the name *alguacils*, for example. From the outset, attempts were made to dampen down any semi-military tendencies. Yet this appeared to have been problematical. When the former Palestine Police Inspector-General Mavrogordato paid an inspection visit in 1932, he noted that the force was still armed and could be called out by the Governor as the first line of defence. Despite this, he saw some evidence of a civil rather than a military organisation.[50] Onreat, in his subsequent report, drew similar conclusions:

> I was soon convinced that there was very little seriously wrong with the Force . . . [M]any of the senior N.C.O.s were up to the standard of the best Asiatic Inspectors I have met and that is no small compliment . . . [So] why is so relatively poor use made of them?[51]

Onraet was referring here to the Colonial Police Service's crack forces in Hong Kong and Ceylon which were intended to adopt British rather than colonial policing traditions. Better use of these non-commissioned officers would free the police of their military responsibilities. It appeared that a higher standard of leadership equated to civil rather than military activities in the Trinidad Police. To enable greater use of civil-style policing, Onraet debated whether a partial restructuring would allow for change. It was here, however, that his theory fell down, and confusion arose as to the precise nature of policing practice. Rather than using the Metropolitan Police code to rewrite the Police Standing Orders, Onraet decided to apply the old RIC criteria. The reasons for this turnabout are not entirely clear, although he believed he would create a 'sound' police organisation, even if one that was heavily imbued with military sentiment. Besides, the training in place was rather more military in style than the administration would have liked. Of a 19-week course, police training took up 139 periods, drill 113 and weapons training 109. Onreat noted 'that military training should not exceed that which has been found necessary', but then emphasised the need to restructure the force along Irish lines. In noting a final recommendation, he stressed that 'Trinidad Police' be changed to 'Trinidad Constabulary', a title which held 'greater prestige' because in line with that of forces such as the RIC.[52]

The ambiguity over what represented a *civil* as compared to a *semi-military* 'constabulary' overshadowed the practicalities of restructuring. Besides, civil disturbances arising from discontent among oil and sugar workers necessitated the use of *stronger* policing during this period. By 1949 the Commissioner had reported:

> Hooliganism and juvenile delinquency are very serious problems in the over-crowded towns. The now famous 'steel bands', which weave subtle harmonies from dustbin lids and kerosene tins, were begun by unemployed men collecting money in the Trinidad streets. At times they have been overdone and have become a public nuisance calling for police action . . . [but] there was no slacking of an ever cheerful effort to do the impossible.[53]

Despite those issues, Trinidad was one of only a relatively few colonies to have established a Police Association, an organisation similar to the British Police Federation. This association represented all non-gazetted police officers and operated through branch boards and a central committee. It was empowered to make representations on matters concerning the general welfare and efficiency of officers. However, it was not at liberty to address issues concerning discipline, promotion, transfer, leave or individual grievances.[54]

Windward Islands

Unlike the Leeward Islands, the Windward Islands consisted of four separate colonies, Dominica, St Lucia, St Vincent and Grenada, under the auspices of one governor. The Windward Islands were not a federation and each island had its own police force. Unlike the colonies previously mentioned, the Windward Islands retained police systems that were essentially colonial in character, with only half-hearted attempts made at enacting civil reform.

In Grenada, serious disturbances occurred in 1951 as a result of strikes on the sugar estates which led to intimidation, incitements to violence, the burning of buildings, theft and the destruction of crops. This had become a familiar story of the post-war Caribbean. In Grenada, however, there were additional political problems resulting from the slow process through which constitutional changes were taking place. As a result, police reinforcements were seconded from St Lucia, Barbados and Trinidad, and assistance was sought from the Royal Navy. The attending officers were quick to deal harshly with the disturbances, using maximum force which resulted in the deaths of three people and the wounding of many more.

The Governor, Sir Robert Arundell, made the decision that the Grenada Police lacked efficient leadership and brought in an officer from Barbados, Brigadier Pickthall, a retired army officer who had police experience with the military administration in Abyssinia. (He was soon replaced by Colonel James, a former Palestine Police officer.) The Government recruited as his deputy Arthur Hughes Jenkins who had previously served as Chief Constable of the Falkland Islands Police. In order to curb the strike, 'anti-subversive' ordinances were enacted, which enhanced police power. On his arrival, Jenkins noted the extent to which the police had been organised on military lines. Indeed it was the 'only armed service' available to defend the territory. He did, however, observe:

> Apart from the small cannon we used for saluting purposes, only small arms were available and training in the handling, care and use of rifles came with the recruit drilling and police training. .303 rifles were available at each police station.[55]

Overall, the experiences of both the Grenada and the St Vincent Police pointed to officers having a dual role of 'a Civil Police and a military force'.[56] Hughes's policing experiences had been of one of those rare colonial constabularies that prided itself on its Britishness. Using *police* as opposed to *military* ranks, the Falkland Islands Police relied on the Falkland Islands Defence Force – a volunteer military unit – to defend the colony. Besides, the police had ample extraneous duties. The Chief Constable was also the colony's 'gaoler' and Superintendent of the Fire Brigade at Port Stanley. The prison accommodation included a padded cell as there was no psychiatric unit on the island. Falkland law was based on English statute law and common law alongside the colony's own ordinances.[57] The Falkland Islands Police was also unique in that it remained an unarmed police force.

Decolonisation 'fiascos': British Honduras and Anguilla

The export of *Britishness* to a number of territories in the British Caribbean had been attempted throughout the region's imperial policing history. The deployment of police officers from the home forces was complicated by a wavering in colonial office policy: on the one hand the colonies should secure self-government with reasonably civilianised notions of law and order, while on the other they should use colonial-style methods to retain control until the appropriate end-point. During the post-war years, British Honduras and Anguilla stand out as cases where the British Government's policy approached the farcical.

A letter from the Governor of British Honduras to Creech-Jones in 1948 highlighted the territory's isolated position. 'The nearest British Colony, Jamaica, is 600 hundred miles away', he wrote. 'Besides the conditions in the two territories are so different that close co-operation in dealing with security problems is not feasible.'[58] Similar to many Caribbean police forces, the British Honduras police force was 'small', having been set up in 1884. Because of the difficulty of travelling around the colony, 'much of the police work [had] to be done by launch, motor-boat or canoe. In the country districts, the policeman [had] to carry out a number of duties in addition to his ordinary police functions such as those of school-attendance officers and even of postman'.[59]

The British Honduras Police did not feature greatly in government reports until the period of decolonisation. An inspection of the force in 1948 showed that it consisted of only 3 gazetted officers, 51 NCO's and 138 other ranks. The colony at that time remained problem-free in British eyes, with 'no sign of an organized subversive movement'. Police strength within CID could be expanded, but at that time this was not pressing. Overall British Honduras policemen were considered to work effectually and to be adequately trained.[60] 'Adequate', however, appeared to have been the watchword, for proposals were regularly made by the late 1950s for the secondment of British police units to assist with training.

For example, in 1961, a request was made for the secondment of four police sergeants, as superintendents, to help restore order following the 'devastation left in the wake of the hurricane'. The suggestion was that they should organise training along similar lines to those of the Malayan Police for a period of two years.[61] It was well-known that police training Malayan-style was heavily paramilitary, following the twelve year emergency. There had been sections of the Malayan Police acting in a frontline capacity alongside the armed forces. Experience acquired in Malaya was hardly conducive to the training of officers along British lines. The following year, the Governor keenly requested that the Colonial Office organise the secondment of Sergeant E. K. Jones. The interest in this officer lay in his colonial experience 'of sorts', as he had been the bodyguard of the Nigerian Prime Minister during his visits to Britain.[62] Once again the emphasis was on colonial as compared to British policing.

By 1966, reports by the IGCP showed that 'likely future internal security commitments' would necessitate an increase in the force's establishment.[63] If the officers were not forthcoming from Britain, then consideration should be given to the setting up of a 'Police Special Force'. Trained and equipped as a paramilitary force, this outfit would resemble the police mobile units that had been attached to most colonial police forces. In the absence of a permanent military force, this special unit would be responsible for internal security and fieldwork, including the management of national disasters, civil disturbances, and would serve as the first line of defence in the event of external aggression. In addition it would act as a police reserve unit in support of the regular force. 'This Special Force will have to be equipped with modern arms, riot equipment, transport, radio etc. and must be not only an effective striking Force but also one which is fully mobile and self-contained.'[64]

Since the Second World War, there had been a number of occasions when detachments of home force units had been posted overseas. In 1945, British police units served in Germany, Austria, Greece and Trieste. In the 1950s, officers were sent to Malaya, Cyprus and Nyasaland. British units were established under the Police (Overseas Service) Act of 1945, which empowered the Colonial Secretary and then the Foreign and Commonwealth Secretary to send members of the home forces for overseas duties. This differed from the secondment of individual officers on contract to colonial government as police advisors, and the case of Anguilla fell into this latter category.

In terms of policing, Anguilla was loosely part of the Leeward Islands Federation. Since 1874, a Leeward Islands police force had been responsible for the policing of each island within this Caribbean group. The Commissioner of the Leeward Islands Police was based in Antigua and responsible for four divisions that corresponded to each grouping. Larger establishments existed in the islands of Antigua and St Kitts–Nevis. The smaller islands, for example the Virgin Islands, relied on only 3–4 policemen directed by a station sergeant. With inadequate training facilities, Trinidad was able to offer certain specialist training courses.[65]

The Leeward Islands joined St Kitts–Nevis and Anguilla in the early part of the twentieth century, and again from 1958 to 1962 to form the British Leeward Islands Federation, which constituted part of the failed West Indies Federation. Anguilla, the Cinderella of the Leewards group, was administered by St Kitts, with a tiny police force comprising twelve officers under the command of a Warden. In February 1967, St Kitts–Nevis–Anguilla became a state in 'voluntary association' with Britain. The St Kitts–Nevis link, under the West Indies Act, fuelled increased public discontent, coming to a head in June 1967 when 250 islanders rioted. During the disturbances, the Warden's house was burnt down and the entire police force was forced off the island to St Kitts. Telecommunications were severed between the two islands as a result. The Premier, Robert Bradshaw, declared the rioting illegal and asked Britain to send in troops to quell the worsening situation. Meanwhile, on 11 July 1967, Anguilla held a referendum on its continued association with St Kitts–Nevis, choosing independence by 1,813 votes to 5. Anguilla had effectively, and illegally, declared its own end of empire. Meanwhile, British, Barbadian, Trinidadian and

Guyanese representatives met in an attempt to end Anguilla's secession. Bradshaw signed an agreement promising to return Anguilla to constitutional relations with St Kitts–Nevis through the formation of a local council. With no end in sight to the tensions on the island Bradshaw and the newly appointed MP Ronald Webster attended talks in London in October 1968. Webster claimed that with the expiry of the interim settlement on 31 December 1968, Anguilla would revert to 'full independence and freedom of action'. As Anguilla's status was governed by the West Indies Act of 1967, the British Government had failed to recognise this fact. Pressure also came from the US administration, with its concerns that Anguilla would become a centre for organised crime.

By early March 1969, there was still no police force in operation on the island. A planned visit by a British ministerial delegation in March required protection from a Royal Navy frigate cruising off the island. On the ground, Inspector Smith and Sergeant Waller from Scotland Yard would provide adequate cover. 'These well-laid plans, in the event, proved disastrously ineffective.'[66] The ministerial party was met by a hostile group of local people which included Webster. Roadblocks were set up, manned by armed islanders. Present too were Webster's 'Keystone Cops', an unofficial police unit, who remained adamant that they could not guarantee the Minister's safety. The extent of opposition to the artificially created state of St Kitts–Nevis–Anguilla had been underestimated, as had been the militancy of Webster and his supporters.

On 17 and 18 March 1969, British troops and police officers from the Met were despatched to Antigua to await the order for their deployment to Anguilla. On hearing of this planned invasion, Jeremiah Gumbs, Anguilla's self-styled UN representative, called for assistance.[67] By 19 March 1969, it appeared that Britain had used the proverbial sledgehammer to crack a nut to regain control.[68] The Anguillans offered no resistance as Britain used troops and 'gunboat diplomacy' to take over the island. At the same time, a detachment from the Metropolitan Police, no doubt the only police force that could supply officers at short notice, arrived on the tiny island some 15 miles long and 5 miles wide, with a population of no more than 5,000. The men of the detachment had been informed that they were 'going to invade' the island, and the officers were issued with Walther automatics 'raided from Special Branch plus the SPG stock'.[69]

The Anguilla Police Unit (APU) was made up initially of members of the Special Patrol Group (SPG) formed to carry out 'special crime operations'. The first wave of approximately four SPG officers landed in Anguilla under the command of Assistant Commissioner Andrew Way, who had previously been seconded to the Montreal Police in 1961 to advise on their reorganisation. They were accompanied by John McKay, a Home Office Inspector of Constabulary and former Chief Constable of the Manchester Police.[70] The following day, forty-five officers commanded by Superintendent Neale left Antigua for Anguilla.[71] While being accountable to the British Commissioner in Anguilla, rather than the Metropolitan Police, the SPG was expected to uphold the British tradition of operating as a Civil Police force. This caused concern within the Police Federation, which was 'disturbed' by the regulations under which the SPG was operating in Anguilla, for they gave rise to questions as to the SPG's legal status. The carrying of arms, therefore, would occur only in 'exceptional circumstances after careful consideration by the senior officer of the unit'.[72] Way believed in 'patrolling areas on the theory that the very presence of uniformed police tends to deter crime and prevent disorder'.[73]

Records show that of the 497 Met officers seconded for short periods to Anguilla there were 11 officers who had served in other colonies, either in the Colonial Police Service or as a member of a British police unit: 5 in Cyprus, one in Jamaica, 2 in Palestine and 5 in Kenya.[74] The majority of the troops withdrew by August 1969, being replaced by detachments of Metropolitan Police officers whose role by this stage was perceived to be largely 'paramilitary'. Negotiations by this time were underway to establish a 'new island police force', which would reduce the size of the APU.[75] By May 1969, the number of officers stood at 95, although the ideal target was no more than 25. This would allow for the development of the APU under the direct supervision of a British police officer with 'colonial' experience.[76] As this process would take some time, it was suggested that the APU's strength remain at around eighty for all ranks until 1971, with the assistance of a detachment of Royal Engineers.[77]

The subsequent transformation of the APU followed a similar path to that of the Jamaica Police some twenty-five years earlier. While the APU had been employed to maintain public order, it had done so on the understanding that arms would be available if necessary, which was hardly the type of image the Foreign and Commonwealth Office really wished portray. Despite British claims that 'it was good to hear that the police no longer carry arms on Anguilla', colonial-style policing was ever present.[78] The future Anguilla Police would include police officers with colonial experience. On 25 August 1969, Superintendent Thomas Crennell, a former officer of the Malayan Police, was despatched to Anguilla despite protestations by senior Metropolitan Police officers. Commander Remnant, for example, was 'wholly opposed to proposals for building up an effective riot control squad trained on traditional Colonial Service lines', for such an initiative would tend to preclude the securing of 'general co-operation' with the public in the event of a riot.[79] However, colonial influences were there to stay, and Anguilla remained a British colony. Crennell became responsible for organising the training of the 'new' Anguilla Police, which initially recruited officers locally to work alongside expatriates as 'police messengers'.[80]

It seems that neither the Colonial Office nor the Home Office could disentangle the colonial from the civil practice of policing. Tentative moves to export a British style were hampered by problems of policing the end of the Empire. Caribbean police forces were typically too small and ill-equipped to deal with public unrest. In the case of British Honduras, the idea of despatching British officers floundered with the practicalities of instructing local officers in paramilitary techniques. Even in Anguilla, it was the SPG that was first deployed, rather than archetypal London policemen. Traditional *colonial* rather than *British* practice was co-extensive with the policing of end of the Empire.

Notes

1   Mavrogordato, 'St Lucia Police Report', 1948, quoted in Jeffries, *Colonial Police*, p. 73.
2   E.A. Burton, 'The Policing of Bermuda from the Earliest Times', *Bermuda Historical Quarterly* (1955), p. 87.
3   Jeffries, *Colonial Police*, p. 60.
4   Howard Johnson, 'The British Caribbean from Demobilization to Constitutional Decolonization', in Judith M. Brown and W. Roger Louis (eds) *The Oxford History of the British Empire*, Vol. 4: *The Twentieth Century* (Oxford: OUP, 1999), p. 599.
5   The British Caribbean included two mainland territories, British Honduras in Central America and British Guiana in South America. Additionally a large number of islands divided for administrative purposes into five areas: Jamaica (with the Cayman Islands and Turks and Caicos Islands as dependencies); Trinidad and Tobago; Barbados; the Windward Islands, comprising the four separate colonies of Grenada, St Vintcent, St Lucia and Dominica; and the Leeward Islands, consisting of the Presidencies of Antigua, St Kitts–Nevis, Montserrat and the Virgin Islands. Today Anguilla, the British Virgin Islands, the Cayman Islands, Montserrat, and the Turks and Caicos Islands remain British overseas territories.
6   Thomas J. D'Agostino, 'Caribbean Politics', in Richard S. Hillman & Thomas J. D'Agostino (eds), *Understanding the Contemporary Caribbean* (London: Lynne Rienner, 2003), p. 104.
7   Johnson, 'Constitutional Decolonization', p. 604.
8   Stephen J. Randall, 'The Historical Context', in Hillman & D'Agostino (eds) *Understanding the Contemporary Caribbean*.
9   Johnson, 'Constitutional Decolonization', p. 608.
10 Randall, 'Historical Context', p. 78.
11 D'Agostino, 'Caribbean Politics', *Understanding the Contemporary Caribbean*, p. 95.
12 Burton, 'Policing of Bermuda', p. 90.
13 Burton, 'Policing of Bermuda', p. 97.
14 Burton, 'Policing of Bermuda', p. 99.
15 The establishment of the Bermuda Police in 1954 was 5 gazetted and 138 all other ranks: Burton, 'Policing of Bermuda', pp. 104–105.

16 Jeffries, *Colonial Police*, pp. 224–225.
17 Herbert Thomas, *The Story of a West Indian Policeman* (Kingston: Gleaner Co., 1927), p. 20. Thomas served for forty-seven years in the Jamaica Police, from 1876 to 1923.
18 The rural police were replaced by part-time district constables in 1899: Jeffries, *Colonial Police*, p. 35.
19 W. Battershill, CO, to Sir Philip Game, HO, 16 Nov. 1944, 'Inspection Jamaica Police', 1944, NA MEPO 2/6093.
20 CO to Jamaica Govt., Memo, 21 Feb. 1945, W. A. Calver, Jamaica Police 1944–45, NA CO 137/856/2.
21 W. A. Calver, 'Report Jamaica Police', 23 Oct. 1945, NA CO 137/867/1.
22 The size of territories and, by extension, the establishment of individual forces directly impacted on police training and any attempts to reorganise and modernise individual forces. Jamaica, Trinidad and British Guiana had their own police training schools. Some islands, for example Grenada, trained their own police but also used outside training schools. By the early 1950s, the smaller forces sent recruits to a new training school in Barbados. Regular conferences were held at which the Police Commissioners of the different Caribbean forces attended to discuss training matters and questions linked to the development of police federations.
23 Calver, 'Report Jamaica Police', 23 Oct. 1945, NA CO 137/867/1.
24 Huggins to G. H. Hall, Colonial Secretary, 15 June 1968, NA CO 137/867/1.
25 G. R. Thomas, CO, Minute, 20 Aug. 1946, NA CO 137/867/1.
26 CO Minutes, July–Aug. 1946, NA CO 137/867/1.
27 'Report of the Commission of Enquiry into the Jamaica Police Force', 1951, para. 44, NA CO 1031/106.
28 M Scott to G. Abbiss, CO Minutes, NA CO 1031/106.
29 IGCP Report on Jamaica Police Force, 1953, Appendix F: Origin Return of Gazetted Officers over the Period 2.248–15.3.51, NA CO 1031/107.
30 HQ Jamaica Constabulary to Capt. T. L. N. Mostyn, Scotland Yard, 5 Feb. 1948, NA MEPO 2/7925.
31 IGCP Report on Jamaica Police Force, 1953, NA CO 1031/107.
32 W. A. Orrett, *The History of the British Guiana Police* (Georgetown: Daily Chronicle Ltd, 1951), pp. 1–7.
33 Orrett, *History of the British Guiana Police*, pp. 21–23.
34 This pattern of recruitment carried through until 1950: Orrett, *History of the British Guiana Police*, pp. 18, 36, 42, 71.
35 De Rinzy quoted in Orrett, *History of the British Guiana Police*, pp. 26–27.
36 Annual Report, 1900, quoted in Orrett, *History of the British Guiana Police*, p. 29.
37 R. S. Howlett, Insp.-Gen. West Indian Local Forces, 10 April 1937, 'Local Forces Inspection Reports British Guiana 1937', NA CO 111/742/17.
38 Orrett, *History of the British Guiana Police*, pp. 53–59.
39 Note on Meeting, Security Matters British Guiana, 28 Oct. 1948, 'Review of British Guiana Police and Security Forces in relation to Communist Infiltration', 1948, NA CO 537/2775.
40 George Abbiss, Minutes, 15 June 1949, 'Labour Situation, Sugar Strikes', NA CO 111/796/6.
41 Enmore Enquiry Commission Report, 1948, paras. 88, 92, NA CO 111/796/6.
42 Minutes, Enmore, para. 92. NA CO 111/796/6.
43 'Review of British Guiana Police and Security Forces in relation to Communist Infiltration', 1948, NA CO 537/2775.
44 IGCP report on British Guiana Police Force, 1953, NA CO 1031/103.
45 Arthur Hughes Jenkins, *A Long Beat: Service to the Crown Home and Abroad* (Denbigh: Gee & Son), p. 224.
46 Hughes, *Long Beat*, p. 244.
47 Grey to J. P. Morton, CO, Secret and Personal, 5 June 1962, NA CO 1037/175.
48 'Expatriate Officers for British Guiana Police, 1960–62', NA CO 1037/175.
49 Onraet, Trinidad Police Report, 1942, NA CO 295/627/5.
50 Mavrogordato, 'The Trinidad Police', *Police Journal* (1932).

51 Onraet, Trinidad Police Report, 1942, NA CO 295/627/5.
52 Onraet, Trinidad Police Report, 1942, NA CO 295/627/5.
53 Police Commissioner's Report, 1949.
54 Jeffries, *Colonial Police*, p. 70.
55 Jenkins, *Long Beat*, p. 171.
56 Jenkins, *Long Beat*, p. 192.
57 Hughes, *Long Beat*, pp. 112, 122, 126.
58 G. A. Hone to Creech-Jones, Secret, 16 Aug. 1948, NA CO 537/2781.
59 Jeffries, *Colonial Police*, pp. 63–65.
60 'Review of British Honduras Police and Security Forces in relation to Communist Infiltration', 1948, NA CO 537/2781.
61 B. H. Taylor, Com., to Stourton, IGCP, 1 Dec. 1961, NA CO 1037/156/4.
62 Stallard to Piper, 27 Feb. 1962, NA CO 1037/156/15.
63 In 1966, the British Honduras Police comprised 9 gazetted officers, 6 Inspectors, 72 NCOs and 295 other ranks, including 10 women police officers; it was 9 constables under establishment: Michael J. Macoun, Dep. IGCP, 'Summary of Comments and Recommendations', British Honduras Police Force Report, 1966, NA CO 1037/257.
64 Macoun, British Honduras Police Report, 1966, NA CO 1037/257.
65 Jeffries, *Colonial Police*, p. 69.
66 Michael Macoun, *Wrong Place, Right Time: Policing the End of Empire* (London: Radcliffe Press, 1996), pp. 154–156. Macoun was present during this visit to Anguilla as the OPA.
67 'Troops and Police stand by for Anguilla', *The Times*, 18 March 1969.
68 Macoun, *Wrong Place, Right Time*, p. 162.
69 Leslie David, 'The Cobras Have Landed! (Anguilla Part 2)', *London Police Pensioner* (date unknown), p. 47.
70 Mckay had assisted in restoring civil police control in Italy in 1944–45: *The Times*, 19 March 1969.
71 'Anguilla Police Unit', 25 March 1969, MEPO 2/11464.
72 'Background Note on Police in Anguilla', 19 March 1969, NA HO, MEPO 2/11464.
73 'Plans for Invasions Anguilla Dropped'. *The Times*, 19 March 1969.
74 'Anguilla Police Unit – Service of Met Officers, 1969', NA MEPO 2/11464.
75 UK Mission, New York, to FCO, Conf. Telegram, 26 April, 1969, NA FCO 63/245.
76 Foreign and Commonwealth Office (FCO) to S. A. Cumber, Acting Comm., Anguilla, 5 May 1969, NA FCO 63/245.
77 Tom Sewell, FCO, Minute, 9 July 1969, FCO 63/245, 'Defence Rotations of Forces in Anguilla, 1969', NA FCO 63/235.
78 UK Mission to UN to Henry Hankey, FCO, 29 June 1969, NA FCO 63/245.
79 Hankey to Sevell, 4 July 1969, NA FCO 63/248.
80 J. H. H. Vaughan, Minute, 5 Jan. 1970, NA FCO 63/248.

CHAPTER FIVE

Policing colonial conflict in the Mediterranean and the Middle East

Policing colonial conflict reinforced the traditions of paramilitary policing. Civil disorder often escalated to emergency levels, marking out a new phase in the policing of end of the Empire and reflecting the social dislocation brought about by the growth of nationalism and the desire for political change. Subduing a territory through the formal conduit of the police allowed colonial rule to continue, albeit temporarily. Brought physically into the line of fire, the colonial police trod a fine line between soldiering and policing.

When a state is threatened it generally creates new laws or powers to legitimise police actions. The colonial police witnessed an increase in their judicial powers throughout this period. Police ordinances were amended in the majority of colonies to include the use of 'twilight powers'. This allowed the police to declare a specific area 'disturbed' without the necessity of the escalatory state of emergency procedures, giving them additional powers of arrest, and the use of curfews and roadblocks. Attempts at juggling emergency and civil styles of policing often led to the creation of auxiliary police units within the security domain with which the darker sides to the end of Empire have been more commonly associated. The hasty withdrawal from Palestine in June 1948 set a precedent in the way in which the policing the end of Empire would take place. Essentially this came about as former Palestine policemen took their experiences to other police forces, which included both the Cyprus and the Aden Police. However, in both cases the Colonial Office tried to impose British policing methods, allied to the secondment of almost 1,000 members of the home forces and the posting overseas of senior British officers.

The Palestine Police: policing the mandate

From the time when British rule had been established in Palestine, the police force was involved in episodic and bloody public security issues. Under the mandate of the League of Nations, controlling Palestine allowed for the co-existence of Arabs and Jews during a period of rapid social change, while dealing with local issues and imperial concerns. From 1920, Arab opposition to the Zionist movement coupled with British promises to establish a national home in Palestine for the Jewish people provided the backdrop for an emergent divided society. The violence that erupted in August 1929 made it apparent that the Jewish and the Arab communities could not live peaceably side by side. From this point, the Palestine Police was constantly threatened with civil disorder. Thus Dowbiggin's subsequent attempts to transform the police into a civil-style operation were thwarted by the need for para-military policing as the security situation worsened. By the time Sir Charles Tegart had been despatched to look at possible reform the scene was set for the security chaos that would ensue. Increasingly the Palestine Police was involved in counter-insurgency operations only to beat a hasty retreat in June 1948 with the end of the mandate. Without adequate intelligence, police operations often floundered, leading to repeated attempts at reform. Really this was more about reinventing colonial policing to cope with the stresses of policing the end of Empire. In many ways the experiences of Palestine were not wasted on the colonial police, as the lessons learnt were channelled through the movement of policemen to the imperial hot spots.

The Palestine Gendarmerie, which had faced rioting and civil disturbances throughout its brief history, transformed into the Palestine Police in 1926. While the name changed, suggesting a greater emphasis on civil police duties, the policing of Palestine thereafter continued in the same vein. With the army and navy deployed during the 1929 riots and the Arab revolt of 1936–39, it was clear that the police provided only a thin line of security.[1] When rioting ensued there was significant 'confusion and commotion', amid which 'Kingsley Heath', who would later become Inspector-General, 'alone gallantly but quite ineffectively charged the crowd on his horse'.[2]

The events of 1929 brought the growing hostility between the two communities to a head. The 'fierce and bloody riots' were felt to have been triggered by religious rather than political issues.[3] The violence that began in Jerusalem spread to Hebron, Nablus and other areas. The Assistant Superintendent at Hebron, Raymond Cafferata, who at one stage had been the only European officer present in the town, witnessed scenes of horrific violence: 'an Arab in the act of cutting off a child's head with a sword' and Jewish homes invaded by crowds 'armed with crowbars, sledgehammers, swords and knives'.[4] He wrote to his mother reflecting that violence would continue and that he would not be surprised if Palestine became a 'repetition of the Irish show' unless the Government ceded to some of the Arab community's demands.[5]

The British reacted promptly to the events of 1929 and set up the Shaw Commission to prepare an investigation. Meanwhile, the Chief of Air Staff and advisor to the Colonial Office on security, Lord Trenchard, recommended greater police deployment throughout Palestine. Some 200 European officers were despatched to swell the ranks of the British Section with a further 290 officers arriving in 1930.[6] While the report was underway, Dowbiggin was summoned to Palestine in January 1930 to advise on police reform.

Dowbiggin would have liked his Ceylon experiment to work in Palestine, namely the creation of a civil, chiefly unarmed, police force operating in a similar fashion to that of the Metropolitan Police. He recommended 'bringing the British police into touch with the Palestinian police' as the segregation between the British and Palestinian Sections created distance and by extension, alienation from the local community. This was a hard task as it required the British Section to cease acting as a strike force and to become engaged in *real* police duties. For Dowbiggin, this involved the prevention and detection of crime, with public order duties taking second place. The gathering of intelligence remained paramount and required close police and military co-operation. To ensure that protection was offered at designated trouble spots, he suggested that military forces be stationed alongside the police within these positions to ensure that an area could be reached in timely fashion. The mounted police would be retained and indeed increased to search remote areas.[7] Dowbiggin also suggested that the number of police stations be increased from 88 to 116 to help quell disturbances and to assist in the gathering of information.[8]

The reform of the Palestine Police would be overseen by one of Dowbiggin's former protégés from the Ceylon Police, Roy Spicer. Poached from the Kenya Police, with which he was serving as Commissioner, Spicer replaced Mavrogordato in July 1931.[9] As hostility between the Arab and Jewish populations increased throughout the 1930s, so that the police were called upon to deal with more public security issues as compared to localised crime prevention. However, Spicer persisted in his attempts to reshape the Palestine Police, as Dowbiggin had intended, with the assistance of his second-in-command and old Kenya colleague Harry Rice. 'Under these two men the force took on a discipline, an impartiality and a sense of urgency which had to be seen to be believed . . . There were no sacred cows, no one was allowed to question or disobey an order once those ideas had been aired and put into the daily routine', commented a former Palestine Police officer.[10]

In 1936, serious rioting broke out once again, which was to continue until 1939. The Peel Commission, sent out in November 1936 to investigate the cause of the so-called Arab revolt, reported back to the British Government in September 1937. Its principal recommendation was the creation of an Arab *and* a Jewish state, dividing Palestine in two. This fuelled Arab discontent still further and effectively paved the way for the British exodus in 1948. As the situation unfurled, so security measures were stepped up. With the Peel Commission sitting, some 25,000 policemen and soldiers were sent out to Palestine, prompting Moshe Shertok's comment that 'no military force of this size had left that country's shores since World War I'.[11] A Jewish supernumerary police force was established at the same time both to assist in the protection of Jewish settlements and to rebalance the numbers of Jews and Arabs in the police.

Former Secretary of State for India Lord Peel, advising on police reform, prompted the arrival in 1938 of Tegart in the guise of unofficial police advisor to the Colonial Office.[12] Tegart was an Irishman and had joined the Bengal Police in 1901 as a junior officer, rising to the rank of Commissioner of the Calcutta Police in 1923. In India, he had gained experience in both security policing and crime prevention and detection, and encouraged his officers to be effective in both spheres.[13] Tegart is said to have had strong views about the political situation in Palestine, accepting of Zionism and encouraging close co-operation between the colonial Government and the Jewish Agency. Indeed, he contracted the Histradrut's construction company Solel Boneh[14] to build his personally designed frontier road with a barbed-wire fence along the northern border, those areas of Palestine that touched the Lebanon and Syria. The same company was involved in the construction of 'reinforced concrete police stations and posts, each with a number of defence towers [and] armoured doors'.[15] These quasi-police forts became known as 'Taggarts' or 'Tegarts'.[16]

In his subsequent report, Tegart argued that 'provided there would be military forces in the country for the next twenty years, what was required was not a Gendarmerie but a really efficient Police Force'. In this manner Tegart drew on Dowbiggin's 1930 report and his own Indian experiences of running security and crime prevention initiatives in tandem.[17] Yet Tegart's report was of significance in that, paradoxically, it argued for the continued militarisation of the force. Locally, this would eradicate some of the weaknesses perceived as inherent within the police and on a wider scale, this would maintain British imperial rule within Palestine. 'There should be an adequate striking force of British Police at all important centres, and it should be capable of being thrown in immediately on the outbreak of serious disturbance', he wrote. In essence, Tegart was advising on the enhancement of the semi-military nature of the Palestine Police. 'British police are eminently suited for employment as Lewis gun teams' he counselled in this respect.[18] Tegart even proposed the creation of a rural mounted division, comparable to the Trans-Jordan Frontier Force, organised on military rather than police lines. Although this recommendation was eventually quashed, it underlined the thinking of the time and the desire to retain a strong militarised police presence within Palestine. The stark reality was that the theory of a civil police force ran counter to the harsh exigencies of the situation.[19] And so, in this vein, Spicer commented in *The Police Journal* that rioting crowds must be prevented physically from coming into proximity with the police. If a baton charge ensued, then it should not penetrate too deeply into the crowd for fear of policemen being isolated. Police equipment was also changed, with a preference for pick-handles rather than short batons, large shields and steel helmets to reduce injury from projectiles.[20]

The Arab revolt of 1936 thus brought about police reform and augmented police strength, though it failed to balance out the number of Arab and Jewish police officers. By 1944, on the eve of Irgun's concerted campaign against British rule, European officers made up well over 50 per cent, with just 20 per cent of Arab and 13 per cent of Jewish personnel.

Translations of seized Irgun Zvai Leumi (IZL) documents from this period by the CID paint this organisation as comprised of 'fighters' for 'national honour and political freedom'. Referring to itself as the National Military Organisation, it demanded that its participants continue 'terror in the towns and fighting in the hills', for the 'rifle outweighed the eulogy'.[21] The way forward to remove 'the misfortune of Jewry was shown by the National Military Organisation with fire and sword'. The IZL supported and hoped to develop its youth organisation, known as the Irgun Hagannah, or Youth Movement, which comprised young people between the ages of 16 and 20 years of age, the majority having spent 2 years in one of the Betar Mobilised Squads.[22] By October 1945, the Hagannah armed wing of the Jewish Agency (representing its Yishuv community) was the largest of these insurgent forces, assisted by the IZL and Lochmei He'rut Israel (LHI) which had begun sporadic terrorist attacks in 1942. The Palestine Police estimated IZL membership at 5,000, LHI's at around 100 members.[23]

The possible reorganisation and modernisation of the Palestine Police along civil lines was reconsidered in 1946 under the auspice of

Sir Charles Wickham, a former RUC Inspector-General.[24] Wickham insisted that policemen 'are civilians' and that 'they resent a military atmosphere, military discipline or being turned into military units where their efficiency inevitably must be judged as soldiers and not as police'.[25] (It should be noted, however, that the Palestine Police had been designated a military force during the war under Section 51(1) of the Police Ordinance.) By the same token, Wickham admitted that it was a 'police responsibility to fight . . . by an intensification of their normal procedure and operation'. He stressed the importance of the role of the police in an intelligence-gathering capacity, one for which they needed to establish 'friendly relations with the public'.[26] Thus although he deplored the use of armoured-car patrols, considering that 'motorised fighting police alienate the public' and resembled 'the Gestapo too closely', he accepted the need for a militarily trained police force, provided that it was brought up to strength and that police recruits received adequate training in police duties.[27]

As with Tegart's earlier findings, Wickham's report presented something of a paradox. On the one hand he recommended moves to civilianise the police and yet, on the other, insisted that the expansion of the force be undertaken through a pool of recruits drawn from the paramilitary strike force, the Palestine Police Mobile Force. The worsening of the situation in Palestine precluded any change to the military nature of the police.

Police memoirs and diaries from the 1946–48 period describe the security force's attempts, albeit in vain, to maintain control against ever-increasing hostility from both sides. Many members of the Palestine Police felt they were poorly equipped to deal with public disorder, let alone take on a counter-insurgency role:

> The primitive riot equipment consisted of a metal shield the size of a dustbin lid with a handle and a loop for one's arm, and steel helmets and truncheons, or the longer *lathi*. [sic] . . . We had to learn the mandatory order inscribed on the large banners which were carried by the riot squads 'Cease this useless bloodshed, go back to your homes, or we will fire'.[28]

In his diary the young British Constable Joe Bryant wrote of how 'policemen are hated like poison out here and any chance of shooting them is welcomed'. He also mentioned 'rumours going about this evening that Britain may drop the mandate of Palestine in which case the police force will be properly in the soup, being fired upon by both sides'.[29] Michael Lang, too, wrote: 'the terrorist is the 'man-in-the-street' and the worker on the land; the scout-master, the teacher, factory worker and shop keeper'.[30] Besides, 'in such situations there is

3 Jaffa riots, 1933

no front line behind which one can feel secure. The newest recruit could be the next victim of an ambush just as easily as a long-serving officer.'[31]

As the mandate drew to a close diary entries reveal daily 'killings' of civilians, members of underground movements and the security forces and the detrimental effect these deaths were having on morale:

> The Arabs mined the Egged [sic] armoured bus on the Rosh Pima road again today and got 4. We heard the explosion and shooting just before we started out with a three tonner and Morris armoured car. I was in the turret of the Morris. When we reached the calvert at Kilo 204 we came upon it and saw the Arabs around in the hills. We stopped short and watched the men in the hills turn, pause and then make off. I thought they they were probably Hagannah men who had cleared out of the bus which was then 50 metres down the road with its nose in a larger crater . . . S . . .was in a hopeless state, he had no idea of what to do and was shouting and screaming at us all, his intention being to open up at the people on the hills.[32]

Thus moves to civilianise aspects of the Palestine Police were pushed aside by the need for a semi-militarised police force that could operate effectively in a colonial war. Thus the need for colonial-style police training remained paramount, and there is no better example of this than the Palestine Police. Its influence with regard to training and paramilitary policing duties was carried throughout the Empire.

[110]

4   Home-made armoured car, Palestine, 1934

Developing counter-insurgency techniques in Palestine: strike forces

The use of police to provide internal defence and security led to the creation of support units known as police mobile, or strike, forces. The training given to these strike forces was heavily militarised and geared to the provision of strong-arm support in situations of public disorder. The Palestine Police Mobile Force (PPMF) provided an early example of this type of unit which was exported throughout the Empire. Created in 1944, it provided a fully militarised unit under the command of the Palestine Police. Its approved establishment stood at 59 gazetted officers and 1,940 other ranks under the leadership of Colonel P. H. Stable.[33] John Rymer-Jones, as Inspector-General, was responsible for securing wartime Cabinet approval for this venture, in the wake of the police's 'disastrous' attempt to search the Jewish settlement of Ramat ha Kovish in 1943, which ended in bloodshed and many casualties.[34] Essentially, the PPMF[35] was formed 'for fear that disturbances might break out on a large scale and that the military forces available in support of the civil power might be inadequate'.[36] It was set up initially with 800 servicemen from Italy, North Africa and Britain, many of whom were on contract to the Palestine Police.[37] The PPMF was organised, trained and equipped along military lines and its personnel wore battle dress from its foundation.

[111]

5   Captain John Rymer-Jones, Inspector-General Palestine Police 1943–46,
from an original pencil drawing

The Government, however, had been keen to stress that the PPMF
was 'not (repeat not) intended to be a military formation separate from
the Palestine Police'. The intention was that it should replace the previous strike force on a larger scale and serve as a recruiting ground for
the regular police.[38] Perceived as *the* crack unit in terms of counter-
insurgency policing, it was largely responsible for the cordoning of settlements prior to search missions and for road patrols.[39] Its paramilitary
nature was highlighted by the weapons available for use by each
PPMF company, of which there were eight. The weapons included 50
2-pounder guns, 100 smoke dischargers, 64 2-inch mortars, 50 3-inch
Brownings and 132 light machine-guns.
    Police mobile, or strike, forces in many other colonies were
modelled largely on the early Palestine version. John Coles used what

[112]

6   Mounted British Police, Palestine, 1946

he had learned as a Palestine Police officer to develop the mobile force detachment at Elmina Castle in the Gold Coast in 1948. Coles stressed that these mobile contingents were used initially for preventative purposes rather than commando-style operations. They did, however, include more than twenty former gazetted Palestine Police officers, experienced in mobile force work, who had been seconded to the colony.[40] The Northern Rhodesian Police also set up a mobile force, in 1949, at Bwana Mkubwa in the Copperbelt region. This unit was specifically officered by men who had served either in the Palestine Police or in the RUC.[41] It was set up along similar lines to those of the PPMF. The Eritrea field force, established in 1945, was considered a perfect copy of the PPMF and was eventually led by former Palestine policemen following the 1948 disbandment.

Outside Africa, there were two important examples of mobile strike forces modelled on the PPMF: Malaya and Cyprus. Lieutenant-Colonel W. Nicol Gray, Commissioner of the Malayan Police, was responsible for development of the jungle squads in Malaya in 1948, the forerunner of the jungle companies in 1950 and subsequently the Police Field Force. While the jungle squads operated in a completely different terrain, they were trained 'gurkha fashion' in the same manner as the PPMF and were led by former members of the Palestine Police. In Kenya, the General Service Unit was inspired by the PPMF. Sir Richard Catling, Commissioner of the Kenya Police during the Mau Mau emergency, had served in both Palestine and Malaya. In Cyprus, the Police Mobile Reserve Division (PMRD) was largely developed and commanded by Hugh (Scotty) Johnstone-Scott, a former Palestine policeman. He remained at the head of this division, comprising ten units, until his retirement in 1960. Each unit was commanded by a colonial police inspector or an assistant superintendent of police (ASP), some having served in the Palestine Police.[42] Chief Superintendent Baxendale, a former member of the Palestine Police who had served in Eritrea,

[113]

Tripitolania and Kenya prior to his posting to Cyprus in 1955, also played a role in setting up this new PMRD. It was disbanded at the end of 1959.[43]

Snatch squads and pseudo gangs

With the development of political and security intelligence in Palestine came the creation of police undercover units. Gray, who became Inspector-General in March 1946, supported the idea of snatch squads and pseudo gangs. Gray, an ex-Marine, found the wartime successes of new organisations such as the Special Air Service (SAS) and the Special Operations Executive highly appealing.

Gray appointed Brigadier Bernard Fergusson, who had served in Burma, as Assistant Inspector-General to form these units, under the banner of the Palestine Police and to be responsible for their training and organisation. Early in 1947, Fergusson was despatched to London to recruit leaders for his squads. He chose two of his former pupils from his instructor days at Sandhurst, Roy Farran and Alastair McGregor. Both men had served in the embryonic SAS.[44] The squads themselves comprised members of the Palestine Police, Army and Air Force.[45] From Spring 1947, Farran's squad operated in the Jaffa–Tel Aviv area and McGregor's in the Jerusalem area, both with great success.[46] Fergusson had intended that these former 'specially trained' servicemen would train the police in modern weaponry and survival techniques as practised by commando troops, alongside their other duties. Yet aside from this there is evidence that, despite repeated warnings from Gray, these squads operated outside the law. Edward Horne noted that they were 'to disappear into the Jewish areas . . . the main object being to flush out terrorist nests and then either arrest or shoot to kill'. He points out that they were, *theoretically*, accountable to the law like any other police officer,[47] but in reality the squads had operational free rein. Farran commented that he had 'to all intents and purposes [been given] a *carte blanche* [sic] . . . a free hand for use against terror when all others were so closely hobbled!' Using the unorthodox 'Grant-Taylor methods' of close-quarter combat, the squads were encouraged to tackle the IZL and the Stern Gang, or Lehi Group. Counter-terrorism and intelligence were seen as entirely the domain of the police, the army being used essentially for guard duty and assistance with cordons and curfews.[48]

In the event, darker aspects of their work emerged with the so-called 'Farran Affair' and the latter's implication in the murder of Alexander Rubowitz, a member of Lehi who vanished in 1947. As a result of the ensuing scandal, the squads were ordered to stand down and all operations in progress were suspended. Fergusson was forced to resign his police commission.[49] In the event, Farran was found not guilty and the murderer of Rubowitz remained unidentified.[50]

The movement of former members of the Palestine Police throughout the Empire

Emergencies required newer forms of policing that brought the traditional paramilitary style into contact with counter-insurgency tactics. The experiences of those responsible for policing Palestine shaped the practice of colonial policing. Methods evolved and then were exported throughout the Empire by former members of the Palestine Police. Importantly, Palestine became *the* unofficial training and recruiting ground for senior colonial policemen.

As discussions regarding the future Colonial Police Service were underway in the early 1930s, so the question of a centre for colonial police training arose. This was in line with the Colonial Office's desire for standardisation. Jeffries was strongly in favour, pointing out that the Colonial Office had a 'good deal of experience recruiting men from the Palestine Police for commissioned ranks in Africa'.[51] Up until 1936, senior officials had debated the merits of the Palestine Police as the focal point for training future commissioned officers,[52] and there was concern voiced in many quarters as to the whether the Palestine Police was the best option. The Ceylon Police also came up for discussion, for under Dowbiggin they had become 'the best training school that we have', providing officers with excellent service records, including 'Mr Spicer in Palestine, Mr Sherringham in Zanzibar [and] Mr King in Cyprus'.[53] Although a Colonial Office minute in 1934 doubted the excellence of the Palestine Police training, finding that 'Kenya['s] white Constables were better than some of the commissioned ranks in Palestine'.[54]

Spicer, as Inspector-General of the Palestine Police from 1931 to 1937, 'pleaded' that the Colonial Office 'should begin to look upon the British Section of the Palestine Force as a training ground for Colonial Police Probationers'. The reason was twofold. First, Spicer considered that recruits to the Palestine Police had always been of the highest calibre: 'We have now', he wrote in 1934, 'a great number of a splendid type of young Britisher who is of good birth, well educated, and suitable in every way for rapid promotion in the Colonial Police Service'. He then outlined the extensive training received by recruits which included criminal law, procedure code, laws of evidence, local laws and ordinances, standing force orders, practical police work and 'instruction examinations in both the vernaculars of this country e.g. Arabic and Hebrew', not to mention the arduous arms and foot drill and equitation. The second reason would appear to have been closer to

Spicer's personal ambitions: he simply wanted to ensure that his 'excellent training ground' provided long-term promotion for every officer. With 650 constables serving in the British Section, there was little possibility for any but a handful to secure promotion in the Palestine Police – a 'gloomy' prospect for those officers. Indeed in the previous year only three had obtained promotion: Corporal Munby seconded to the Seychelles Police as Commissioner; Sergeant Alderson to the commissioned ranks of the Bermuda Police; and Constable Ford who had been promoted in the Palestine Police to Acting Superior Officer.[55]

The Colonial Office carefully considered Spicer's requests. In response, it was agreed that not only did the Palestine Police recruit from 'young men of good birth and education', but each officer received 'a thorough grounding in Police work'. Thereafter they would be suitable for promotion and secondment to other colonial constabularies where 'Colonial Governments would certainly not be the losers by getting trained men for the same salary as new probationers'.[56] As a result, some 100 members of the British Section left to take senior police appointments in other parts of the Empire between 1933 and 1939.[57]

Rymer-Jones, Inspector-General from 1943 to 1946, discussed the possibility of Palestine becoming the senior officer-producing unit for the Colonial Police Service once more with the Colonial Office. Rymer-Jones stated that, as a result of his actions, this became official policy from 1943 to 1947.[58] The Palestine Police provided an important training and recruiting ground for future colonial policemen.

Overall from 1926 to 1947 almost 10,000 men passed through the training depot.[59] Figures gleaned from a number of sources have shown that between 1920 and 1946, of the 58 most senior-ranking officers (inspector-general, deputy inspector-general, assistant inspector-general and senior superintendent), the majority rose to the most senior ranks in the Colonial Police Service, about 12 becoming Commissioners of Police.[60] Peak recruiting from the Palestine Police seems to have occurred after 1935 and up until disbandment, when approximately 108 former members of the Palestine Police rose to the most senior ranks in 49 police forces. Of these the majority were colonial police forces, although five British and a small number of non-British police forces recruited from the Palestine ranks. Senior officers aside, from 1935 to 1948, approximately 2,731 former Palestine policemen (of all ranks) found employment in other colonial territories, Commonwealth countries and a few other territories. The last Palestine policeman, R. G. W. Lamb, went on to serve in the Falklands and was present during the Argentine invasion in 1982.[61] Approximately 1,483 of the total number mentioned served in the Colonial Police Service.

The influence of the Palestine Police reached its zenith following its disbandment on 15 May 1948.[62] Approximately 1,400 Palestine policemen obtained postings after disbandment, which almost coincided with the declaration of a state of emergency in Malaya (June 1948) and the measures undertaken to strengthen the police.[63] The Government requested that police recruits have 'special experience in combating terrorism', and suggested an intake from the Palestine Police.[64] As a result, a Special Constabulary numbering approximately 500 former Palestine policemen was established.[65] In the event, some 404 served in the Malay Police Force, with 70 former Palestine policemen killed as a direct result of counter-insurgency work. Those policemen were used for training and organising special constables on the estates and mines, as leaders of jungle squads and as technicians in the Malay Police wireless and transport service.[66] They were regarded as particularly useful in jungle operations and counter-insurgency work.

The difficulties of policing Cyprus 1955–60

With the end of the mandate in Palestine and with troubles brewing in Suez, close attention was paid to Cyprus: strategically, the island's military base was well-placed in relation to the both the Middle East and the Mediterranean. By the mid-1950s the future constitutional development of Cyprus was threatened by the campaign for the island to be joined with Greece, or *enosis*, undertaken by Greek Cypriots and opposed by the Turkish minority.

In terms of policing, the Colonial Office recognised only in 1948 that the Cyprus Police needed to be more efficient overall, better organised, equipped and trained. With a worsening of the security situation, reform came mainly in the form of British policemen seconded from the home forces.

Policing the ethnically divided population of Cyprus had never been easy. During the period of conflict that ensued, the EOKA leader George Grivas drove a deeper wedge between the general public and the police in his attempts to attack the colonial administration. The communalisation of the Cyprus Police was used as a means to measure the balance of power between the Greek and Turkish communities.[67] In 1949, a Colonial Office official noted:

The only police the Cypriots knew before were the Turkish Police of Ottoman days, and I have no doubt that they were extremely rough and ready and arbitrary in their ways . . . So long as a police force behaves like that the population will never regard the police as their friends and servants and co-operate with them as 99 citizens out of 100 do here [in

Britain] . . . The Cypriot government may not realise the price they are paying by not establishing a 'cleaner' tradition of policing.[68]

Yet in a manner commensurate with other colonies, it took a declaration of a state of emergency on 26 November 1955 to bring about an increase in police establishment and the force's subsequent reform. As the situation in Cyprus escalated towards an emergency, Police Commissioner George Robins feared that morale was too low to retaliate against Grivas's full-scale attacks, designed to terrorise the police and kill as many as possible. 'I must emphasise', he wrote, 'that events in Malaya and Kenya prove how much more costly it is in the long run to give the police too little too late.'[69] A strengthening of the Cyprus Police was envisaged by mid-1955, and Robins was sent to the Canal Zone to vet applications from police officers for Special Branch and communications posts.[70]

It was not until May of the following year that the island was under police control. Even then, the Colonial Office was convinced that the British way forward was best. In 1956, J. W. Deegan from the Colonial Office wrote that the police continued to be regarded 'as a sort of "alien, imperialistic strong arm". I am sure in time it would gain the confidence, respect and co-operation of the public.'[71]

The Governor, Field-Marshal Sir John Harding, pushed for an expansion of the Cyprus Police, including the creation of Police mobile reserves, drawn principally from the Turkish-Cypriot community. *Britishness* would be introduced in the form of the leadership provided for this new unit and by adding to the ranks of the regular police through recruitment from the home forces.[72] British police would then 'assist' the Cypriot police in the transitional period following the cessation of emergency regulations. It was felt that the 'colonial policemen, i.e. from the Federation of Malaya, were not as a general rule the type needed in Cyprus in the long term,'[73] and that personnel with a background in civil-style policing would offer better community policing in the longer term. However, for the duration of the emergency, those officers would find themselves in a potentially counter-insurgency role. That in itself would become problematical for the Home Office.

In 1955, two British policemen were sent out to Cyprus.[74] The Home Office became rapidly concerned about British officers, having been exposed to policing Cyprus, then returning to more 'normal' duties in Britain.[75] The Colonial Office, on the other hand expressed the view that had been held since 1948: the Cyprus Police should be reinforced with British policemen to bring 'civil order' within the realms of emergency policing.[76] By early 1956, the Colonial Office was pressing for additional British policemen to be sent to Cyprus. After some delay, 150 officers were seconded under the command of Inspector Lockley of the Metropolitan Police.[77]

Later that year, Commissioner Robins of the Cyprus Police and his deputy, John Biles, were *forced* to resign.[78] Robins was replaced by Lieutenant Colonel George White, Chief Constable of the Warwickshire Police, on a two-year secondment.[79] The replacement of these senior colonial policemen came about for two reasons: it was in direct response to Colonial Office attempts to export Britishness; and Harding wanted to bring in his own men in view of the security situation to eradicate ongoing turf wars between the army and the police – a familiar theme of colonial conflicts of the end of Empire. The resignations of Robins and Biles were forced rather than sought on grounds of ineptitude. Sir Robert Armitage, then Governor of Cyprus, had even acknowledged Robins's achievement in reforming the previously poor intelligence system.

Robins had been determined to modernise the police force and to work effectively with the British security services to ensure anti-terrorist operations were carried out effectively.[80] However, in terms of the relationship between the administration and the police during this period, Armitage had declared shortly after his arrival in Cyprus that 'there is a lack of coordination between the forces and the government'.[81] He held numerous meetings between the police, the armed forces and the administration in an attempt to overcome the apparent differences. The problems of operational co-ordination were never properly resolved.[82] Martin Clemens, Defence Secretary in Cyprus during this period, stated that Robins was loath to discuss security matters with him. Moreover, 'he just did not co-operate with anyone. I believe that all concerned (army and administration) felt the same.'[83] He added: 'With terrorism on your hands, everyone must co-operate . . . Every military problem needed a civil response and every civil problem affected the military.'[84]

This was particularly true in terms of sharing intelligence. Some senior police officers felt that the army used *police* intelligence rather than its own for operational gain. This destroyed valuable intelligence links the police had built up on the ground. Mr Robinson, brought in by Armitage to head up the Special Branch, 'did not take kindly to military indiscretions in dealing with intelligence'.[85] Robinson had, after all, been involved in 'cleaning up Limassol' and arresting EOKA suspects, including the 'whole Cotsapas family'.[86]

On 17 September 1955, serious rioting took place in Nicosia which culminated in the use of the South Staffordshire Regiment. Colonel 'Tiger' White, the army's senior public relations officer, told the press on the following day that the police had failed to work with the army in suppressing the disturbances. 'Four times, between 10.20 and 11.20 p.m. the army had asked the police whether they required assistance and were told that it was not needed.' White defended the army, and since the police and administration were not represented at the press conference, they took the blame. Armitage revealed that 'there was no proper tie-up between the military and police', despite all the steps he had taken to get effective co-ordination of operations. Robins offered his resignation at that stage but was told by Armitage that 'Governors were expendable but not Commissioners of Police'.[87] Despite plans for closer co-operation between the army and the police, the situation worsened. The decision was taken that Armitage was to stand down and be replaced by Sir John Harding. By August 1956, two other heads had rolled – those of Robins and Biles.[88]

The sacking of Robins, and Biles's imminent departure for Zanzibar, left the Colonial Office in a quandary. White demanded that the new deputy have considerable seniority and experience, but Stourton commented that any 'officers who would be suitable are either drawing much more pay already, or it may well be that such officers do not feel like putting their heads on what may well become a chopping block . . .'.[89] White's view was wholly supported meanwhile by Brigadier George Baker, Harding's Chief of Staff, and by Harding himself.[90] Despite the issues raised, neither Harding nor White had experience of colonial policing. Harding wanted the police to be involved in army-style operations. Paradoxically, this conflicted with Colonial Office thinking at the time, which was of exporting Britishness to the Cyprus Police. When a last minute offer was made for him to remain in Cyprus, Biles's position was that the 'political interference' which took place at the hands of the administration and army made it impossible for him to consider staying. The attempts by the Colonial Office to construct a 'non-colonial policy' through the use of British policemen made the job of colonial policemen untenable.[91]

Nevertheless, the export of the fabled *British* police ethos became central to the policing of Cyprus. White was keen to point out that UK policemen were 'indispensable' for use during the Cyprus emergency and felt there was a need to retain experienced sergeants and inspectors. 'Really experienced men of these ranks do not exist in the colonial police service', he claimed.[92] By October 1956 the number of British policemen was once again deemed insufficient,and calls were made for a further 132 officers, including 12 dog-handlers, 9 replacements for officers on per-manent sick leave and 9 officers to work as guards in the internment camp. The Colonial Office declared a preference for Metropolitan Police and Birmingham policemen or perhaps a few drawn from the Scottish forces. This was no doubt influenced by Harding's praise of the earlier contributions made by Metropolitan Police officers in Cyprus.[93]

In the event, the Cyprus administration became loath to repatriate the UK Police Unit, particularly in view of the continuing postponement of independence. Sir Hugh Foot wanted to retain as many as possible of the British officers in Cyprus:

> I shall see as many of the members of the UK Police Unit as I can to press them and persuade them to stay. I may be able to work out a scheme by which those who have served longest here can take leave in the UK on condition that they are subject to immediate recall. Looking further ahead, we might wish very soon to appeal to the home police forces to release men who have served here before to come back for a further period of service in Cyprus.[94]

Foot was particularly keen to retain certain Special Branch officers, for example Chief Superintendent Barlow, who had returned to London to take up employment as Investigating Officer with the Ministry of Supply.[95]

Foot insisted that the duties and function of the UK Police Unit would be different from those performed during the emergency. He considered that reinforcements of about 110 men, of whom 70 were to have uniformed duties, would be adequate.[96] Wherever possible these civil police officers should 'no longer carry guns', which was seen as tendering an olive branch to the local communities. By 1960, the UK Police Unit stood at 182 officers.[97] From that point, it was decided to send a 'block of 100–150 men' by appealing to chief constables directly to release named officers with previous service in Cyprus.[98] As a consequence the Colonial Office wrote directly to all chief constables and police authorities requesting permission that certain members of the UK Police Unit extend their residential service in Cyprus for an initial period of three months. This would be renewable on a month-to-month basis thereafter by mutual agreement. The officers concerned had already been approached and a majority, from thirty-five police forces, accepted the offer.[99] Seven counties provided one policeman each, 6 provided 2, another 6 provided 3, and 2 provided 4 apiece. Eight borough forces supplied one man each, one 2, and another 3; the Met gave 19. The implication of these proportions is that the various forces were encouraged to find suitable men on a *pro rata* basis.[100]

The members of the UK Police Unit who served for a period of time in Cyprus and who had returned to their parent force by 1960 also appear to have been provided by quota, with one exception. They included 33 Special Branch officers from 21 forces, and 431 uniformed officers from 103 forces. The nineteen CID officers came from just four forces (Durham, Kent, Lancashire and the Metropolitan Police), suggesting that the detectives were selected to transfer to existing teams. Almost 1,000 British policemen served some time in Cyprus.[101]

The case of the Aden Police

The Aden Police faced difficulties similar to those of both the Palestine and the Cyprus Police prior to the British withdrawal in 1967.[102] During the final decades of colonial rule, the Aden Police was increasingly faced with resistance to British rule in the form of inter-community disturbances, industrial unrest, student demonstrations and rising 'violent resistance labeled terrorism by the British'.[103] Aden was of strategic value to the British in a similar way to Cyprus, a 'link in the chain of imperial colony fortresses'.[104] It had become part of the Empire on its capture in 1839, in an attempt to protect British interests in the Middle East. Officially the port of Aden only was under British control; the remainder, known as the Aden Protectorates, was a small group of states, each ruled by its monarch. These became later divided into the twenty-four states of Eastern and Western Aden Protectorates. Within this area the Aden Police had no jurisdiction. In the western region, each state had its own security force of Government Guards, under British and Arab officers. Local forces of 'tribal guards' or tribal police operated throughout, some groups being financially supported by grants from Britain. In the eastern section, police and security work was carried out by the constabulary and other forces working within a particular state. Security in the Protectorates was perceived as a wider problem than it was in Aden Colony. Principal concerns revolved around keeping the trade routes open 'by the old-fashioned method of placating unruly and tiresome individuals with rifles and ammunition and money'.[105]

Although a part of the Arabian Peninsular, Aden and the Protectorates were administered by the Bombay Presidency until 1937 when they were transferred under the auspices of the Colonial Office. By that time, Aden's military defence had been transferred to the Royal Air Force, which had proved to be a more effective and less expensive way of policing Britain's recent acquisitions in the Middle East.[106] Keeping the Protectorates politically stable was of strategic value in creating a buffer zone between Aden–Yemen and Saudi Arabia.

An Aden Colony police force had existed since the 1850s.[107] Prior to that period, the first Governor of the Aden settlement, S. B. Haines, had recruited a small unit, made up of 9 Arabs and 2 Indians, to police the port from 1839. This quasi-police force was augmented the following year when Bombay dispatched several police constables. By 1855, the police numbered 160, among them the first draft of European consta-bles.[108] From April 1932 until March 1937, the Aden Police was admin-istered as a 'Chief Commissioner's Province' under the control of central government in Dehli, becoming a colonial police force proper in 1937. Aid to the civil power had come from one British and one Indian infantry battalion. With a move at this time to use the RAF rather than the army, principally for financially reasons, the need for an 'armed' as distinct from a civil police arose.[109] As with the Indian Police, the Bombay Government saw a need for two police units oper-ating side by side. An armed branch of the police would be recruited, resulting in an establishment set at 2 British officers, 14 inspectors, 4 *jamadars* (the Indian rank equivalent to assistant sub-inspector), 200 armed police and a further 292 constables.[110]

The armed police, principally recruited from the Protectorates, were set up in a similar manner to the RIC, housed in military barracks outside the main town, Crater. Recruits into the Civil Police were some-what different to the Armed Police counterparts in terms of background and education. The civil police were recruited from Aden Colony as well as the Protectorates and tended to be literate in Arabic. A small number had some command of English and were recruited directly into the Inspectorate. Jeffries noted that there were even two locally recruited gazetted officers in the civil police by 1950.[111] Attempts were made to improve training and standards between 1947 and 1967 by sending offi-cers to Britain to attend courses at Hendon or Ryton-on-Dunsmore. Some expatriate officers also attended language courses at the School of Oriental and African Studies. Inspectors could expect to receive training with other colonial police forces, notably in Kenya or the Sudan.[112]

The potential for social disorder was present in every colony at the end of empire, and Aden was no exception. Managing the Arab com-munities alongside ethnic minorities provided the backdrop against which growing nationalism would provoke serious unrest.[113] In his autobiography, former Governor Sir Tom Hickinbotham explained:

> There are in the Colony three races who have no special love for each other. The Jews are disliked and despised by the Arabs whom they fear, while the Arabs in their turn dislike the Somalis who are, at the best of times, a truculent lot. Therefore, we were always liable to have trouble between the Arabs and the Jews which might well spread to the Hindu community, or between the Somalis and the Arabs, or between all three, and in no time we were having a devil of a storm, which with firm mea-sures would pass as quickly as it began.[114]

Indeed public order disturbances occurred in Aden in 1931 and 1947, with strikes taking place between 1956 and 1960. Thereafter the colony was placed under a state of emergency. In each case officers were forced to revert to their role as paramilitary policemen. The events of December 1947, following the November announcement of partition plans in Palestine, 'put a match to the sensitive tinder that is Aden. The result was horrible because of the appalling speed with which order dissolved into chaos and murder.'[115] Whereas the 1931 disturbances had been successfully contained, in this instance the 100 Armed Police and 60 Civil Police from Crater were overwhelmed by the scale of events. Sections of the Jewish and Arab communities soon became involved in a display of 'faction fighting', while the police 'did their best to keep order, including in their measures a small amount of carefully controlled rifle fire'.[116] Full-scale rioting ensued, with attacks on Jewish property, looting and fires raging all over Crater. When the police failed to contain the situation, the Aden Protectorate Levies – raised after the First World War as the 1st Yemen Infantry to police the roads – were deployed to bring order to the colony. The Levies arrived on the scene and fired at the crowds of rioters, but they too were unsuccessful in quelling the disorder, so that two British destroyers had to deploy naval officers and members of the North Staffordshire Regiment. When the situation was finally brought under control the scene was one of chaos: 38 Arabs and 76 Jews had been killed, and many more wounded. Extensive damage to property had occurred, particularly in the Jewish quarters, with most Jewish shops looted and destroyed. As a direct result of these events a section of the Jewish community uprooted itself to Palestine, leaving only 700 members of their community in place. Harry Trusted, the Commissioner of the inquiry into the events of 1947, placed no direct blame on the actions of the police. The finger was pointed instead at the Levies who were reported to have been 'trigger happy' in their uncontrolled use of both rifles and machine-guns. The presence of British troops in Aden was advocated for internal security purposes.[117]

A report in 1951 recorded that the force establishment stood at 311 Armed and 407 Civil Police, of whom the great majority were classified as 'Protectorate Arabs', the remainder being drawn from the Indian, Somali and Yemeni populations.[118] The role of the Armed Police had been outlined the previous year as that of 'the first line of defence in the event of civil disturbances', being 'thoroughly trained in riot drill and the use of tear smoke . . . [and] in the use of arms', including the Lewis gun.[119] The number of police officers was clearly insufficient, however, in dealing with the events of 1947. Moreover, the report queried the usefulness of augmenting the numbers of the Civil Police as compared to the Armed Police. This issue was raised when the Aden Police was inspected by IGCP Muller for the first time in September

1951. Muller became more preoccupied, however, with the question of police corruption and the lack of adequate transport, rather than with how future outbreaks of public unrest should be contained. He saw the 'serious' problems created for the police by 'the large number of passenger and cargo ships calling in the port [and] the problem of dealing with touts and preventing the nuisances common to all such ports'.[120] Muller also noted a marked difference between the Civil and the Armed Police, and the lack of the contact the latter maintained with the general public. Around the time of Muller's visit, the colony had been relatively quiet, and the Armed Police were 'regularly practised in carrying out a scheme to meet an emergency'. Muller appeared confident that they could deal with threats to internal stability. The CID, in terms of its collation of political intelligence, dealt adequately with 'deportations of undesirables, most of whom happen to be criminals'. Indeed Muller's real criticism was reserved for the police's 'unenviable reputation for corruption',[121] though in the event, little progress was made on that front.[122]

The following year, the British Government attempted to halt the wheels of decolonisation, by bringing the individual states of the Protectorates into one federation. Approving the federation in 1952, the Governor of Aden, Sir Tom Hickinbotham,[123] noted that it would serve three aims. First, it would increase political solidarity in the Protectorates, binding the regions to Aden; second, it would prepare the population for self-government; and, most importantly, it would reduce Britain's expenditure in the region by creating a financially independent state.[124] This met with the support of the Colonial Office which saw that a federation would allow the British greater control of the area, while dampening nationalist activities throughout the Middle East. Secret correspondence between the Colonial Office and Aden Colony provided evidence of the 'growing problem' with security and culminated in the posting, in March 1953, of a Security Liaison Officer (SLO). As a result Muller twice requested a review of the Aden Police's Special Branch and its subsequent 'building up'[125] This news appears to have come as something of a surprise to the Aden Government which had not discussed proposals for 'building up the Police Special Branch', which at that time was incorporated within the CID.[126]

The general pattern of 'too little, too late' certainly applied to the Aden Police. Muller had been keen to augment the Special Branch rather than the regular police. (Templer's report on colonial security in 1955 heavily criticised police intelligence in Aden.) By the late 1950s industrial unrest had spread throughout the colony. Abdallah al-Asnaj, leader of the Aden Trades Union Congress, demanded an end to the British occupation and the union with the Protectorates. With the increase in strikes and public disturbances came the need for additional police officers and the formation of a unit of riot police, the Police Mobile Squad. Created in 1959, this unit consisted initially of a sub-inspector, a sergeant, 2 corporals and 18 constables.[127]

Sir Bernard Reilly (Governor of Aden, 1938–40) had previously written to the Treasury urging an increase in police pay to 'meet the needs of the situation'. The Government of Aden was dealing with a 'serious outbreak of strikes . . . probably economic in their origin [but] being exploited for political motives and aggravated by persistent anti-British propaganda from Cairo'. The constant risk faced by the police of serious public disorder created 'heavier responsibilities' which threatened their morale as 'an efficient, well-organised and contented force'.[128] All recent disturbances, triggered principally by industrial disputes, had been quelled by the armed police.[129] However, it was hoped that police numbers could be increased across the board. This would include the appointment of an ASP for Special Branch as 'events in the colony over the last two months have shown certain defects in the overall security position necessitating a revision of the police establishment'.[130]

In partial response, the Colonial Office sent several senior figures, Lord Lloyd, J. C. Morgan and J. H. Robertson, on an official visit to Aden in May 1956. Their specific brief was to gauge reactions to the long-range policy on Aden. Lord Lloyd was to outline this policy to the Governor of Aden and the leaders in the colony and the Protectorates, emphasising the colony's strategic importance east of Suez. During the visit Lord Lloyd also met with Police Commissioner Maclean to discuss police strength.[131] With the ongoing Suez crisis, Britain's most pressing priority in the region was military. The 'Sandys White Paper' outlined Aden's new policy direction the following year. To maintain Britain's position in the Middle East after the permanent loss of the Suez base, there remained three alternative locations: Cyprus, Kenya and Aden.[132]

Following a meeting at Government House, Lord Lloyd reported that the established police strength of 500 was 'adequate' to meet the current needs. Of that number, 315 made up the Armed Police. The problem Lord Lloyd saw was not to do with the number but with the training and experience of those officers. He noted that only that morning '80 men had been in a state bordering on mutiny but had returned to work'. Their problem was that 'they had never done a proper day's work', resulting in boredom. Were internal security issues to arise, then 'he could not be sure' that the police would cope. Besides, their Commandant, an Indian officer named Khan Sahib Mohammed Khan, was shortly to retire and should be replaced by an experienced

British officer. The debate was whether recruitment should be from colonial policemen or members of the home forces.[133] Maclean accepted Lord Lloyd's report without a murmur, producing the names of four officers who, he had heard, would be suitable material for Aden – all of them senior colonial policemen: Seaby from the Gold Coast, Eccles and Patrick from Kenya and Coventry from Tanganyika.[134] The matter was taken up with Muller who agreed that three 'expatriate' ASPs should be recruited, one of whom would join the Special Branch. Clearly the use of *British* policemen had been forgotten by this stage, though not the financial constraints, a familiar theme of policing the end of empire. Lamenting 'how difficult' the Standing Finance Committee was proving to be over the possible 'expatriate staff', E. D. Hore commented that 'we deserve a bouquet rather than a brickbat for what we have achieved for the Police this year'. The Colonial Office would need 'to deliver' additional ASPs so that the Aden Government could 'see its way through'.[135]

This gradual process saw some strengthening of the gazetted section of the Aden Police but it failed to prepare the force adequately for the serious disturbances that would follow. By 1962, proposals for a 'substantial' increase of 8 gazetted officers, 14 inspectors and 191 ranks at a cost of £65,000 had reached the Standing Finance Committee, where it was met with the usual uphill struggle as the Treasury attempted to place the financial burden on the Aden Government. By 1963, the prospect seemed more realistic, particularly when Governor Trevaskis hinted to the Colonial Office that the merger of Aden with the Protectorates had increased government revenue.[136] This allowed for the 'immediate' recruitment and subsequent training of 52 police officers as of April 1963, paid for by Aden while the Colonial Office vote had made an additional provision of £10,000. By this time, the Ministry of Defence had become embroiled in arguments over financing police expansion. Their view on Aden outlined 'the major function of the base [to be] defence over a wide area in the middle east'. A 'strong Federal internal security force' was needed to contain any threat emanating from the Yemen.[137] In the event, the Treasury stood firm in its belief that payment for additional police officers should come directly from the coffers of the Aden Government. The stick used was the perceived unwillingness of the Aden Government to allow federal forces into Aden to assist in maintaining order.[138]

The debate surrounding finance directly affected two important areas of the police during this decolonisation period: one touched on localisation of the police; the other concerned compensation for retiring European expatriates. By the early 1960s, senior officers were complaining that the 'importation' of gazetted officers would be interpreted as 'an attempt to slow down Adenisation',[139] a process that had been underway for some time. 'Local' ministers were clearly opposing any prospective appointments on that very basis. Exceptions would only be made if expatriate officers were clearly designated as 'specialists' within the CID or the Special Branch. Paradoxically, senior expatriate officers were needed at this time to manage growing sections of both the Civil and the Armed Police. Any confidence in the Government's ability to maintain law and order had been eroded by police inadequacy in assessing security threats and 'dealing with them quickly and firmly in their early stages'.[140]

To deal with the ongoing crisis, the Colonial Office suggested, as it had done in Cyprus, that approximately 12 officers should be seconded from Britain on 18–24-month contracts. Concern was raised by the Home Office at the prospect of members of the home constabularies being subjected to colonial unrest. In the event, however, a handful of Met officers were seconded to Aden for short periods. They included Inspector C.O. Myhan, chosen for his military background, who became Deputy Superintendent for the duration of his stay.[141] Preference overall was given to the recruitment of experienced colonial policemen. This once again countered the notion of exporting members of the home forces.

The withdrawal from Aden: a 'nasty whiff of the Palestine scuttle about it'[142]

On 11 February 1959, the six states in the Western Protectorate united as the Federation of South Arabia. The Colonial Office viewed the Federation as bringing political stability to the region. Lennox-Boyd, the Colonial Secretary, commented at the opening ceremony that it was his 'earnest hope that while growing in strength the young Federation will also grow in size, and that it will not be long before other States in the Protectorate join it'.[143] Indeed the majority of the western states eventually joined, as well as Wahidi State from the Eastern Protectorate.

However, in establishing a Federation, a situation was created whereby interest was generated in Arab nationalism, causing the security situation to deteriorate further. Opposition from the South Arabian League, the National Liberation Front, the National United Front and the Front for the Liberation of Occupied South Yemen caused serious public unrest.

With Aden merging with the Federation in the early 1960s, the Legislative Council decided that no political group was permitted to march in protest. Following the arrest of Abdullah al-Asnaj, the leader of the People's Socialist Party – the political wing of the Aden Trades Union Congress – and the suspension of the pro-PSP newspaper *Al Haqiqa* for inciting protest against the merger, Aden's security forces were placed on alert. On the day of the debate, a near general strike began in Aden, with demonstrations taking place throughout Crater. The police were again unable to quell rioting and British troops were called in to bring the situation under control. The rioting resulted in the deaths of two protestors and several injured. In subsequent days, the decision of Governor Sir Charles Johnston was to go on the defensive. The way was clear for Aden to transfer from a being a crown colony to a new state within the Federation.[144]

Because the issue of the Yemen had wider implications for the country's future, the National Liberation Front, with its Yemeni membership, was *unofficially* supported by the Egyptian Government to shift from a political to an armed struggle at this time. Local tribes were issued with weapons to encourage them to join in the attacks on the British and the federal Government. Just as had happened in the policing of so many colonies at the end of empire, the detection and prevention of crime in Aden was overshadowed by police involvement in counter-insurgency duties. A grenade attack against High Commissioner Trevaskis in December 1963 pointed to the Federation's underlying fragility. The Federation responded by declaring a state of emergency, as also did Aden, and closing the border with the Yemen. Aden's Police Commissioner offered a £5,000 reward for information leading to the arrest of the perpetrators and ordered the deportation of prominent Yemeni political activists. The deaths of George Henderson, the Deputy High Commissioner, as a result of the grenade attack, and of members of the Federation leadership were seen as a precursor to a worsening in the security situation. 'The days of relative calm had ended and the active struggle for South Arabia had begun.'[145]

In February 1966, Prime Minister Harold Wilson announced the British Government's intention to hand over power to the Southern Arabian Federation in 1968. Mounting terrorist activity during the subsequent campaign further consolidated British policy. By the end of 1964, 39 people had been killed or injured in Aden alone as a result of terrorist attacks. That number would increase five-fold by the end of 1965.[146] Arab-speaking members of Aden Police's Special Branch were the primary victims of terrorist attacks from this time, although many members of the general public were also affected. By the end of 1966, 61 people had been killed and 426 wounded;[147] the Special Branch lost many of its members. 'British and Arab officers of the Special Branch were to be almost eliminated, one by one, until the original team had virtually ceased to exist.'[148]

The Federal Regular Army and the Aden Police were known to be infiltrated by the National Liberation Front, and it was at this time that rumours began to circulate about police brutality and torture in relation to interrogation methods: 'The British Government publicly denied the allegations of torture even though members of the Government responsible for Aden were aware of the activities in the interrogation centres and accepted them as a necessary evil.' Sir Roderick Bowen, barrister and former Liberal MP, was sent to investigate the charges. In the subsequent Bowen Report the allegations made against the police were reported as true though somewhat exaggerated.[149] The morale and reliability of the Aden Police was debated in both Foreign Office and Colonial Office circles. The 'value' of the police in engaging in anti-terrorist activities was perceived to be 'negligible' and 'under political stress easily intimidated'. As a result the army was relied on to carry out anti-terrorist activities, resulting in 'sorely strained Police/Army relations'.[150]

Aden's decreasing value to Britain was also shown after the diplomatic crisis caused by Southern Rhodesia's unilateral declaration of independence (UDI). The logistical problems of using Aden, the military base nearest to Rhodesia, made it practically impossible for Britain to react militarily to Rhodesia's UDI. By December 1965, the Joint Intelligence Committee turned its attentions to the wider ramifications of Britain's future withdrawal from Aden.[151] The decision was made to eliminate the military base, and that marked the end of Britain's presence in Aden.

The last British soldier left Aden on 28 November 1967, but not before the 'final whiff' from the Aden Police. Still under-strength and having operated in difficult circumstances, the Armed Police mutinied on 16 June 1967, on hearing rumours of British troops firing on soldiers of the South Arabian Army. Almost 140 officers took over the troops' barracks in the middle of Crater. As British troops attempted to infiltrate the area and regain control, thirteen soldiers were killed. Crater was secured by early July, but by that stage colonial rule in Aden had come to a bitter close.

The examples drawn from Cyprus and Aden have shown how British endeavours to reform the police came, typically, too late in the day. Essentially the type of reform differed between the needs of the colonial governments' and the Colonial Office's wishes. In the case of the former, police reform was based on practicalities: there were insufficient police officers and equipment to deal with the ongoing situation. These issues were dealt with by the Colonial Office, in these two cases, by meeting their criterion for reform: the transformation from a colonial to a civil style of policing. While the ongoing situation precluded the complete removal of the military aspects of policing, in seconding police officers from the home forces it was hoped that a gradual change would occur in police traditions. In Cyprus, in particular, the replacement of a senior colonial police officer with a *British* officer was proof enough. In the event, however, home-trained officers were not as suitable as those trained in colonial policing. Colonial Office theory was far removed from the practicalities of policing the end of Empire. In both Palestine and Aden, the situation simply boiled over, leaving the security forces no option but to scuttle back home, but not until the military sides to policing had been strengthened, rather than diluted, with the advent of newer forms of auxiliary force. It seemed as if there was no possibility of transplanting *Britishness* to territories where the tradition of colonial policing was deeply embedded within society and the end of Empire marked by increased resistance to colonial rule.

Notes

1   Martin Kolinsky, *Law, Order and Riots hin Mandatory Palestine, 1928–1935* (New York: St. Martin's Press, 1993), p. 79.
2   Sir Hugh Foot, *A Start in Freedom* (London: Hodder & Stoughton, 1964), p. 19.
3   Foot, *Start in Freedom*, p. 42.
4   Cafferata report, p. 4 quoted in Kolinsky, *Mandatory Palestine*, p. 51.
5   Cafferata to his mother, 29 Nov. 1929, quoted in Segev, *One Palestine, Complete*, p. 325.
6   Sir Arthur Wauchope, High Commissioner, to Colonial Secretary, Despatch, 29 Oct. 1930, NA CO 733/180/2/24.
7   Dowbiggin, 'Report on the Palestine Police', 1930, paras 140, 10.
8   Dowbiggin, 'Report on the Palestine Police', 1930, paras 156–157.
9   Colin Imray, *Policeman in Palestine* (Bideford: Edward Gaskell, 1995), pp. 6–7.
10 Imray, *Policeman in Palestine*, pp. 8–9.
11 Segev, *One Palestine, Complete*, p. 415.
12 Memo from H. F. Downie, Colonial Office, 19 Oct. 1937, NA CO 733/355/8/2.
13 Horne, *Job Well Done*, p. 236.
14 Segev, *One Palestine, Complete*, p. 428.
15 Horne, *Job Well Done*, p. 236.
16 Michael Lang, *One Man in His Time: The Diary of a Palestine Policeman 1946–48* (Lewes: Book Guild, 1997), p. 3.
17 Sir Charles Tegart, Report on Police Reorganisation, Section III, NA CO 733/383/2/32.
18 Sir Charles Tegart, Report on Police Reorganisation, Section I, NA CO 733/383/75742.
19 MacMichael to MacDonald, 4 Aug. 1938, NA CO 733/383/2/11.
20 Spicer, 'The Recent Palestine Riots: Some Police Lessons Learned', *Police Journal*, 7 (1934) pp. 350–355.
21 Translations undertaken by Palestine Police CID, 'Information of the Country Rule', No. 107 (5 Nov. 1939), District CID, HQ Nazareth, Biles, Family Papers.
22 R. H. B. Biles, District CID, HQ Nazareth, 'The Jews in Palestine', 1940, Biles, Family Papers.
23 Tim Jones, *Postwar Counterinsurgency and the SAS 1945–1952: A Special Type of Warfare* (London: Frank Cass, 2001), p. 19.
24 Report by Sir Charles Wickham, 2 Dec. 1946, NA CO 537/2269/49.

25 Wickham, 2 Dec. 1946, NA CO 537/2269 /53.
26 Wickham, 2 Dec. 1946, NA CO 537/2269/49.
27 Wickham, 2 Dec. 1946, NA CO 537/2269/50.
28 Howard Mansfield, Memoir, Palestine Police, p. 20, Family Papers.
29 J. D. Bryant, Diary entry, Monday 11 Nov. 1946, Bryant, Family Papers.
30 Lang, Sarona, 30 June, 1946, *One Man in His Time*, p. 16.
31 Lang, Tel Aviv, 14 Oct. 1946, *One Man in His Time*, p. 41.
32 Bryant, Wed. 14 March 1948, Bryant, Family Papers.
33 Palestine Secret DespatchV/1320/HH, 30 Sept. 1946, NA CO 537/1696/2.
34 Taken from an interview with Edward Horne (Palestine Police, the Met, Act. Insp., rtd, 1941–74), May 2001.
35 The PMF totalled 59 officers, 28 warrant officers and staff sergeants, 2,000 ranks and 481 tradesmen. It operated for a total of two years before a lack of recruits forced its abolition to enable members to enter the regular police. At disbandment, its actual effective strength stood at only 724. Throughout its brief existence, the PMF had never reached the total establishment of 1940. At its peak, membership had totalled just below 1,000. Palestine Secret Despatch V/1320/HH, 30 Sept. 1946, NA CO 537/1696/2.
36 Cunningham to MacMichael, Secret Despatch U/1520/44, 30 Sept. 1946, NA CO 537/1696/29.
37 Trafford-Smith, CO Minutes, 28 Nov. 1946, NA CO 537/1696.
38 Harold MacMichael to Colonial Secretary, 15 Jan. 1944, NA CO 733/451/2.
39 Taken from an interview with Edward Wells (Palestine Police, HKP, Kenya Police, Chief Insp., rtd, 1946–65), May 2000.
40 Coles, RHL MSS Afr. s. 1784, Box I, f. 34. Martin Clemens, Defence Secretary in Cyprus during the emergency, recalled that 'there were very few Colonial police-men, other than Palestine or Malayan who had the experience of modern aggres-sive politics. In any case I believe volunteers were asked for, and we did get a few, mostly ex Palestine': Clemens in correspondence with the author, 30 Dec. 2001.
41 John J. I. Hawkins, RHL MSS Afr. s. 1784, Box XVI, f. 4.
42 Peter Hewitt (Kenya, Cyprus, Nyasaland and Papua New Guinea Police, rtd, 1953–72) in correspondence with the author, 30 July 2002. Hewitt commanded one of the PMR units in Cyprus during this period.
43 Horne (interview), May 2001; Hewitt (interview), July 2002.
44 Gerald J. Green (ex-Palestine Police) to Edward Horne, 10 Aug. 1998, Horne, Family Papers; Roy Farran, *Winged Dagger: Adventures on Special Service* (London: Collins, 1948).
45 Known as 'snatch' squads or 'Q' squads owing to operations involving the 'snatch-ing' of terrorists. It has been estimated that some 400 Irgun and Stern members were arrested in 1947: interview with Ronald G. Postlethwaite (Palestine Police, 1945–48, RSM, rtd, Royal Signals, 1950–72), Nov. 2004.
46 Bernard Fergusson, *Trumpet in Hall* (London: Collins, 1970), p. 227.
47 Horne, *Job Well Done*, p. 565.
48 Farran, *Winged Dagger*, pp. 348–351.
49 Fergusson, *Trumpet in Hall*, p. 228.
50 *Palestine Post*, 3 Oct. 1947.
51 Jeffries, Minute, 23 July 1931, NA CO 850/40/7.
52 A. B. Acheson, Minute, 13 March 1934, 'Unification of Colonial Police Service', NA CO 850/40/7.
53 Minute signed G. J. F., 21 April 1934, 'Question Appointment of an Inspector-General Police', NA CO 850/54/20.
54 Flood, Minute, 14 May 1934, NA CO 850/54/20.
55 Spicer to Chief Secretary, CO, 30 Jan. 1934, NA CO 850/40/7.
56 Chief Secretary's Office: J. Hathorn Hall, Palestine, to A. C. C. Parkinson, CO, NA CO 850/40/7.
57 A. J. Kingsley-Heath, who became Assistant Inspector-General during Alan Saunders's leadership of the Palestine Police, is said to have repeatedly pressured

the Colonial Office to accept that the Palestine Police was the senior colonial officer-producing force during the 1940s: taken from an interview with Peter Kingsley-Heath, 20 May 2002. Binsley noted his encounters with members of the Palestine Police in the late 1930s who were 'part of the scheme for using the Palestine Police as a training ground for future senior officers of the Colonial Police Service': Binsley, Autobiography, unpublished, Binsley, Family Papers, p. 253.

58   Rymer-Jones gave this information to Edward Horne in 1973: Horne (interview), May 2001; Rymer-Jones's son, John, in interview with the author, Oct. 2005.

59   There was at this time only one woman serving in the Palestine Police, Violet Graham, who became Matron of Bethlehem Women's Prison, 1930–46: Horne, *Job Well Done*, pp. 386–387.

60   Palestine Police Old Comrades' Association Archive, Horne, Family Papers.

61   Horne (interview), May 2001.

62   The official stand-down took place at Buckingham Palace on 20 July 1948.

63   It would appear that some former Palestine policemen found employment in the RAF Police: Air Ministry Minutes, R. C. Kent, 14 April 1948, NA AIR 2/10228.

64   Creech-Jones, Cabinet Memo, 'The Situation in Malaya', 1 July 1948, NA CAB 129/28, CP (48)171.

65   The Colonial Office sought to recruit 500 police sergeants and a 'number' of gazetted officers for rapid secondment to Malaya: *Police Review*, 19 July 1948, NA PREM 8/1406, CP (48) 190.

66   K.W. Baxter, Colonial Office, to H. Clough, Treasury, 19 May 1950, NA CO 850/267/10.

67   Robert Holland, *Britain and the Revolt in Cyprus, 1954–1959* (Oxford: Clarendon Press, 1998), pp. 60–61.

68   J. S. Bennett, CO Minutes, 28 June 1949, NA CO 537/4982.

69   Robins to Colonial Secretary, 24 Jan. 1955, RHL MSS Medit. s. 9, ff. 1–2.

70   The total revised establishment of the Cyprus Police was put forward as one Commissioner, one Deputy Commissioner, one Force Inspecting Officer, one Civil Secretary, 3 Assistant Commissioners, 7 Senior Superintendents, 19 Superintendents, 43 Assistant Superintendents, one Director of Music, one Fire Officer, 150 Chief Inspectors, Inspectors and Sub-Inspectors, 450 NCOs and 2,800 Constables: Biles to Robins, 24 Nov. 1955, John Biles, Family Papers.

71   Deegan, CO Minute, 21 Nov. 1956, NA CO 1037/5.

72   The Police Overseas Services Act of 1945 made provision for the maintenance of British *civil* police forces in certain countries and territories outside the UK.

73   Lt. Col. G. C. White, Commissioner, to CO, letter commenting on 'Proposals New Constitution Cyprus', 1956, NA CO 1037/5/14–15.

74   'UK Police Unit in Cyprus, 1954–56', NA CO 1037/52.

75   Holland, *Revolt in Cyprus*, p. 100.

76   Robertson, CO, to Russell Edmunds, Treasury, no date (1956), NA CO 1037/53.

77   CO Minute, signature illegible, 1 June 1956, NA CO 1037/5.

78   Both Robins and Biles were experienced colonial policemen: Robins had served in the Ceylon Police, Biles in the Palestine Police and then in the Nigeria Police.

79   Biles (interview), March 2001; Colonial Secretary to O.A.G. Cyprus, Secret Telegram No. 989, 5 June 1956, NA CO 1037/5/35.

80   Colin Baker, *Retreat from Empire: Sir Robert Armitage in Africa and Cyprus* (London: I. B. Tauris, 1998), pp. 126–127. This was taken from Baker's interview with Robins on 13 June 1992. See also Robins Papers, RHL MSS Medit. s. 9, and in particular his report 'The Development of the Cyprus Police Force', 24 Jan. 1955.

81   Baker, *Retreat from Empire*, p. 151.

82   Biles (interview), March 2000.

83   Clemens in correspondence with the author, 30 Dec. 2000.

84   Clemens in correspondence with the author, 22 Feb. 2001.

85   Baker, *Retreat from Empire*, p. 152.

86   Biles to Robins, 24 Nov. 1955, John Biles, Family Papers.

87   Baker, *Retreat from Empire*, p. 163, quoted in an interview with Robins, June 1992.

88 Clark, *Colonial Police and Anti-Terrorism*, p. 319; Biles, Police Diary, Family Papers.
89 Stourton to Mullen, 26 July 1956, John Biles, Family Papers.
90 Biles in correspondence with the author, 5 April 2000.
91 Biles in correspondence with the author, 5 April 2000.
92 White to CO, 'Future Strength and Reorganisation of the Cyprus Police', Oct. 1956, NA CO 1037/5.
93 F. A. Newsam (HO) to Chairman, Standing Joint Committee, 6 June 1956, NA CO 1037/53.
94 Foot to Colonial Secretary, Telegram 86, 31 Jan. 1960, NA CO 1037/158/2.
95 Foot proposed to offer these officers the rank of inspector as an inducement on their return to Cyprus: Foot to Colonial Secretary, Telegram, 6 March 1960, NA CO 1037/158/24 and 15 Feb. 1960, NA CO 1037/158/19.
96 Foot to Colonial Secretary, Telegram, 20 Feb. 1960, NA CO 1037/8/20.
97 Sir J. Martin, CO, to W. H. Cornish, HO, 10 Feb. 1960, NA CO 1037/158.
98 S. D. Cornelius, CO Minute, 9 Feb. 1960, NA CO 1037/158.
99 D. M. Amber, CO, to Chief Constables, 16 Feb. 1960, NA CO 1037/158/8.
100 Foot to Colonial Secretary, Telegram 116, 13 Feb. 1960, NA CO 1037/158/7A.
101 E. St Johnston *One Policeman's Story* (Chichester: B. Rose, 1978), p. 243.
102 This section considers the case of the Aden Police rather than the wider spectrum of civil police and armed constabularies that existed across southern Arabia. Research into the Aden Police remains limited. See John Mathew Willis, 'Colonial Police in Aden 1937–1967', MA Arab Studies, Georgetown University (1996), Willis, 'Colonial Policing in Aden, 1937–1967', *Arab Studies Journal*, 5:1 (Spring, 1997). However, Willis's study focuses on the how the Aden Police maintained what he calls 'disciplinary order' in an attempt to bring social and political reform. This is principally a social study with little mention of the emergency situation leading up to independence. For a study of British foreign and colonial policing at the end of Empire see John William Allgood, 'Britain's Final Decade in South Arabia: Aden, the Federation and the Struggle Against Arab Nationalism', PhD (University of Texas at Austin, 1999).
103 Willis, 'Colonial Policing', p. 59.
104 Gillian King, *Imperial Outpost Aden*, Chatham House Essays 6 (Oxford: OUP, 1964), p. 6.
105 Sir Tom Hickinbotham, *Aden* (London: Constable & Co., 1958), p. 96.
106 For an in-depth survey of the development of air policing within the Empire see David Omissi, *Air Power and Colonial Control: The Royal Air Force 1919–1939* (Manchester: MUP, 1990).
107 Aden Police, Annual Report, 1951, NA CO 1015/380.
108 Z. H. Kour, *The History of Aden, 1839–72* (London: Frank Cass, 1981), p. 95.
109 Allgood, 'Britain's Final Decade', p. 10.
110 Cliff Lord and David Birtles, *The Armed Forces of Aden 1839–1967* (Solihull: Helion & Co., 2000), pp. 8–67.
111 Jeffries, *Colonial Police*, Appendix 1, pp. 224–225.
112 Willis, 'Colonial Police', p. 63.
113 A 1955 census gave the population at 138,441, of whom 106,400 were categorised as Arabs (locally born and Yemenis), 15,800 as Indians, 10,600 as Somalis, 800 as Jews and 4,400 as Europeans. By 1963 the total population had increased to approximately 220,000: King, *Aden*, p. 41.
114 Hickinbotham, *Aden*, p. 82.
115 Hickinbotham, *Aden*, p. 87.
116 Jeffries, *Colonial Police*, p. 201.
117 *Report into the Commission of Enquiry into Disturbances in Aden, December 1947* (London: HMSO, 1948), pp. 6–25.
118 Aden Police, Annual Report, 1951, NA CO 1015/380.
119 Aden Police, Annual Report, 1950, NA CO 1015/380.
120 Muller to Hickinbotham, Governor, Secret, 16 Nov. 1951, NA CO 537/6949.

121 'Report Aden Police by Inspector-General Colonial Police', 1951, NA CO 1015/379.
122 Hickinbotham to Lyttleton, Colonial Secretary, Secret, Savingram No. 458, 16 May 1952, NA CO 1015/379/7.
123 Hickinbotham had spent most of his career in Aden. He became first assistant to the Resident and later to the first governor, Sir Bernard Reilly.
124 Hickinbotham to Lyttleton, Secret, 25 Oct. 1952, NA CO 1015/166.
125 Sir B. Reilly, CO, to T. Hickinbotham, Governor, Aden, 28 March 1953; Muller to Luke, Minutes, 24 March 1953, NA CO 1015/379, 12 May 1953, NA CO 1015/379/14.
126 Hickinbotham to Reilly, 1 May 1953, NA CO 1015/379/13.
127 Aden Police Report, 1959, pp. 2–4.
128 Reilly to W. Russell Edmunds, 28 April 1956, NA CO1037/27.
129 'Armed Police – Aden', 1956, NA CO 1037/24.
130 A. H. Dutton, Financial Secretary, CO, Memo to Standing Finance Committee, no. 38, 21 May 1956, NA CO 1037/22.
131 'Long Range Policy in the Aden Protectorate and Aden Colony', Memo, 22 Sept. 1955, NA PREM 11/2616.
132 For a detailed discussion of the 'Sandys White Paper' see Philip Darby, *British Defence Policy East of Suez 1947–1968* (London: OUP for the Institute of International Affairs, 1973), pp. 94–133.
133 'Discussion Matters Aden Police Arising Lord Lloyd's Visit May 1956', NA CO 1037/23.
134 Minutes, Robertson to Robertson, 5 June 1956; Muller to Stourton, 7 June 1956, NA CO 1037/23.
135 Hore to Robertson, CO, 11 June 1956, NA CO 1037/22.
136 Robertson, CO Minute, 19 Feb. 1964, NA CO 1037/225.
137 T. M. Jenkins, CO, to F. G. Burnett, Treasury, 21 Jan. 1963 and note of a meeting held at the Treasury, 13 March 1963, NA CO 1037/22.
138 C. J. Hayes, Treasury, to C. S. Roberts, CO, 20 March 1963, NA CO 1037/225.
139 'Adenisation' here is referring to localisation of the gazetted ranks.
140 'Proposed Increase in Police Establishment Aden 1962–1964', Confidential and Personal Telegram, K. Trevaskis, Governor, to Colonial Secretary, 21 Dec. 1962, NA CO 1037/225.
141 'Officers Recommended for Special Duty in Aden, 1966', NA FO 371/185311.
142 'This has, I admit, the nasty whiff of the Palestine scuttle about it. However, we are giving ourselves more time for an orderly withdrawal and are announcing our intention to withdraw before we are clearly being driven out': Sam Falle, Minute, 14 Jan. 1966, NA FO 371/185180.
143 Lennox-Boyd, Policy paper on Somaliland and Aden, 24 Dec. 1958, NA CO 1015/1911.
144 Allgood, 'Britain's Final Decade', pp. 95–132.
145 Allgood, 'Britain's Final Decade', pp. 171, 282.
146 Allgood, 'Britain's Final Decade', p. 199.
147 David Ledger, *Shifting Sands: The British in South Arabia* (London: Immel Publishing, 1983), p. 87.
148 Julian Paget, *Last Post: Aden 1964–1967* (London: Faber & Faber, 1969), pp. 134–136.
149 Allgood, 'Britain's Final Decade', pp. 326–327.
150 'Note on the Morale and Reliability of the Aden Police', 4 July, 1966, NA FO 371/1185311.
151 Report by the JIC, 'The Effects in the Middle East and Africa of an Announcement of British Withdrawal from South Arabia in 1967 or 1968', Secret, JIC (65)92 (Final), 23 Dec. 1965, NA CAB 148/49.

CHAPTER SIX

Policing conflict in British colonial Africa

In British Colonial Africa throughout the post-war years notions of crime prevention became overshadowed by the need to maintain order. This was particularly the case in colonies facing emergency situations and increased public unrest. Under-strength, under-resourced colonial police forces turned to the old-fashioned methods that worked best, and in that way a greater use of semi-military policing eroded any Colonial Office endeavours to instill British policing practice.

Peculiar to some areas of British colonial Africa was the concept of indirect rule, which necessitated the presence of native authority, or tribal, police as distinct from the regular police. These local policemen were accountable, through the native authority, to the administration and were involved primarily in issues of tribal law and custom. In carrying out these duties, they accompanied the district officers on tax-collection safaris, guarding cash or stock received as tax, operating as orderlies at chiefs' or tribal elders' courts and routine patrolling within the designated reserve areas.

Indirect rule became a feature of the colonial state and was developed during the early part of the twentieth century by Sir Frederick Lugard. When northern Nigeria became a British protectorate in 1900, Lugard became its first High Commissioner and then, some twelve years later, Governor-General of a united Nigeria. He provided some theoretical underpinning to a system whereby a native administration enabled a group of 75 'residents' and a small army to control a population of some 7 million within a territory of 300,000 square miles. British rule was maintained at minimum cost by delegating power from the centre to existing systems of local government. John Lawrence, one of Lugard's residents, explained that this system

leaves in existence the administrative machinery which had been created by the native Councils, native Courts of Justice, by which European

influence is brought to bear on the native indirectly, through his chiefs . . .
and by which the European keeps himself a good deal in the background.[1]

While systems of rural administration differed radically throughout
British colonial Africa, the Lugardian concept of indirect rule became a
model that colonial administrators sought to emulate.[2] These notions
of indirect rule naturally impinged on policing functions.

Indeed the native authority ordinances, implemented throughout
much of British colonial Africa, stated that the first duty of the native
authority was the maintenance of law and order.[3] Indirect rule constituted the greater part of rural administration and policing in the vast
majority of African territories prior to 1947. By the same token it
caused tensions between the idealised notions of paternalism and the
need to retain control of a given territory, as became apparent in the
latter days of the Empire. In rural areas, day-to-day public order was
kept by the chiefs and the NAP. The more serious breaches of public
order, such as large-scale public disorder, murders, rapes, crimes involving Europeans and misdemeanours, for example witchcraft, that did not
contravene native customs were dealt with by the regular colonial
police. As with the expansion of rural administration, the development
of the NAP was uneven, resulting from a lack of policy direction from
Whitehall, a scarcity of funds, and from the differing approaches of
colonial governments within each territory. Generally, the district
administrators in the field made decisions regarding its development,
which resulted in differences in the type, size and organisation of
the NAP forces.[4] It also impinged on their relationship with the local
community.

William Johnson concluded in his 1949 report on the colonial police,
that reform within this area was necessary, in view of the 'very variable
standard' of policing that provided 'no surety of a fair and impartial
policing and would be no safeguard against internal disorder'. With the
trend towards self-government this existing ' "patchwork" of policing
will become an increasingly vital problem'. It was necessary to ensure
the development of an impartial (i.e. free from tribal and political influences) and efficient police service alongside the development of 'political consciousness'.[5]

The attitude of the Colonial Office towards the NAP offered an
interesting insight into British colonial policy during the decolonisation era, pinpointing their concerns as to colonial styles of policing.
The future of the NAP was raised at the first police commissioners'
conference in 1951. The Colonial Office questioned whether NAP
forces should be absorbed into or replaced by the regular police. The
variegated structures and roles of the different forces prevented a

7   Inspection of the Nigeria Police at Port Harcourt, 1956

conclusive response, although the general view tended towards gradual absorption.[6]

Grassroots policing

A broad consideration of the policing of British colonial Africa at its grassroots level provides some insight into the policing of the end of the Empire. Colonial policemen in all territories engaged in what they described as *normal* police duties: the prevention and detection of crime and the maintenance of public order, unless they were precluded from doing so by an emergency situation. Yet the post-war period saw a marked change in the level of public disorder, manifested in unrest and lawlessness, which encouraged the tradition of colonial policing. Generally speaking, policing occurred in four contexts: in urban areas, European settled or farming areas, native reserve areas and the far-flung rural outposts. Here the police operated paramilitary practices to a far greater extent. The Kenya Police, for example, was responsible for the protection of tribes in the Northern Frontier Province against armed incursion from Ethiopian and Somalian peoples. As Derek Franklin noted:

[138]

8 Remembrance Day ceremony, with officers from the Field Force, Gambia,
1959

> Clashes in the Northern Frontier, whether trans-border or purely inter-
> nal raids, could be very violent and result in many deaths. Cattle raids
> where 20 to 30 armed men might abscond with several hundred head of
> cattle were not uncommon. The race would then be on by both the secu-
> rity forces and the local tribe so afflicted, to get at the raiders before they
> reached Ethiopia and sometimes Somalia.[7]

Policing within the native reserves was characteristic of British colonial
Africa. In Kenya, not one European officer of the Kenya Police served in
the African reserves until 1943, when the Police Act formally extended
their range of jurisdiction into three native districts: Kiambu, Nandi and
Narok.[8] In the post-war years the jurisdiction of the Kenya Police was
very gradually extended throughout the reserves. However, jurisdiction
over the native areas had been granted so late that the Kenya Police
found themselves rather more of a token presence than a regular police
force. Crime rates, however, remained lower than in other areas. In the
force's report for 1948, the incidence of crime in the five largest reserves
showed that over half were cases that came under local or special laws,
including, for example, drinking offences. On the other hand in the
settled and urban areas in the same year, 15,170 instances of identifiable
crime were reported, of which over 12,000 were burglaries, house break-
ins, robberies and thefts, excluding stock thefts.[9]

   Crime aside, an important activity of the regular police was the day-
to-day gathering of grassroots intelligence. Prior to their formal entry

[139]

9   The Queen visiting Enugu accompanied by members of the Nigeria
Police, 1956

into the reserve areas, such work had been undertaken, somewhat hap-
hazardly, by tribal police and district officers. The poor quality of the
intelligence from these areas regarding the growth of the Mau Mau in
the late 1940s is said to have contributed to the Government's com-
placency about this issue.[10] Indeed, in his 1955 report on colonial security, Templer perceived the exclusion of the regular Kenya Police from
the Kikuyu Reserve as a costly mistake.[11]

Overall, the belated introduction of regular policemen into the
native reserve areas was not particularly welcomed. Sir Richard
Catling, former Commissioner of Police, talked about 'some fairly
protracted jousts' with the provincial administration over the role of
tribal policemen whose status became anomalous following the
granting of full jurisdiction to the Kenya Police. With the onset of the
emergency came the need for more thorough training along the lines
of the regular police. By the late 1950s, the provincial administration
had founded a training centre at Nairobi Airport,[12] but plans to incor-
porate the tribal police into the Kenya Police were shelved until a later
date.

What did the practice of *colonial* policing in Africa involve? Former members of the colonial police recalled that prior to the Second World War period policing practice was essentially limited to minor local issues, drill, frequent inspections of police stations and kit, ceremonial duties and supervision of building works.[13] Weekly letters and diaries of ex-colonial policemen reveal that such routine policing included, in the main, dealing with tribal disputes, tax-collection enforcement, petty theft and burglary, bank and shop robberies.[14] These also referred to traffic offences, unlicensed sale of merchandise, resisting arrest, contravention of regulations, illicit brewing of beer, drunk and disorderly behaviour, stock theft and poaching, farm patrols, juvenile crime[15] and minor industrial strikes for which a small number of armed police generally sufficed. In Nigeria, for example, from the establishment of the Nigeria Police on 27 February 1930 to the onset of the Second World War there were only two events necessitating a major law enforcement commitment. The first occurred in the Zinna area of Adamawa and was sparked by resistance to tax collection; the second was also caused by taxation unrest, and occurred in the Okigwi and Bende Divisions in 1938.[16]

In British colonial Africa, serious crime meant essentially murder (as opposed to manslaughter), witchcraft and the purchase and use of hard drugs. When John Biles was Senior ASP in the Nigeria Police, posted to Benue Province, he commented in a weekly letter to the Commissioner in 1951 on the scarcity of serious crime:

> The Judge has been in Makurdi since Tuesday. Although he has not many cases to hear this time and we have only had one conviction for murder so far. There seems to have been a spate of defilement cases during the past few months. As may be expected in such cases, the only offence lies in the fact that the girl is under age. It is a pity that one can take no action against parents who send their small daughters out hawking.[17]

Violence and manslaughter following heavy drinking were not uncommon. Beer was cheap with no excise duty payable and, along with home-brewed varieties, was frequently consumed – Africans were not permitted to purchase or consume imported spirits unless they held a permit issued by the district commissioner. As a result, the smuggling of alcohol became commonplace.[18] Franklin talked about the problems caused by the brewing of illegal beer in Kenya, known as *pombe*, and spirits, 'nubian gin and the like'. A few chiefs and headmen were granted permission to issue permits for the brewing of beer, but not of spirits, despite 'a feeling that the brewing of home made beer would rob the exchequer of revenue'. Overall illegal brewing remained commonplace, and the police 'tended to turn a blind eye as long as the brewers

[141]

were not what we would call bad hats. Spirits brewed mostly in towns was another matter and the culprits would be taken to court.'[19]

In order to control serious crime, some territories enforced a curfew in the major towns, making it an offence for any African to be out on the streets after a certain time unless in possession of a pass authorised by his or her employer.[20] Former colonial policemen have claimed that in some areas, regardless of whether those involved were African or European, serious crimes was investigated in much the same manner. The reality was noticeably different in colonies with large European settler populations, and particularly when emergency situations occurred; certainly the colour of the perpetrator in such colonies affected the manner in which the crime was investigated. Many members of the European community saw no reason to be prosecuted for minor traffic offences or theft, and anecdotal evidence points to the European settlers' dislike of police involvement. Franklin noted:

> I can remember disruption of my police patrol when we arrived on the farm of a rather uppity farmer in the Nanyuki areas. His farm was just outside my areas on the banks of the River Usao Nyiro. The river was my boundary but sometimes I had to cross his farm area by a local bridge. He would then rant and rave at me, my men and anyone else he could think of. He reached even more notoriety when he was stopped by a Police road-block where his licence and vehicle were checked. He insisted on recording the numbers and also asked for the full names of each *askari* [constable]. Apparently not being satisfied with these details, he insisted on delving into the *askaris'* shorts, where he said their force numbers should be inscribed. Not surprisingly, the *askaris* objected to being debagged on the public highway and T . . . was arrested, charged with assault and eventually convicted.[21]

It was not just Europeans who attempted to evade justice: African chiefs were noted for their attempts to 'bribe' the police into covering up petty crimes that had occurred among their tribes.[22] Minor corruption was also reported among the rank and file, particularly in connection with traffic offences. The matter of corruption within the colonial police has been highlighted by the high-profile cases which occurred in Hong Kong, but there is some documentary evidence to suggest that this occurred also in African colonies. Biles, while serving in the Nigeria Police, reported in June 1951:

> The new wireless building is looking fine and should be completed very soon. The Contractor was 'so grateful for my constant interest and supervision and advice' that he left 50 [Nigerian] pounds on my desk yesterday, as a 'present'. I was so shaken that I was speechless for a minute. I then told him that if he didn't get out of my office with his money within five seconds he would find himself in my lock-up. When I recovered my

temper a little I wondered whether I should not have led him on a little and then run him. It only makes one wonder exactly how the Yard Superintendents in various Provinces can afford so much beer![23]

Colonial police practice was frequently linked to the specific economic activity of a given colony. In northern Rhodesia, the police dealt with crimes arising from a migrant worker population employed in the copper mines. Police stations were clustered around the central railway line and settled areas within the copper belt, and when civil unrest – railway sabotage and the use of explosives, unheard of in other parts of colonial Africa – occurred in the 1950s, it was typically triggered by strikes in that region.[24] The continuing strikes and demonstrations during the period necessitated the frequent use of the mobile strike unit and assistance from the British South Africa Police.[25] The practice of the Sierra Leone Police revolved partially around protection of the diamond mines and detection of diamond smuggling.[26] Ted Eates, when serving in the Sierra Leone Police, noted in his weekly letter to the Commissioner in 1954 that illegal mining was

> a pressing matter for our attention. It appears that large numbers of persons are mining at several places on the SEWA River without any attempt at concealment. [We] will send a spare ADC and about 10 men to carry out an offensive reconnaissance to find out the extent of the mining and how we can get at the offenders, without their making off into the bush. According to some opinion, however, if they are disturbed by the police they will stand and fight . . . It seems that permanent patrols, say two half units or the equivalent, will be required to patrol the diamondiferous areas in this Province.[27]

Successes in the detection of smuggling were, however, occasionally reported. The following year Eates described

> a 'Boys' Own' expedition to Baoma to arrest Dip Mansour, allegedly the chief illegal diamond buyer. The surprise was complete and we found Mansour sitting at a desk with money, stones and scales in front of him. There was complete pandemonium for a few minutes in the darkness while the Police detailed to surround the house tried to catch his fleeing clients and he tried to scatter the diamonds on to the floor, without success.[28]

In the Gold Coast, police protected parties engaged in 'cutting out' cocoa 'swollen shoots' and assisted in the destruction of diseased bushes,[29] while in Uganda they dealt with mixed ethnic armed-gang robberies, known locally as *bakondo*, perpetrated on both Africans and Asians.[30] Illicit ivory-trafficking and gun-running were also problems in Uganda.[31] Often *colonial* practice necessitated unusual police work, something that has provided a wealth of anecdotal evidence of, for example, policemen being required to kill or capture a variety of wild animals in both urban and rural areas.

In the main, colonial police practice encompassed an array of extraneous duties, and these responsibilities gave rise to additional police powers that increased police accountability to colonial governments. Their functions included the monitoring of weights and measures, vehicle and driving-licence inspection, government census, licensing of dogs and firearms, and film censorship. In many territories the police were also responsible for immigration and passport control, and the prison and fire-brigade services. In some territories, the commissioner of police was also the sheriff and the senior police officers deputy sheriffs. They carried out warrants, including the death warrant, and served writs and summonses. Distaste at having to carry out capital punishment was widespread. 'Hanging disturbed me greatly', noted Peter Mills who served in the Kenya Police; 'execution by shooting would be far more humane'.[32] Philip Milton explained his belief that 'a policeman is there to bring people to justice by the law and put them before the Magistrate but that is when his duty stops . . . You cannot be an executioner as well as judge and jury.'[33] Robin Mitchell agreed with this point of view, commenting: 'I had attended executions in the Sudan and I had hated them. I hated almost more having to sign, in the ease and security of my office, a piece of paper which represented the irreversible step towards ending a man's life.'[34] In many territories senior police officers were empowered to appear as public prosecutors in the High Court in the place of crown counsel, some officers finding that the prosecutor role took over from their role as policemen, so that work revolved around court appearances rather than police patrols[35] – any police officer could appear as the prosecutor in the lower courts.[36]

The 'colour bar'

Colour and cultural–social bars naturally touched the police, with forms of racial discrimination particularly evident in colonies with large European settler populations, Kenya and Southern Rhodesia being prime examples. Discrimination was certainly more of a feature in East African than West African colonies, Nigeria, where racial segregation was not practised and where social mixing between Africans and Europeans was accepted, being a good example of the latter.

Policemen themselves felt somewhat intimidated by the upper echelons of European society, as David Hewson, a former member of the Kenya Police, pointed out: 'Except for the most senior officers of the Kenya Police, ordinary force members were near the bottom of the heap, and as such, we were constrained to watch our "Ps" and "Qs" whenever treating with the higher white socialites.'[37] Members of the regular police were, in the main, cautious in their dealings with Europeans. Peter Hewitt wrote candidly of his experiences as a youthful Police Inspector in Kenya:

> [N]o bumptious upstart of a 'Cook's tour' police inspector was going to ask to see . . . [the settler's] driving licence or to arrest him for attempted murder for having hastened the departure of a cheeky garden boy with a few well aimed shots past his head! 'You are here in case we should want you and may come when invited . . . and even then you will kindly leave your notebook behind.' Most of us soon got the message.[38]

Colin Imray talked vividly about Kenya being a 'settler country'. European settlers, in the post-war years, saw the colony as 'their country and they would brook no interference'.[39] In their defence, a number of expatriate police officers claimed that they faced 'enormous pressure' from the European community to prosecute Africans for the smallest of crimes, including, for example, the theft of a maize cob or a milk bottle, often taken because of hunger.[40] Another example regularly cited centred on the regular checking of the *kipande* (identity card) of Africans, while, by contrast, a principle of laissez faire was applied when it came to either Europeans or Asians, despite the fact that every person residing in Kenya was obliged by law to carry formal identification. In the experience of some former members of the Kenya Police, Africans were 'enforced to obtain and carry about that document', but not so Europeans.[41] The *kipande* system could be perceived as an informal means of imposing social segregation

Overall, divisions in the Kenya Police between the officer corps and the ranks reflected the segregation in Kenyan society. It was nigh impossible for an African or Asian to rise above the rank of police inspector until in 1961 the proximity of independence forced accelerated *localisation*. This process included a 'higher' training course at Kiganjo for members of the Kenya Inspectorate. 'Localisation' did not differentiate the population's races, and the term was later replaced by 'Africanisation', which made no distinction between Kenyan, Ugandan or Tanzanian Africans, only to be superseded by 'Kenyanisation', embracing Kenya's citizens irrespective of race. Officers who were originally from either Uganda or Tanzania were 'Kenyanised' by inter-country transfer or were retired.[42]

David Rowcroft, who joined the Kenya Police in 1955, recalled that it was only in the three years prior to independence that European officers were required to identify African candidates for possible career advancement and accelerated promotion. He gave the example of Corporal Joseph Mudambi Kora who served under his command at

Kangundo police station. Kora was recommended for advancement training and within a year was in charge of his own station. He eventually rose to the rank of Assistant Commissioner of Police and was in charge of the police training school.[43] Catling, as Commissioner of the Kenya Police, perceived that Africanisation of the regular police had occurred too late, with the promotion of the first African to gazetted rank happening only in 1960, which compared unfavourably with other African colonies. Moreover, Africanisation of the Special Branch was not contemplated until 1959.[44]

Where Asian officers were concerned, there were only 5 Chief Inspectors and 34 Inspectors and Assistant Inspectors by 1948, despite a rising Asian population.[45] Avtar Matharu, who joined with the rank of constable in 1953, was the third Asian to be promoted to the rank of ASP by 1963, among a group of approximately fifteen local officers. Two other officers, Bhajan Singh Bohi and Haza Ra Singh, had served almost thirty years in the Kenya Police prior to their promotion into the gazetted ranks in 1954.[46] Even then, the promotion of those officers caused something of a stir: with a debate raging over their promotion prospects in February 1954, the Kenya Government admitted to the Colonial Office that both officers were serving on a pay scale of £300–684, which was three-fifths of the European scale for an ASP.[47]

Reinforcing notions of paramilitary policing

In 1948, Johnson commented that the colonial policeman 'will act as soldier although wearing a police uniform'.[48] The military traditions of colonial policing increased in the post-war period with the general colonial upheaval and were noticeably bolstered by an intake of recruits who had served in the armed forces and the Palestine Police. They felt at ease with military-style training and particularly enjoyed team sports, an essential element of any colonial policeman's recreation. Geoffrey Morton, who became Commissioner of Police in Nyasaland in 1953, had started his policing career in the Palestine Police in 1930. In his memoirs he described how his early Palestine training stayed with him throughout his policing career. He wrote: 'at the end of our training we were all pretty efficient soldiers, and could slope and present arms and perform complicated drill movements with a polish worthy of a crack regiment. In addition, we were able to fire our rifles and revolvers with reasonable accuracy . . . and the Lewis gun'.[49]

Paramilitary training for African police personnel remained a priority through to the late 1950s. For example, in Nyasaland the locally recruited policemen received no training in *normal* police practice and a recruit only passed the training course when he had qualified as proficient in the use of weapons. In Northern Rhodesia, 38 per cent of training time was given to drill and weaponry practice, 37 per cent to law and police duties, 9 per cent to learning local languages and 4 per cent to administration.[50] In Sierra Leone, emphasis was placed on drill and musketry training, while in the Gambia training was 'based on police work combined with military principles', consisting of fire and close-order drill, physical exercise, small arms practice, observation techniques, as well as evidence-giving in court and traffic control.[51] The Palestine example was reflected in all territories, where policemen were encouraged to become crack shots:

> There have been two marksmen, eighteen first class shots and eighteen second class shots. This [was] an improvement on last year when there were only one marksman and fourteen first class shots. With perseverance, we shall be able to make the newer recruits into second class or at least third class shots. We have managed to get forty-eight men through their annual musketry course before the rains started. I shall give musketry a rest for a while, apart from periodic aiming practice, trigger squeezing and muscle exercizes for the younger constables.[52]

This particular style of training was repeatedly criticised by the colonial administration. Attempts had been made from the early 1930s to downplay the importance of military-style training, but this was eventually overtaken by the outbreak of the Second World War. In Nigeria, in January 1937, the administration, following the recommendations of Commissioner Alan Saunders, decided to remove 'company drill' and 'bayonet fighting' from the training programme. This was to be replaced with 'riot drill', which formed part of what he had described as 'primary police duties' and would be of greater use when dealing with public disturbances than military instruction. Saunders had insisted that the Nigeria Police should be trained along the lines of an 'Armed Civil Police Force', and that required a higher standard of training in the prevention, detection, investigation and prosecution of crime, while maintaining a disciplined approach to the use of arms to suppress public disorder.[53]

It was not, however, until 1950 that Johnson, as the Colonial Police Advisor, was able to force limited changes on training programmes to ensure that European recruits received greater instruction in traditional British police practice. The more important reforms came in the number of officers trained in Britain. Efforts to improve officer and inspector training courses were repeatedly made at the conferences of Colonial Commissioners of Police, though the conferences did not look at ways of developing the training of the rank and file and failed to end the traditional military styles of training.[54] Nevertheless, more colonial policemen received their initial training in Britain from the late post-war period onwards Colin Limb joined the Colonial Police Service in early 1950. He was sent to Mill Reece for the first 6 months and then to Hendon Police College for a further 3 months, prior to a posting to Nigeria. He reported that he trained with 8 future colonial policemen and approximately 100 British policemen. When he arrived in Nigeria, he was given foot and arms drill, weaponry instruction and the language tuition[55] he had not received in Britain.[56]

Policing public disorder

Throughout this period, colonial police practice involved a greater than hitherto use of force to deal with an increase in civil disturbances. In some colonies, the resulting emergency situations forced a revision of their riot drill procedures. At the Gold Coast in 1949, for example, the new 'Riot Drill' pamphlet incorporated the practical knowledge of other colonial police forces and the expertise of the Palestine Police.[57] 'I was very glad to see the new Force Order regarding revolver drill, which appears to be identical with what we practised in Palestine', noted John Biles in 1950.

More importantly, it included the 1948 experience of the Gold Coast Police during the Accra disturbances and the ensuing emergency. Richard Edelsten, who served in the Gold Coast Police at this time, has described the changes to riot drill in detail in relation to the movement of officers within an area of civil disturbance. First, they would advance in a broad arrowhead formation with an armed party in the rear. Then they would position themselves on three sides of a square, with baton-carrying officers facing outward and armed officers in the centre. Next, officers would advance in triangular formation, the baton-carrying officers forming the sides and the armed officers in the centre.[58] When he became Commissioner of the Zanzibar Police, Biles stressed the importance of differentiating between a rout and a riot: a rout generally occurred on the back of an unlawful assembly, whereas a riot could be the result of a rout, i.e. an advancing crowd, which failed to be adequately checked by the police.[59] Typically batons and tear-smoke were used in cases of unlawful assembly and for routs. Riots could well necessitate the use of armed force. Philip Milton, who served in the Nigeria Police, noted that a 'baton party' was typically made up of 25–50 men. The 'gas party' generally stood behind the baton party with tear-smoke guns.[60]

In most circumstances waves of baton-carrying officers attempted to take control of an area and set up blocking procedures. The first advance into the crowd typically occurred when these officers were within fifteen yards of the crowd. Batons were aimed at collarbones, arms and legs, to avoid serious injury.[61] In the more serious situations, baton and gas use would be relinquished in the front line to armed policemen, each of whom would load a single round, and, if the crowd still failed to disperse, would raise their rifles to the aim position. This would be followed by a volley at the order 'Fire!', the order being repeated as necessary, based on the so-called principles of minimum force. The authorisation was provided by the local magistrate, but the senior officer present 'gave the target' and the order to fire.[62]

Riot-drill theory differed from its practice. Morton noted that the colonial policeman was faced with a difficult decision as to the form of *force* to use, when to use firearms and how many rounds to fire.[63] Colin Limb, who served in the Nigeria and Nyasaland police forces, considered that the responsibility of the policeman who takes these decisions was far greater than that of the soldier,[64] for 'if he opens fire too soon, or fires too many rounds, or if his policemen (God forbid) get out of control and start firing indiscriminately in spite of their careful training, he alone will have to answer for his actions and theirs at the subsequent judicial enquiry'.[65] All in all, on the basis of reports made by colonial policemen, it seems that the form of riot procedure used depended entirely on the officer in charge. George Willis, who served in the Nigeria Police, commented that in the run up to independence, rioting increased and intensified in terms of the violence that ensued and that the management of riots changed accordingly. He perceived a general unease among officers dealing with riots about the necessity of increased force as a result.[66]

Civil disorder grew markedly in the post-war years throughout British colonial Africa, reflecting both the growth of nationalism and a desire for political change. Many ex-colonial policemen remarked on the increased level of civil disorder, which was linked to a rise in serious and violent crime. Attempts at civil policing were frustrated, on the one hand, by the need for containment of public disorder and civil disobedience and, on the other, by a serious shortage of manpower and resources.

The public disturbances witnessed throughout the African colonies were triggered by factors that had been present over previous decades, many of the incidents sparked by long-standing tribal, religious and trade disputes, and political or taxation issues. Conflagrations often revealed the weaknesses inherent to the colonial police. Maurice Akker served in the Zanzibar Police and was present during the 'Kiembe Samaki' events of July 1951, when local Shirazi protests erupted into serious rioting. The outburst had grown out of local concern over land appropriation for the construction of an airport and was triggered in the short term by opposition to compulsory cattle inoculation.[67] A small police detachment, led by Akker and principally formed by members of the ceremonial band, opened fire on rioters without the usual procedure, as outlined above, killing several. Rioting worsened throughout

10 Riot-drill training, Taveta police station: 'Attention!' Kenya, 1961

the day and was not contained by the Zanzibar Police. In the event, a detachment of the Tanganyika Police had to be called in to provide assistance. This event was of significance in Zanzibar's future in that it aroused fierce anti-colonial sentiment among the local population.[68] Biles, who became (1957–63) Commissioner of the Zanzibar Police, described officers as feeling more comfortable with ceremonial duties and somewhat 'unused' to civil disorder. Up until a declaration of a state of emergency in 1963, the force remained small and ill-equipped.[69]

In some cases, tribal unrest occurred as a result of increases in taxation. The Oshogbo dispute, in Nigeria in 1957, was triggered initially by market women protesting against an increase in water rates and led to the partial destruction of the local police station. A police unit used tear gas to disperse the crowd. Willis, who was present during these disturbances, considered them similar to many others during this period, and commented that rioting could no longer be easily contained by a small number of policemen with a 'large dose of good humour'.

11   Riot-drill training, Taveta police station: 'Ready!' Kenya, 1961

A minor disturbance was prone to flare up in to a full-blown riot, with Africans resorting to the use of home-made Dane guns, poisoned arrows, spears and machetes.[70] In controlling many riots in Nigeria during this period, the police used 'maximum', i.e. lethal, force.[71]

The decolonisation era was marked by a rise in politically motivated civil unrest. The Kano riots in Nigeria in 1953, for example, were triggered indirectly by the Action Group whose members had attempted to hold a rally in Kano which opposing political groups tried to prevent. In the course of four days' rioting involving 'murderous mobs, agitators, perpetrators of criminal acts including murder, mutilation, arson and looting', 36 people were killed and more than 200 injured.[72] Disturbances broke out throughout the Western Region of Nigeria in 1956 as a result of the death of Alhaji Adelabu, the Western Region Assembly's leader of the opposition. Popular opinion held that his death, in a road traffic accident, had been caused by witchcraft. The disturbance that followed led to multiple deaths as rioters used spiked knoberries and machetes to attack their opponents. The police were forced to summon reinforcements, with a total of ten riot units committed to action.[73] Independence saw continued political disturbance in many parts of Nigeria. The first serious rioting occurred on 24 March 1960 and required the deployment of riots squads to Gboko,

Lafia, Makurdi and Katsina Ala. Later that year serious unrest occurred among members of the Tiv tribe, many of whom were killed.[74]

Uganda, too, was beset with violent disturbances and a string of emergencies up until independence in 1962. The Bukedi disturbances, in the eastern province in 1960, are remembered as the worst in Uganda's colonial history. Michael Macoun, who became Commissioner of the Uganda Police in 1959, recalled that he was confronted with the first of many such emergencies shortly after his arrival, and public disorder would plague the Uganda Police for the next six years, the 'prelude to the chronicle of violence'.[75] Many riots were directed primarily against the local authorities as a result of mounting dissatisfaction with the graduated tax assessments made by the chiefs. Macoun himself considered these assessments both 'arbitrary and inequable', affecting the poorer segments of the population. The Roman Catholic Democratic Party exploited the population's general discontent. Politico-religious elements became interwoven with discontent at rising taxation. The provincial administration failed to recognise the lack of support for the chiefs and pressed ahead with the new graduated tax. As a result, the rioters directed their anger at all local authorities, and every county and parish headquarters was attacked, together with local authority police stations and barracks. Protectorate security forces were drafted in to assist the local police, but together they were unable to contain the rioting. A 'disturbed area' was declared, which brought in a battalion of the Uganda Rifles (4th KAR) in aid of the civil power.[76] The police annual report concluded that the several days' rioting had resulted in 15 deaths, 1,763 arrests and 594 convictions.[77] A commission of enquiry was appointed and the system of graduated taxation was reviewed as a result of the riots. Many chiefs were relieved of their posts and a network of central government police posts was established throughout the district.

The strong-arm men

The police mobile strike force (or riot-control unit) was a means by which colonial governments could control rising public unrest in the post-war years. The units were strategically located colony-wide to enable rapid deployment. Their very existence was a challenge to imported civil styles of policing, involving as they did the paramilitary practice of riot-control techniques. As public disorder increased throughout the 1950s, the use of this type of unit rose taking on a galaxy of new names, which included the police field force, police service unit, police mobile unit and police motorised company. In general, one inspector, one NCO and eight men formed a unit, its role to control public disorder, though such units could also be used for ceremonial and guard duties during quieter times.

The weapons of these units were initially truncheons and firearms; all members carried riot shields and had been trained to perform a series of riot manoeuvres. By the 1950s, tear gas was in use to speedily disperse or contain a crowd;[78] use of other so-called 'non-lethal' weapons was developed during the 1960s – for example, the Hong Kong Police fired baton rounds of wood in place of live ammunition.[79]

In May 1948, the Elmina mobile force was set up on the Gold Coast under the command of ASP Coles. He noted that this strike force was called out on more than fifty occasions to assist in controlling disorders or to prevent disorders from occurring. Coles described this side to police practice as 'positive police action' and told of how order, during the Elmina riots of 9 May 1948, was restored in 7 minutes and was followed by 29 arrests and convictions.[80]

In Uganda, the heavily militarised police service unit and later, in 1952, the 'special force' were increasingly used to combat civil disorder.[81] The Nigeria Police made use of its 'riot control squads' to deal with public disorder up until the early 1960s. In 1958, the new Inspector-General, Sir Kerr Bovell, undertook a reorganisation of the Nigeria Police. This included the formation of specific police mobile units based on his policing experiences in Malaya. In the early 1960s, officers from these units were sent to Malaya for training.[82]

In Kenya, in 1948, the so-called 'emergency company'was founded, and renamed the General Service Unit (GSU) in September 1953. The GSU was a 'strike' force, to act in support of the regular police at times of public unrest, and did not undertake normal policing duties. At the height of the emergency the GSU numbered some 1,100 men, divided into 32 platoons,[83] with approximately 47 European officers. Dispersed throughout the colony, its task was to provide each affected area and province with its own mobile striking force. Heavily armed and organised along military lines, the GSU operated more as an army platoon rather than a police unit, each platoon being equipped with Bren guns, rifles, 2-inch mortars and small arms. John Burton, who served from 1955 to 1957 in the GSU, stated that members were better equipped than soldiers: 'I had operated with the army who were still equipped with Sten guns and we had the Patchett and later the .9mm Sterling SMG. Later still the GSU went from the .303 rifle to the FN and SLR.'[84] The maximum period of service within the GSU was supposedly two years, after which the officer was transferred back to normal police duties; Richard Catling hoped that this limit would prevent a GSU member from becoming too *militarised* in his outlook.

John Fforde, when appointed Commissioner of the NRP in 1951, used his counter-insurgency training from Palestine to introduce the concept of the mobile unit. Fforde had an arrangement with the civil aviation authorities by which mobile unit detachments could be flown anywhere at short notice. A permanent base for the mobile unit was opened at Kamfinsa in 1963.[85] The Nyasaland Police's mobile force was established in 1954 from the existing riot squad, and was set up with some 250 policemen, organised into platoons of 36 members, each led by 2 officers who either had experience of the Malayan emergency or were from the British South Africa Police. The Nyasaland Police mobile force, like other mobile units, was armed and travelled in armoured trucks. It was called out frequently during the 1950s to deal with increasing hostility among the general population.[86]

Policing at the sharp end: the case of Kenya

The Mau Mau state of emergency in Kenya was the only counter-insurgency campaign faced by the British in post-war colonial Africa. Official concerns at the apparent growth in the scale of violence culminated with the approval of Emergency Bills by the Kenya Legislative Council on 1 October 1952. The Kenya Police was given additional powers, which included arrest and detention of suspects without trial, the creation of prohibited areas, imposing curfews and powers to deport any foreign national suspected of assisting the Mau Mau. On 21 October, the declaration of a state of emergency coincided with the launching of 'Operation Jock Scott'. From that point, it was estimated, some 15,000 Kikuyus entered the Aberdare and Mount Kenya forests under the Mau Mau leadership of Dedan Kimathi, Stanley Mathenge and 'General China'.

The Kenya Police was faced with many obstacles as a result of the emergency. In terms of the policing structure, many units were operating in parallel or actually in opposition to one another. (The regular police operated alongside the Kenya Police Reserve (KPR) and a number of units attached to the Special Branch.) Policing the emergency eventually overshadowed crime prevention and detection within the areas affected by Mau Mau. By 1953, the police were involved in more complex counter-insurgency work, including investigations into oathing among settler farm labour, links between the forest gangs and their sympathisers, the protection of loyalists and informers, escorting large numbers of Kikuyu to protected villages and guarding detention centres. In some areas, the police were wholly responsible until army reinforcements arrived. As the emergency continued, police intelligence skills expanded into the field of tracker combat team and pseudo-gang work.[87]

Overall the police were below the strength[88] required to deal with the situation at hand and were forced to rely on an influx of some 2,000

European Assistant Inspectors on 2–3-year contracts who were referred to somewhat glibly as 'Kenya Cowboys'.[89] Despite an increase in numbers, the police were often under considerable strain. Operation Anvil, for example, to remove all non-employed Kikuyu from Nairobi in April 1954, sorely tested police resources and may well have failed had it not been for a joint police–army effort.[90] In comparison with so many colonial police forces, there was too significant a shortfall in funds to provide adequate equipment and training and to house new police recruits. Most police stations were built on a shoe-string budget and relied on the local population being dragooned into supplying free labour and cheap, or free, building materials.[91]

The 1953 Police Commission had recommended an increase in the number of African recruits. However, this too posed a problem in terms the tribal makeup of the Kenya Police, with too few Kikuyu members and difficulties in their recruitment.[92] Within the Kenya Police there was a policy of never staffing more than roughly 30 per cent of a station or post with members of the local tribe. Thus, in 1945, 4,949 Africans in the Kenya Police came from over 41 Kenya tribes, over 9 Ugandan tribes, over 7 Tanganyikan tribes and a handful of other foreign tribes. Of these tribes the greatest number represented were the Kamba, Luo, Lumbwa, Kavirondo Bantu, Somali and Meru, the Kikuyu accounting for only 112 members.[93] By the time of the Police Commission's recommendation, the number of Africans in the police had risen to 9,828, although the number of tribes represented had shrunk to around 40.[94] The number of Africans peaked at 11,289 in 1955 because of the ongoing emergency.[95]

As the military campaign intensified, operational command passed to the military and the Kenya Police became one leg of a 'three-legged stool' of army, administration and police.[96] John Bailey, a former member of the Kenya Police, explained that the murders of Eric Bowkerno and Jack Meiklejohn in late 1952 altered the attitude of both Europeans and Asians towards the situation in Kenya. As a result Bailey believed that the policy of minimum force allied to public co-operation was replaced by an 'aggressive attitude'.[97] From the declaration of a state of emergency until its conclusion, all European police officers were required to carry side arms both on and off duty. The increased use of firearms was extended to the European settler communities, who were advised by the police to 'have your gun loaded and ready for instant action'.[98]

Police back-up

From an outside perspective, the policing of the emergency appeared complex as a result of the variety of the units operating, which included uniformed police, CID, strike forces, special forces, reserve and auxiliary forces. Catling had, however, stressed that the different police departments had specific roles that should not overlap if policing were to be effective. Thus theoretically Special Branch was responsible for 'the identification and containment of subversives', CID was responsible for the investigation and prosecution of crime and the GSU was the police strike force or back-up. Communications and movement of men and equipment were the task of Police Signals, Police Transport and the Air Wing.[99] While this may have been advantageous in theory, in practice it created units that operated with a great deal of autonomy.

The Auxiliary Police Force (which had been staffed by national servicemen) had initially been brought to a close on 24 February 1947. However, it was deemed necessary that a force of this kind should remain in place to assist the regular police in the event of an emergency. In March 1952, Africans were enrolled as special police to serve in police posts within operational areas, continuing to use their traditional weapons of spears, bow, arrows and *pangas*, until later that year. The picture became more complex when the role of the Home Guard (which became the Kikuyu Guard) was considered. The Home Guard was comprised of 'loyal'[100] Kikuyu and, to a lesser extent, members of the Embu and Meru tribes. Members of the Home Guard were sent to posts in close proximity to police stations, many posts being commanded by European settlers under the mantle of temporary district officers.[101]

The use of combat tracker teams and pseudo-gangs to 'capture' and, in some instances, 'turn' insurgents was utilised during the Mau Mau emergency, and once again reinforced the paramilitary nature of colonial policing. Initiated in Palestine in the form of snatch squads, this concept was then further developed during the Malayan emergency by the so-called 'jungle squads'. In Kenya, the principal role of the police became bound up with combating the Mau Mau, particularly in the central forest areas of the colony known as the White Highlands. Entry into many areas became prohibited as the situation intensified. Under emergency regulations, any person found in those areas who was not a member of the security forces was liable to be 'shot without question'. In some forest perimeters, deep trenches were dug as part of the Government's forced labour programme. Police posts, police stations and Home Guard units in rural areas were staffed by regular police and members of the KPR. The regular police attempted to isolate the Mau Mau from local villages and prevent food and supplies from reaching them,[102] objectives that necessitated regular patrols and ambushes.[103]

The combat tracker teams also served to protect the European

12   Sir Richard Catling inspecting the Kenya Police, c. 1959

farms in the so-called 'settled areas', preventing the maiming and
slaughter of stock, and creating ambushes. When a Mau Mau raid
occurred, patrols were sent out to track the gang. This early use of
tracker teams, often using sniffer dogs, was largely unsuccessful
owing to 'the skill of the Mau Mau in confusing their tracks, the incidence of wild game spoiling the spoor and the time delay in the reporting and subsequent follow up of the incident'. However, in terms of
making 'contact' with gangs, the police were rather more fortunate.[104]
As the combat tracker teams developed, so the use of pseudo-gangs
came to the fore.

Tracker teams typically comprised one European and 8–10 *askaris*;
members of the Kenya Regiment could also be present. Teams were
armed with MK5 .303 rifles and a Bren gun. The team had one landrover
equipped with VHF radio, a lorry, three tents and a water trailer.
Uniform was abandoned, for

> we dressed as per Mau Mau, with a mixture of 'skins' from forest animals
> and very old khaki trousers. Darkening of the face, and any other exposed
> bits, was carried out with a mixture of burnt cork, boot polish and, when
> available, actor's make-up. Heads were always covered and, to retain
> maximum protection from prying eyes, the European stayed well in the
> back ground when contact was made with other gangs. Any close contact

[157]

13 Inspector Derek Franklin with a Combat Tracker Team, Ndathi, Kenya, 1955

with a Mau Mau would not survive even the most professional of make-up, so one slunk at the tail end . . . to help kill any civilised scent we all rubbed our hands in some very rough (and pungent) African 'Kariko' (tobacco). Our aim was to try and establish contact with a local gang hoping that we could entice them into a meeting.[105]

The purpose of this disguise was to penetrate Mau Mau gangs,[106] their capture being of primary importance for the intelligence it would reveal and the prospect of 'turning' members into police informers. Those Mau Mau members who either refused to go back into the forest as informers or were deemed unsuitable were interned in detention camps. Camps were typically staffed by members of the Kenya Police and the administration.[107] As the emergency unfolded, so some combat tracker teams effectively ceased operating solely as 'trackers', becoming pseudo-gangs. Using Kikuyu 'pseudos' was considered better bait than members of the Mkamba, Wkamba or Samburu who often made up the tracker teams. Eventually some pseudo-gangs became known as 'Blue Doctor Pseudo Teams' under the leadership of Ian Henderson. These evolved in the Lower Tharaka area from 1957, continuing through until 1959 as Mau Mau activity on Mount Kenya and the Aberdares decreased. After 1957 their main preoccupation was the capture of Dedan Kimathi and Stanley Mathenge.[108]

The KPR

The creation of the KPR in 1948 gave some European settlers the idea that it could become 'the nucleus of a burgher force'.[109] David Anderson has described the KPR as a 'white *gendarmerie*', who 'frequently took independent actions against Mau Mau "suspects"'. In Nairobi small groups of KPR formed their own 'strike squads', possessing their own weapons and ammunition. In the early months of the emergency the regular police found it exceedingly difficult to 'control these renegade groups'.[110] Certainly members of the regular police believed that the KPR operated with an autonomy they found less than desirable. Hewson recalled:

> I came back from patrol one day to the police station and found six pairs of hands lying outside. My constable said the mounted section KPR had been up in the forest and they couldn't bring the bodies back so they brought the hands. But legally they were only allowed out on 'search and destroy' missions if approved by the operations centre. They weren't allowed to go on killing sprees.[111]

By 31 December 1952, the KPR comprised 4,786 Europeans, 1,144 Asians and 2,673 Africans.[112] As the overriding majority within the KPR, the Europeans settlers became a law to themselves, compromising their regular police duties in the operational areas of the Central and Rift Valley Provinces and in Nairobi's Special Area. As an unpaid unit, the KPR had its own hierarchy and rank structure with a predominantly European officer corps. Akker, who served as a Superintendent in the Kiambu district in 1954 recalled:

> The K.P.R. seemed to do as they pleased. They had their own HQ and full-time reserve officers all over the place. They initiated their own operations, put up Police posts on their farms, submitted enormous mileage claims and did their own interrogations often in a very questionable way. It must be remembered that a large number of K.P.R. were ex Army, ex Navy ex R.A.F. Senior officers ... They all knew the Governor of course.[113]

With the creation of mounted police sections, personnel were drawn not only from the regular police but from the settler-led KPR and the Kenya Regiment. Their operational successes against Mau Mau gangs in the Naivasha, Laipia, Nanyuki and Nyeri settled areas were said to be reasonably high. However, the operational independence of some units meant that KPR opertives were perceived as more akin to cowboys than to policemen, indulging in their own private vendettas against Mau Mau.[114] The KPR was afforded the same independence within its tracker combat teams, which operated principally in the

Thomson's Falls area. Led initially by European settlers like Kenneth Cunningham and Peter Becker, a former 'white hunter', this unit, comprising a combination of KPR, Kenya Police and European farmers, was partially responsible for weeding out Mau Mau from this area.[115] Moreover, there was 'nothing to stop a farmer' shooting a Mau Mau suspect: 'After all the emergency was on!'[116]

The problem was solved only through attempts to end the KPR's autonomy. Sir George Erskine, Commander-in-Chief of the security forces from June 1953, was authorised by police headquarters to curb the KPR's policing powers because of his concern over 'indiscriminate' shootings and by '£5 rewards for "kills"'. As a result, many settlers professed a dislike of his motives and actions. 'Kenya is a sunny place for shady people . . . I hate the guts of them all', Erskine wrote to his wife.[117] There is no doubt that 'strong-arm methods' caused considerable anxiety to those regular police who behaved with greater restraint. There was a proportion of the settler population, however, who saw the emergency as *their* war, and Erskine's 'orders of the day', issued against unwarranted attacks on civilians and the ill-treatment of prisoners and suspects, were not accepted by the settler communities in the same way as they were by the security forces.

Unlawful behaviour was, in the main, infrequently investigated and brought to trial. A case came before the Nairobi Magistrates' Court, on 10 December 1954, which involved a former District Commandant, Derek Laurence Searle, and Inspector George Horsfall of the Kenya Police. Both were charged with perjury that involved evidence given at the trial of an African who had been sentenced to death for possession of a firearm. (The African was subsequently released following a successful appeal.) Searle and Horsfall eventually received eighteen months' hard labour following an appeal to the Supreme Court.[118]

Emergency situations brought out the more sinister aspects to policing the end of the Empire, particularly in colonies boasting European settler communities, and parallels can be drawn between Kenya and Southern Rhodesia. The use of settler-led part-time reserves to bolster the regular police had a triangular effect within policing that had dire consequences for the community and did much to tarnish the reputation of members of the regular police. What became apparent across the whole spectrum of post-war policing was the increase in levels of public disturbance which, in turn, reinforced notions of paramilitary-style policing, as exemplified by the 'mobile' forces that emerged during this period, in contrast to the ideal of civil-style police forces.

Notes

1 Charles Temple, *Native Races and Their Rulers: Sketches and Studies of Official Life and Administrative Problems* (London: Frank Cass, 1968), p. 30.
2 J. D. Fage, *A History of Africa* (London: Routledge, 1988), p. 414.
3 Paper entitled 'Local Government and Law and Order' given at CO course on African administration and local government, 20 August–1 September 1951, para. 13, NA CO 879/155.
4 Some areas did not have formally established NAP, for example Eastern Nigeria and Nyasaland, but a system of messengers, commonly referred to as court messengers or district messengers whose policing practices appeared somewhat similar to other territories. Overall policing practice appeared to have been shaped rather more by the field administrators than through official policy: see 'Local Government and Law and Order', para. 13, NA CO 879/155.
5 W. C. Johnson, Police Advisor to the Secretary of State for the Colonies, 'Report on the Colonial Police Service', 28 Dec. 1949, NA CO 537/5440.
6 Report of the 1st Conference of Colonial Commissioners of Police, 1951, p. 7, NA CO 885/119.
7 Derek Franklin, Memoirs of a Colonial Police Officer, 1953–1981, unpublished, Franklin, Family Papers, p. 37.
8 The drafting of regular police into the native reserves did not begin in earnest until 1950, apart from small numbers stationed at provincial and district headquarters, responsible for guard duties. Sir F. D. Corfield suggested that the main reason for this was a lack of adequate funding: Colonial Office, *Historical Survey of the Origins and Growth of Mau Mau* (London: HMSO, 1960), hereafter referred to as the Corfield Report, ch. 12, p. xiv. For example by the end of 1952, the total number of regular police in the whole of the Central Province had risen by 160 to 723 and the Kenya Police Reserve by 624 to 1,500: Corfield Report, ch. 12, p. xvii.
9 Kenya Police Report, 1948, pp. 5–6.
10 John Burton (Kenya Police, Div. Comm., rtd, 1954–66) in correspondence with the author, 4 Aug. 2000.
11 Templer, 'Report on Colonial Security', May 1955, NA CAB 129/76/352.
12 Taken from an interview with David Hewson (Kenya Police, Chief Sup., rtd, 1951–75), March 2000.
13 'We differed from UK police practice in that, in addition to normal police duties, junior officers were trained in foot and arms drill . . . to inculcate smartness, alertness and togetherness': Eates (interview), May 2005.
14 Eates, Hadow, Biles, weekly letters drawn from West Africa, 1950–55, Family Papers.
15 Eates noted that the police supervised punishment meted out to juvenile offenders under the corporal punishment ordinance. This included the punishment of beating for which the juveniles remained in police custody until the sentence was executed: Eates to Commissioner, Sierra Leone Police, 9 Oct. 1954, Eates, Family Papers.
16 Shirley, *History of the Nigeria Police*, pp. 39–63.
17 Biles to the Commissioner, Nigeria Police, 30 June 1956, Biles, Family Papers.
18 Biles reported gin-smuggling in Loko, the 'principal place in the Province for illicit alcohol smuggling': Biles to Commissioner, Nigeria Police, 9 June 1951, Biles, Family Papers.
19 Franklin, *Memoirs*, p. 37.
20 Geoffrey Morton, *Just the Job: Some Experiences of a Colonial Policeman* (London: Hodder & Stoughton, 1957), p. 239.
21 Franklin in correspondence with the author, Oct. 2000.
22 A common bribe offered was a bottle of whiskey: Milton (interview), July 2000.
23 Biles to Commissioner, 1 June 1951, Biles, Family Papers.
24 Clayton, *Thin Blue Line*, pp. 66, 75.
25 Clayton, *Thin Blue Line*, p. 76.
26 Eates (interview), June 2001; Clayton, *Thin Blue Line*, p. 204.

27 Eates to Commissioner, Sierra Leone Police, 25 Sept. 1954, Eates, Family Papers.
28 Eates to Commissioner, Sierra Leone Police, 30 July 1955, Eates, Family Papers.
29 Clayton, *Thin Blue Line*, p. 23.
30 Clayton, *Thin Blue Line*, p. 105.
31 Hadow (interview), Jan. 2002.
32 Chistopher Lawrence Hiscox, *The Dawn Stand-To* (Bideford: Lazurus Press, 2000), p. 275. Similar comments have been made by former members of the colonial administration. Sir Hugh Foot noted that 'the cold killing of the wretched murderer in Acre remains far more terrible than any killing . . . As a Governor I have had to sign many death warrants': *A Start in Freedom* (London: Hodder & Stoughton), p. 55.
33 Milton (interview), July 2000. Milton noted that while the prison was responsible for 'physically' carrying out the execution, the policeman present gave the instructions to the executioner.
34 Robin Mitchell (Nigeria Police, Assist. Sup., rtd, 1955–65), taken from 'Law and the Administration of Justice: A Police Perspective', *IHR*, 27–28 May 1999.
35 Milton (interview), July 2000.
36 'The Colonial Police Service, Duties and Responsibilities', John Biles, Family Papers.
37 Hewson (interview), March 2000.
38 Peter Hewitt, *Kenya Cowboy: A Police Officer's Account of the Mau Mau Emergency* (London: Avon Books, 1999) p. 79.
39 Imray, *Policeman in Africa*, pp. 161–162, 167, 173–174.
40 Hewson (interview), April 2000.
41 The *kipande* was introduced in 1915 as the Registration of Native Ordinance and instituted in 1920, requiring that every African male over the age of 15 to register with his local administrative officer and be issued with a finger-printed certificate of identity. The *kipande* provided basic personal details and acted as a record of employment: Native Registration Amendment Ordinance (no 19 of 1920), *Kenya Gazette*, 18 Aug. 1920.
42 Taken from an interview with Avtar S. Matharu (Kenya Police, Assist. Sup., rtd, 1953–67), June 2002.
43 Taken from an interview with David Rowcroft (Kenya Police, rtd, 1955–63), Nov. 2000.
44 Taken from an interview with Sir Richard Catling (Palestine Police, Malayan Police, Kenya Police, Com., dec., 1935–63), June 2000.
45 Kenya Police Annual Report, 1955, p. 2.
46 Matharu (interview), June 2002.
47 Evelyn Baring, Governor, to Lyttelton, Colonial Secretary, Telegram, 19 Feb. 1954, NA CO 1037/39.
48 W. C. Johnson, Police Advisor to the Secretary of State for the Colonies, 'Report on the Colonial Police Service', 28 Dec. 1948, NA CO 537/5440/5.
49 Morton, *Just the Job*, p 19.
50 N. J. Small, 'The Northern Rhodesia Police and its Legacy, *African Social Research*, 27 (1979), p. 533.
51 Morrison, 'Policing in Anglophone Africa', p. 62.
52 Biles to Commissioner, Nigeria Police, 7 May, 1951. Biles, Family Papers.
53 Tamuno, The Police in Modern Nigeria, pp. 181–182.
54 Morrison, 'Policing in Anglophone Africa', pp. 231–232.
55 Members of the colonial police were obliged to pass language exams in order to apply for promotion within three years of their posting. They were also required to pass exams in 'law, colonial regulations and financial instructions', for example, in order for their appointment to be confirmed. Many officers were proficient in a number of languages and were able to take courses at the School of African and Oriental Study in London during their home leave: Eates (interview), May 2005.
56 Limb (interview), Aug. 2000.
57 Biles, ASP Nigeria Police, Benue Province, to Commissioner, 18 Dec. 1950, weekly letter, Biles, Family Papers.

58 Richard Edelsten (Gold Coast Police, Assist. Sup., dec., 1944–57), 'Riot Drill', Gold Coast Police Pamphlet (1949), RHL MSS Afr. s. 1784, Box II, f. 1.
59 Biles (interview), March 2000.
60 Milton (interview), July 2000. George Willis (interview), Sept. 2000, noted that a riot squad was closer to 50 men in the run-up to independence:, .
61 Edelsten, RHL MSS Afr. s. 1784, Box II, f. 4G.
62 Milton (interview), July 2000; Eates (interview), May 2005.
63 Morton, *Just the Job*, p. 49.
64 Milton (interview), July 2000.
65 Morton, *Just the Job*, p. 49.
66 Willis (interview), Sept. 2000.
67 Clayton, *Thin Blue Line*, p. 214.
68 Clayton, *Thin Blue Line*, pp. 214–215.
69 Biles, in correspondence with the author, 21 March 2001.
70 Willis (interview), Sept. 2000.
71 Taken from an interview with Bob Bradney (Nigeria Police, Assist. Sup., rtd, 1953–64), Nov. 2000. Bradney mentioned a number of riots during which the Nigeria Police used 'maximum' force; for example, the Eruwa riot in Oyo Province in 1953 when shots were fired at the police followed by the police returning fire, with one rioter being killed and several injured.
72 Clayton, *Thin Blue Line*, pp. 56–57.
73 Clayton, *Thin Blue Line*, pp. 52–53; Bradney (interview), Nov. 2000.
74 Milton (interview), July 2000.
75 Macoun, *Wrong Place, Right Time*, p. 37.
76 Macoun, *Wrong Place, Right Time*, pp. 44–45.
77 Macoun noted that 12 were killed and 1,200 arrests were made: *Wrong Place, Right Time*, p. 45.
78 Hadow (interview), Jan. 2002; Willis (interview), Sept. 2000; Milton (interview), July 2000.
79 Northam, *Shooting in the Dark*, p. 131.
80 Clayton, *Thin Blue Line*, p. 23–24.
81 Hadow (interview), Jan. 2002.
82 Bradney (interview), Nov. 2000.
83 Morrison, 'Policing in Anglophone Africa', p. 133, cited in a press handout, 'The Kenya Emergency – Report by the War Council', 20 Oct. 1954, Kenya National Archives, INF 6/278.
84 Burton in correspondence with the author, August 2000. Burton was later transferred back to the GSU in 1959 in the Northern Frontier Province.
85 Clayton, *Thin Blue Line*, pp. 72–73.
86 Clayton, *Thin Blue Line*, pp. 97–99.
87 Franklin (interview), Oct. 2002.
88 In 1951, the European Inspectorate numbered 125. It rose to over 1,000 at the height of the emergency in 1955. It then decreased to around 666 by 1961, of whom 153 were Chief Inspectors and 513 were Inspectors: Hewson (interview), March 2000.
89 Hewitt, *Kenya Cowboy*, pp. viii–ix. The European community referred to these inexperienced policemen as 'green boys': from an interview with Don Clarke (Kenya Police, Chief Insp., rtd, 1953–64), Sept. 2000.
90 Clayton, *Thin Blue Line*, p. 166.
91 Roger Dracup (Palestine Police, Kenya Police, Assist. Sup., rtd, 1947–60) in correspondence with the author, June 2000. Mention is given of the 'goat bag' (Kenya Police equivalent of a black box) from which funds were taken for building and supplies.
92 Clayton, *Thin Blue Line*, pp. 160–162.
93 Kenya Police Report, 1945, pp. 2–3.
94 Kenya Police Report, 1953, p. 4.
95 Kenya Police Report, 1955, p. 2.
96 Clayton, *Thin Blue Line*, p. 158.

   97   John Bailey (Kenya Police, Div. Com., rtd, 1954–66) in correspondence with the author, Nov. 2000.
   98   Directive 'Your Turn May Come', published by the Department of Information, Nakuru, for the Provincial Emergency Committee, 1952: Peter Hewitt, Family Papers.
   99   Catling, RHL MSS Afr. s. 1784, Box IX, f. 21A.
  100   The Kikuyu Guard has been described as a 'loyalist movement': Corfield Report, ch. 12, p. iv. Mention has also been made of its infiltration by Mau Mau. Taken from interviews with Ted Evans (Kenya Police, Special Branch, rtd, 1954–73), July 2000 and James Colquoun (District Officer, Kenya, rtd, 1954–56), May 2001.
  101   Foran, *Kenya Police*, p. 209, James Forster (Kenya Police, Insp., rtd, 1954–56) in correspondence with the author, 29 May 2000.
  102   Percy Turner Wild, *Bwana Polisi* (Braunton: Merlin Books, 1993), pp. 9–10.
  103   The official figure of Mau Mau losses from October 1952 to August 1955 was 13,320–9,514 killed, 1,907 captured and 1,899 surrendered. Deaths within the security forces were 32 Europeans, 26 Asians and 525 Africans. Civilian casualties were far higher: Foran, *Kenya Police*, pp. 216, 226.
  104   Derek Franklin, *A Pied Cloak: Memoirs of a Colonial Police (Special Branch) Officer* (London: Janus, 1996), p. 45; Kenneth Cunningham, 'Tracker Combat Operations', Kenya Police, Oct. 1955, MSS Afr. s. 1784 (21D).
  105   Franklin, *Memoirs*, pp. 23–24.
  106   Wild, *Bwana Polisi*, p. 14.
  107   For an in-depth account of the detention camps see: Caroline Elkins, *Britain's Gulag: The Brutal End of Empire in Kenya* (London: Jonathan Cape, 2005). Elkins considers that 'the number of Africans detained was at least two times and more likely four times the official figure, or somewhat between 160,000 and 320,000 (p. xi). Regarding the Mau Mau trials and an overall account of British justice in Kenya during the emergency see: David Anderson, *Histories of the Hanged: Britain's Dirty War in Kenya and the End of the Empire* (London, Weidenfeld & Nicolson, 2005).
  108   Franklin, *Pied Cloak*, pp. 72–86.
  109   Clayton. *Thin Blue Line*, p. 154.
  110   Anderson, *Histories of the Hanged*, p. 85.
  111   Hewson (interview), April 2000.
  112   Foran, *Kenya Police*, p. 136. In 1955, its total strength rose to some 9,076.
  113   Akker, RHL MSS Afr. s. 1784, Box 20, f. 3.
  114   Hewson, 19 April 00. For detailed account of KPR brutality see Elkins, *Britain's Gulag*, pp. 79–82.
  115   Foran, *Kenya Police*, p. 202.
  116   Franklin (interview), Oct. 00.
  117   Quoted in Brian Lapping, *End of Empire* (London: Guild Publishing, 1985), p. 27.
  118   *Kessing's Contemporary Archives*, 4–11 June, 1955, p. 14248.

CHAPTER SEVEN

Policing colonial conflict in Southeast Asia

Threatening the survival of the British Empire during the post-war years was the spread of communism and the growth of the cold war. Southeast Asia appeared to be the immediate communist target, with British rule in Malaya, Singapore and Hong Kong coming under threat.

By the late 1940s, Malaya had become one of Britain's highest dollar earners, producing high-calibre tin and rubber for the world markets. Its export earnings were a cash cow to counterbalance the post-war 'financial Dunkirk'. Any successful communist push into Malaya would thus threaten Britain's global economic interests, already teetering on the brink of collapse. The threat to Malaya's stability came in the guise of the Malay Communist Party (MCP) which was supported principally by immigrant Chinese. Having assisted the British during the war in their fight against the Japanese as the Malay Anti-Japanese People's Party (MPAJA), their struggle after 1945 quickly became an anti-imperialist one and was undertaken by the Malay Races' Liberation Army (MRLA) under the leadership of Chin Peng. The picture was somewhat complicated during the pre-emergency period by an additional group, the Malay Overseas Chinese Self-Defence Army (MOCSDA). Consisting mainly of Kwangsai Chinese, this small group was based in Upper Perak and Kelantan, proclaiming loyalty to Chiang Kai-shek.[1]

Until the MCP's legal status was removed in 1948, its early efforts revolved around trade union activities, including the organisation of demonstrations and strikes in opposition to the Malayan Union. By mid-1948, the MCP was intent on forcing the British out of Malaya. During the same period, Malaya witnessed the growth of a new political party, the United Malays National Organisation (UMNO), supported by the Malayan sultans and a large cross-section of the population. UMNO was also resistant to the idea of the Union, the upshot of which was the creation of a Malayan Federation in February

1948 and the prospect of colonial rule for some time to come. Yet the advent of a Federation had coincided with two conferences of Asian communist parties held in Calcutta in March 1948. There was documentary evidence in party papers seized from Burma that the Burmese Communist Party had decided to launch its own civil war. It was strongly suspected that similar orders had been given in Calcutta for an 'armed revolt' in Malaya. The MRLA's military machinery was set in motion. That month, a combined military–police operation was launched against the MOCSDA at five separate locations in Perak.[2] By May 1948, the emergency was unofficially underway, although it took the murders of three European rubber planters at Sungei Siput in Perak, for an official declaration to be made in June 1948.

The Malayan emergency 1948–60: jungle-bashing

The Malayan Police played a crucial role during the ensuing conflict that spanned over a decade.[3] By 1952, 100,000 regular and auxiliary police, 189,000 Home Guards and 45,000 Kampong Guards were assisting the armed forces, often in a frontline capacity. The previous year, the Home Guard, a largely unarmed force had been amalgamated with the Kampong Guard, armed typically with shotguns. The Kampong Guard had been engaged in semi-military policing since the onset of the emergency. Located usually in the old villages, rather than the newer villages, they were responsible for guard duties and defence.[4] The Malayan emergency increasingly became a war with civilian dimensions, and it was the general population and the police who suffered the majority of the casualties – by 1957, 2,890 police and 3,253 civilians had been killed.[5]

The role of the police became one of 'stamping out a well-organised armed force which adopts terrorism and guerrilla tactics'. By isolating the MRLA from its sources of supply – the Min Yuen (the MRLA's intelligence and supply wing), the police would be contributing to the success of the Briggs Plan.[6] However, this became just one of the ways in which the security forces' tactics of coercion and enforcement, on the one hand, and 'winning hearts and minds', on the other, caught the peoples of Malaya in the 'middle between two millstones'.[7] The police, too, were trapped between the practice of *civil* policing – the 'hearts and minds' policy – and *paramilitary* policing. Government measures to reorganise aspects of police practice on *British* lines clashed with the reality of a conflict situation in which the police were often frontline targets. As the emergency unfurled, the *colonial* side to policing was strengthened, and that contrasted with the secondment of Arthur Young to undertake a civil overhaul of police duties.

[166]

Initially, the Malayan Police was unable to prevent the situation from worsening, being under-strength and ill-prepared to deal with the type of 'jungle warfare' the MRLA had developed, basing insurgents in remote jungle areas to strike, when opportunities arose, at plantations, mines and police stations. In the early stages of the emergency, Chinese 'squatters' living on the fringes of the jungle supplied food and intelligence. In addition, the Min Yuen was responsible for assassinations carried out by 'specialised Killer Squads . . . the only crime of their victims is that either they have in some way opposed the Communist cause, refused to give money, food or shelter, or have killed a guerrilla, Party official or Min Yuen agent'.[8]

Although the Malayan Police had been privy to some of the lessons learnt during the Second World War. 'By 1946, lessons from the European resistance movements were available' to Malayan police commissioners, and these may have provided information as to how the 'communist terrorists' could be dealt with; however, until 1948 the Malayan Police seem to have found little relevance in such 'lessons' and instead concentrated on going back to basics in terms of training and organisation.[9] Over 500 former Palestine Police officers, including a new Commissioner, Nicol Gray, bolstered the police's depleted ranks, bringing their much need counter-insurgency experiences, but also creating tensions within the force as the new personnel made their presence felt. Many of the British officers were of 'pre-war vintage; most had been prisoners of the Japanese and anyone who had not "been in the bag" was looked down on and seen as intruders [sic]'.[10]

Problems within the police were only partially alleviated as their numbers swelled from 12,767 in early 1949 to a peak of 36,737 by 1953. The Malayan Special Constabulary rose from 10,000 in August 1948 to 44,878 by mid-1952.[11] Templer attempted to increase the number of Chinese serving in the uniformed police from 800 to 2,000 in 1952 in an effort to make the force more representative of the population at large.[12] Needless to say, the Palestine contingency, comprising some 'rough types and adventurers', provided the badly needed experience in counter-insurgency policing which contributed to winning the shooting war, but was hardly conducive to winning hearts and minds.[13] Many were used to train the auxiliary police in the protection of mines and estates and to form the backbone to the new jungle-squads.

While counter-insurgency operations were primarily the army's responsibility, the police gradually built up their own operations, intensifying their paramilitary role. Early examples included the creation in 1949 of a police 'pseudo-guerrilla unit' based on Palestine experiences. When the police lacked the training to deal with a given situation, they were helped by army officers and NCOs. They provided 'on-the-job' tuition based on 'ample experience' of Imperial Policing mainly from India and the Middle East, the focus being on Palestine-style settlement cordon-and-search and population controls.[14] At the same time, the Colonial Office despatched a number of 'experts' to assist in the fight against 'communism',[15] including roving members of the Security Service like Alex Kellar. By 1952, major operations code-named SWORD and SPEAR were mounted using the combined military and police efforts to either kill or flush out and capture insurgents. By the time that police jungle companies had been set up, the army was able to hand large areas over to the police for their direct control. Thus the police were involved on the edges of the jungle to enforce civil measures, including curfews, restrictions on shop hours and the use of vehicles, as well as intercepting any terrorist movements. War executive committees were established at both state and district level to oversee operations chaired by administration, army and police members.[16]

A number of special, or irregular, forces using both army and police were created to counter the hit and run tactics of mobile guerrilla forces entrenched within the jungle and also to guard the frontiers. From the onset of the emergency, members of the Forestry Department and the Malayan Civil Service (MCS) with 'jungle experience' were posted to border areas. Known as the Malayan Frontier Force, they came under the leadership of John Watts from the MCS. The group was soon absorbed into the regular police and became known as the Frontier Branch, with the responsibility of patrolling the border areas. Members were trained at the British Army's 'Jungle Warfare School' at Nee Soon in Singapore. Eventually a jungle training centre was set up at Sik in Central Kedah.[17] The 'jungle warfare wing' known initially as jungle squads, then jungle companies and, latterly, as the Police Field Forces, operated deep within jungle areas. These undercover police units operated in a similar manner to infantry units with the use of both Sten and Bren guns.[18] During the early part of the emergency, the Ferret Force, initially comprising 136 police and military officers, became an important source of intelligence and provided operational support. This led to the creation of special jungle squads of 20 operational units each with 15 men. The purpose of these long-range squads was to live in the jungle and establish links with the Aborigines who would provide intelligence regarding the whereabouts of the guerrillas.[19]

The aboriginal tribes were seen as potential troublemakers, having become 'contaminated by the MPAJA' during the Second World War, hence, for example, the use of control and intimidation in dealing with the Orang Asli people who had been forced by the insurgents to grow food and act as spies and guides, partly as a result of their location and partly because of their relationship with the MPAJA.[20] A widespread bombing campaign coupled with heavy-handed attempts to resettle this aboriginal people merely alienated them further.[21] Closer ties with the Aborigines were established through abandoning resettlement. In its place, Templer ordered the construction of jungle forts to provide security for the Aborigines and a nucleus for intelligence-gathering and operational activities. The first fort was built near Kuala Lipis by Sergeant Monty Gay, a former Palestine policeman.[22] From this point, a string of jungle forts were erected within the aboriginal tribal and hunting grounds, which allowed the police jungle companies to remain for long periods within remote areas. Once the jungle companies were established, the authorities built helicopter pads, airstrips and police forts in many areas

A former Commander of 20 Jungle Company based at Ipoh in Perak State explained that the Aborigines had perceived the MCP as heroes who had fought to free Malaya following the Japanese invasion. It took time and persuasion to break this pattern and convince the Aborigines to work with the British. Once a relationship had been established, the Aborigines were used as trackers and guides, and 'were invaluable to our operational success in the jungle as they could tell you anything about the layout of the land and where the communists were hiding'.[23] Templer considered that convincing the Aborigines to change sides was an important factor in winning the shooting war and in implementing the hearts and minds policy.[24] Search and destroy missions would be undertaken either by the jungle squads independently or in conjunction with regular forces.[25] Anecdotal tales of this bloody conflict contained repeated references to the militarised nature of policing and its successes.[26]

By early 1950, the army was assisted by over 200 new police jungle squads[27] while operating alone in the deep jungle. A combination of policing, resettlement, large-scale operations and prolonged small unit patrolling, with an emphasis on the latter, was endorsed by the War Office and the Chiefs of Staff. Field Marshal Slim wrote that he had 'always been' of the opinion that such methods were the right ones, as they were 'found' in similar operations in the past, Greece and Burma probably being on his mind.[28] Certainly there was a demand for tried and tested techniques like those used in Palestine, particularly with Templer's arrival in Malaya in February 1952, and concerted attempts at a hearts and minds policy.

Hearts and minds

Templer was appointed as both High Commissioner and Director of Operations. His priorities lay in reforming the administration, the police and the intelligence services. Assistance came from Young who had previously worked for Templer in the British Military Government in Germany in 1945.[29] Templer's reshaping of the administration meant that 'all the dead wood was swiftly and ruthlessly removed from the Administrative tree – some to be thrown away for good, some relegated to the lower branches'.[30] This involved Young replacing a disgruntled Gray on 25 January 1952, the latter having repeatedly disagreed with senior police colleagues over the role of the Malayan Police.

Gray had believed that counter-insurgency should be the primary task of the police, repeating his Palestine experiences; civil duties assuming second place. The old Malay hands disagreed with the growing importance of the jungle war and were concerned about the deteriorating relationship between the police and the general public. Young was also faced with a schism within the European ranks of the Malayan Police: the first group, occupying the most senior administrative posts, was composed of the 'old Malayan Police group'; the second group consisted of those officers who had served in India, having been seconded to Malaya after independence in 1947;[31] the third group was made up of former Palestine Police officers who had been seconded in 1948 and had considerable counter-insurgency experience; and the final group was comprised of members of the home police forces despatched to bring all things British to Malaya. Having conducted a review of the police and all aspects of their work, Young remarked that it could be summed up in two words: 'organised disorganisation'. Unable fully to reconcile the differences between the groups, to distinguish between the shooting war and normal police duties, Young made headway in other areas. These included improving the arsenal of weapons, bringing in new MK 5 rifles, greater numbers of Bren and Sten guns as well as .300 American carbines, which proved more effective for 'fast jungle shooting'. Policing reforms were, however, underpinned by Young's desire to distinguish between the 'shooting war' and 'normal' police duties.[32]

Templer also drew a distinction between paramilitary and civil police duties. Shortly after his arrival in Malaya, he declared that 'normal civil government and the business of the Emergency are two separate entities'.[33] The Malayan Police would continue to assist the counter-insurgency campaign, while providing a new 'civil' police service to the population at large. Police officers were, therefore, supposed to 'go off on [their] rounds, visiting police stations and posts, police deployed on plantations, to see village chiefs and so on'; however, 'because virtually the whole area was classified "red", my travelling had to be done by armoured personnel carrier'.[34]

Templer's interest in bettering relations between the police and the general public also placed an onus on the population. He believed that the public should assist the security forces, for 'without the co-opera-tion of the ordinary man-in-the-street the Emergency would continue indefinitely'. This became rather more than just a public relations exer-cise. In February 1950 'Anti-Bandit Month' began, during which members of the public aided the police with the manning of road blocks and carrying out screening programmes. Young noted that over half a million adults enrolled in this scheme, providing 'a complete refutation of the Communist propaganda that the bandits had the support of the Malayan people'.[35] In reality, however, Templer's and Young's brand of 'hearts and minds' clashed with the realities of policing an emergency. In essence, Templer's policy necessitated holding out a carrot in the one hand while brandishing a large stick in the other.

Templer was able to bring about a change for the better in the situa-tion in Malaya during his two years stay.[36] He recognised that by bring-ing the emergency under control, steps could be taken towards future self-government. Emergency regulations provided the Government with powers to raise a force of special constables, to arrest and detain without a warrant, to register the population and to try all but capital offences *in camera*. Emergency powers enabled the Malayan Government to take more drastic measures and allowed pressure to be brought to bear on the state governments. Emergency Regulations 17D, 17E and 17F were promulgated to allow the rounding-up of squatter populations.[37] The harshness of punishment and the level of restric-tions on movement, economic life and the purchase of day-to-day com-modities intensified as the conflict wore on, clashing with any notions of 'hearts and minds' civil styles of policing.

The Malayan Police was involved, for example, in the collective pun-ishment of villages, a policy approved by the British Government in November 1950. Fines were imposed on villages like Pusing, Perak and Bukit Selambau in Kedah for failure to supply information about guer-rilla activity.[38] The Tanjong Malim incident was an example of just how far coercion could be taken. On 25 March 1952, R. M. C. Codner, an Assistant District Officer, 7 police officers, an engineer and 3 members of a repair party were ambushed and killed following an attempt to rein-stall Tanjong Malim's water supply, which had been the target of an attack. Templer decided to 'clamp down hard' in the first major inci-dent that he faced in Malaya. No information regarding the attack was forthcoming from people in the town, who, it was assumed, had sup-ported the attack. Templer's course of action was to impose collective punishment – a twenty-two-hour curfew daily – until information was forthcoming.[39]

During the next few months, similar measures were taken against towns and villages close to the locations of major incidents. Snap road-blocks were often set up and manned by British troops. Villages were then searched on the slightest suspicion and curfews enforced on a twenty-two hour basis. Added to the curfews and a reduction in rice rations was the imposition of a collective fine. In August 1952, following the death of a Chinese man in Permatang Tinggi, the police questioned the villagers, but they refused to provide any information about the incident and no local intelligence was forthcoming. As a result, sixty-two villagers – men, women and children – were sent to detention camps and the village was then destroyed.[40]

Another effective stick wielded by the Government and supervised by the police was food control. Malaya did not produce enough rice for its population and the resettlement programme allowed for strict supervision of the distribution of food and other essentials such as medicine. Lieutenant-General Briggs had set up a Federal Joint Intelligence Advisory Committee in May 1950 to coordinate all intelligence functions, and this organisation was responsible for the development of 'food denial operations', which caused 'relentless, sustained pressure on a Communist group accompanied by constant military and police harassment . . . [and eventually resulted] in its total collapse'.[41] The Chairman of the Johore State War Committee, however, reported that food denial had a 'harmful effect on the good-will and co-operation of the public out of all proportion to the effect on the bandit supply problem'.[42] The implementation of the hearts and minds policy would address this issue. The support of the local population was essential to the intelligence-gathering process.

Under the so-called 'Briggs Plan', Chinese squatters and other people exposed to the MCP were moved to new settlements. The implementation of this plan was extremely slow and tied up large number of policemen. By 1952 there were 509 settlements comprising a population of 461,822.[43] The resettlement placed a strain on Malaya's police:

> Many of the Malayan special constables hated the darkness and kept their patrolling of the perimeter fences down to an absolute minimum. Any potential food-suppliers had little difficult in keeping watch on the movements of these patrols. It was therefore a simple matter for them to slip away from one of the buildings and deposit a parcel of food on the outside of the fence at a time previously arranged with the terrorists.[44]

In terms of the police's relationship with the public, the plan was something of a double-edged sword. The police were attempting to isolate the Chinese communities from the MCP through the creation of new villages, while preventing any contact between the two parties. Former members of the Malayan Police have insisted that they forged good relations with the Chinese communities through this process.[45] The

Malayan emergency rumbled on until 1960, three years after the colony had attained its independence. By the 1960s, problems linked to the threat of communist expansion had surfaced within Britain's Southeast Asian jewel, Hong Kong.

Hong Kong headaches

In June 1968, following the most serious public disturbances in the history of the colony, the Commissioner of Police, Ted Eates, reported that the situation in Hong Kong continued to be 'dominated by relations with China'. The long-term aim of China centred on encouraging 'the Communists in Hong Kong [to] dominate decisions and policies of the Government, without losing the benefits, e.g., of access to the free world, an intelligence base and source of foreign exchange'. As a result, insurgents in Hong Kong had attempted wherever possible to discredit the police, whose routine was hampered by 'irritation or worse, owing to crowding, and competition for space'. The police's system for dealing with hawkers was 'out of hand' and traffic was chaotic owing to 'poor driving standards'. At the very top of the list of 'headaches' was corruption, which was to become a focal point of media attention and official investigation by the 1970s.[46] Eates described corruption as one of the main reasons for public dissatisfaction with both the Government and the Royal Hong Kong Police (RHKP).[47] Having successfully contained the 'communist' threat in 1967, acquiring the title 'Royal' in the process, the image of the force was to be one of corruption in subsequent years.

Yet throughout much of its history the Hong Kong Police (HKP) was perceived as a highly efficient force. Jeffries noted that 'in police matters as in everything else, Hong Kong is unique'. Alongside the Ceylon and the Palestine Police, the HKP had always been considered one of the finest colonial constabularies. Certainly the manner in which the serious public disturbances of 1966 and 1967 were contained was an indicator of its abilities. Previous reform had sharpened its riot-control capabilities. Throughout the early 1960s, efforts had been made to improve public relations by keeping the populace informed about police aims and methods, so that, by winning hearts and minds in this manner, the public would be encouraged to accept the HKP and cooperate in the fight against crime.[48] The 1968 reforms contributed to general improvements in the force, only to be marred by the corruption scandals of subsequent years. Nevertheless, the RHKP stands out as a hybrid of old-fashioned *colonial* and *civil* police practices.

Hong Kong was ceded to Britain by the Chinese Government in 1841. The colony's first Chief Magistrate, Captain William Caine,

14   Howard Mansfield patrolling with the Malayan Police,
Siamese border, 1954

became responsible for law and order, which encompassed the police. The area was increased to include the Chinese city of Kowloon, on the mainland side, and, in 1898, extended to the New Territories, including a large number of islands, on a lease of ninety-nine years. For the purpose of policing, Hong Kong was divided into three: the island of Hong Kong, Kowloon and the New Territories, covering a total area of 398 square miles. By the 1960s, Hong Kong was referred to no longer as a colony but as a 'territory'. Each area had a tendency towards one style of policing. Within the urban centres of Hong Kong and Kowloon, there was greater emphasis on civil policing, while in the New Territories colonial police practices prevailed.

'A big force in a small area instead of a small force in a big area' was how the HKP was described by a former Commissioner. This allowed for a 'tighter grip geographically'. Besides, there was traditionally a strong military presence in Hong Kong which permitted swift aid to the civil power when needed and plenty of government funds were available:

> In West Africa, getting money for the police was like getting blood out of a stone. I suppose because there was no tax base. Hong Kong raised revenue and income tax. Financing the police was not such problem. We had better buildings, better transport and communications and so on than other places.[49]

From the outset, the HKP was well equipped in terms of weaponry, transport and general equipment as compared to other colonial police forces.[50] (In later years, the force would be used as a testing ground for new equipment.) Its officers were also better paid than those of other colonial forces. It was generally tough to gain entry into the HKP, in a way similar to the Malayan Singapore or Ceylon Police, with recruits typically coming from a lower age bracket.[51] Once a person had been

15   Passing out parade, Police Training School, Hong Kong, 1968

accepted into the police, he was expected to train to the very highest level, from basic foot drill though to training in law and order.

As a port, Hong Kong's particular feature was its continual movement of people. It was an important centre for migration, to the extent that the colony suffered from overcrowding; there was therefore a need to maintain public order. The removal of squatters, restriction and control of unlicensed street-hawkers and strict enforcement of traffic regulations were duties which served to distance the public from the police.[52] 'Pressure policing' was how one officer referred to this type of policing, which saw a high ratio of uniformed officers on the streets of Hong Kong and Kowloon.[53] It was not until after the 1967 disturbances that the public viewed the police in a better light, and their reputation improved drastically.

Hong Kong's first police force had consisted of ninety-three soldiers seconded from British and Indian regiments. On 1 May 1844, a Police Ordinance was passed creating a formal colonial constabulary over which Charles May presided as Captain Superintendent of Police. It is thought that May intended to model the HKP on the lines of the Metropolitan Police. Yet as a result of the general lawlessness that prevailed in the colony at that time, he was unable to follow this plan, although there did begin a closening of the ties between the Metropolitan

Police and the HKP. From 1841 until 1945, officers and inspectors were recruited in Britain on short to medium term contracts ((i.e. 3–5 years) from the home forces. The Colonial Office noted in 1949, for example, that nine officers were due to be transferred back to their original forces.[54]

In terms of the recruitment of rank and file, the HKP established a tradition of using outsiders for certain specific duties, namely public disorders and traffic. In this way, the old RIC tradition of 'policing by strangers' came to the fore. Recruits were drawn initially from India and later from Wei Hei Wei, a British enclave on China's north coast. The Hong Kong Government believed that the colony's security should not be placed in the hands of locally recruited Chinese police officers.[55] A similar view had been held in Ireland, where RIC officers were posted to areas away from their home towns. By 1950, therefore, the rank and file were split between the Hong Kong Chinese and a small contingency of around 1,000 Asian officers and recruits from northern China. Both the Asian and Shantung Wei Hei Wei officers spoke little or no Punti, the local Cantonese dialect. The northern Chinese recruits were generally given one of two duties: traffic or emergency. This was not just because, speaking Mandarin rather than Cantonese, their ability to communicate with the general public was generally limited; they were also typically taller than the average Hong Kong Chinese, and thus physically seen as more able to deal with these duties.[56]

Similarly Asian – Indian and Pakistani – officers were used almost exclusively in the emergency units that were called out to deal with both public disorder and emergency situations. By 1950, it was recommended that 'the policy of recruitment of Pakistanis or time-expired Gurkhas should be reviewed immediately'. As a result, a request was made to the Pakistan Government for permission to recruit 300 officers to augment the emergency squads and to lift the ban imposed on recruitment since January 1949.[57] The Pakistan Government responded favourably to this request.[58] In general, the recruitment of Pakistanis and Indians to deal with public disorder was highly popular within the European contingent of the Hong Kong police: 'They were extremely good at dealing with drunken expatriate soldiers, for instance', commented Ivan Scott, who served in the HKP as a gazetted officer from 1955–87, 'because generally they were bigger than your average Chinese officer. Besides they wore the same uniform as us and held the view that your Queen is also my Queen.'[59] Essentially though, the emphasis was on retaining control of the local population in true colonial style, which could not be easily entrusted to Hong Kong Chinese officers:

> To begin with nobody knew how Hong Kong Chinese policemen were going to react against their own people. So the Pakistanis, for example,

were brought in as a wedge if the Chinese refused to 'fight' against their own people. The Wei Hei Wei officers were used in the same way. In the end we did not need these wedges as the Hong Kong Chinese were absolutely fantastic.[60]

In the longer term (i.e. by the 1980s), Asian and northern Chinese officers were no longer recruited into the HKP.[61] Yet this was a slow process and prevented the early localisation of the police and remained a source of friction between the police and the local population up until the 1960s. Overall the traditions of riot policing owed much to the Asian and northern Chinese policemen who had been so closely involved with its development. As Michael Ko chun commented:

> I believe that the police really came out on top at that time. In some countries, riot police end up by acting like rioters themselves. In Hong Kong, when face to face with rioters they were often spat upon but they did not lift a finger unless asked to do so. The training had made them this way.[62]

The police tactical unit, formerly the police training contingent, used for crowd control and rioting, was a particular colonial feature of the HKP. A self-contained mobile strike force, it had an establishment of roughly fifty men in each company, over and above divisional strength. By the early 1960s, five companies could be deployed within a short space of time. Within each unit were snatch squads, responsible for going into a crowd to make arrests whilst members of the tactical unit held the line. It was during the 1967 disturbances that the Hong Kong strike forces earned a reputation for first-class efficiency, and made increased use of colonial styles of policing. However, improvement to practices of policing public disturbances came about after the Star Ferry riots in the 1950s.

Policing 'a storm in a teacup': the Star Ferry riots

After the Second World War and the liberation of the Japanese camps, some officers returned to the HKP. Overall a dearth of police officers led to recruitment from the home forces and, after 1948, former members of the Palestine Police. The frontier with China, after 1949, was increasingly targeted by those Chinese eager to escape communism. It was after this period that political agitation came to the fore, with 'disillusioned workers' flocking to join a burgeoning trade union movement.[63] 'In 1949', noted former Assistant Commissioner C. L. Scobell, 'the Chinese Communist Party armies overran China up to the Hong Kong border and drove KMT remnants into Hong Kong as refugees.

Some of these were also recruited into the Hong Kong Police, anti-Communist sentiments and all.'[64]

Following the re-occupation of Hong Kong after the Second World War, internal security arrangements were regarded as bordering on the merely 'adequate'. The advent of communist China in 1949, coupled with escalating tensions as a result of the cold war, heightened security issues within Hong Kong. Certainly, pro-communist elements in the colony were roused by Mao's teachings and began to mobilise support. It was not, however, until the 1960s that the real shock-waves from Mao's Cultural Revolution reached Hong Kong and threatened to destabilise colonial rule. With the onset of cold war tensions and serious public disturbances, colonial methods of policing came to be preferred.

The serious rioting that occurred in 1952 and, again, in 1956 were clear indicators that neither the riot squads nor the regular police were adequately equipped or trained to prevent the escalation of problems without the assistance of the army. As a result, a number of reforms, in terms of riot-control methods, were introduced to the HKP with considerable success. 'With the large increases in population, one thing the Hong Kong Police had to learn to do well was how to deal with huge crowds. This they did and drew the attention of Western world police forces that were interested in improving riot-control methods in their own cities.'[65]

The Kowloon disturbances – referred to locally as the Star Ferry riots – were not directly linked to either the communist or the pro-KMT movement. The problem was sparked by the ferry company's decision to increase second-class cross-harbour fares. However, the disturbances were no doubt symptomatic of a deeper malaise within Hong Kong society as a result of the growing schism between nationalism and communism. Prior to the application of the fare increase, the Chinese press had drawn attention to rumours that discussions were underway; the Government was urged by one paper to allay public fears, for 'how could a family of five mouths afford extra expenses of several tens of dollars a month?'[66]

Prior to the subsequent demonstrations and riots that took place in April 1966, Sau Chung took up a prominent position between the subway and the turnstiles, wearing a black jacket which bore the words 'Join the hunger strike to block fare increase'. Sympathy with his cause was soon building among the press and the general public, resulting in widespread demonstrations in Kowloon and Hong Kong Island. By the third day, 2,655 uniformed police officers, including almost 1,000 members of the riot squads, had been fully mobilised. On 6 April the demonstrations turned violent and serious rioting broke out. Outside

Yau Ma Tei police station, for example, some 300 young men were shouting and screaming:

> It was menacing with its angry roar, so Mr Fergus, Superintendent of Police, initiated the precautions known as 'attack on station' and took his company outside and ordered a baton charge on the crowd.[67]

The crowd was successfully dispersed, but meanwhile, in neighbouring areas, similar problems were occurring involving crowds of over 1,000. Throughout Kowloon the police used baton charges and tear-smoke to disperse the rioters that night with the assistance of emergency units. By the following day, the numbers of police officers had increased to 3,600, with 1,167 operating within riot squads. Disturbances of this nature continued for a further three days and nights, with the police using a combination of curfew and riot-control tactics to contain affected areas, assisted by auxiliary police units and the military.

This 'storm-in-a-teacup' situation led to police being deployed in accordance with their new riot-control tactics and they established their reputation as a 'class one' colonial constabulary.[68] Yet their reputation spread to other police forces rather than to the Hong Kong population at large. Allegations were made against the police during the course of the government inquiry. They were accused, first, of having caused 'the peaceful demonstrations to degenerate into riots' and, second, of having carried out 'unjustified arrests' and acting with 'violence' towards individual members of the community. The inquiry concluded that these 'rumours' were ill-founded and that, on the contrary, the police had shown remarkable restraint in suppressing the rioting. This was illustrated by only 'a total of 93 rounds of ammunition [being] fired [with] one death and three injuries from gunshot wounds'.[69] (There were ten police casualties as a direct result of events.) The police had well and truly evolved from the experiences of the 1956 riots. They would be adequately prepared for the events of the following year.

The Hong Kong disturbances, May–December 1967

In 1966, the Commissioner of the HKP reported that 'Hong Kong's recent history has been remarkably orderly and free from major disturbances', though, he pointed out, the force should not be allowed to 'rest on its laurels'.[70] This was a timely warning, for between May and December of the following year the police were involved in duties that could hardly be described as routine, and precluded any notions of civil policing.

A confidential report, distributed on a restricted basis to government departments and not released to the press, attributed the 1967 disturbances to the 'effects of the cultural revolution, and in particular the intense patriotism and the devotion to Chairman Mao Tse Tung and his teaching, [which] were bound to spill over into Hong Kong'.[71] While the Government had professed that it 'was not engaged in a "war" with the communists', the global cold war context remained a prevailing factor. Hong Kong Territory was undoubtedly influenced by communism. 'This was hardly surprising given the atmosphere of the Cultural Revolution and the manner in which communists and nationalists used Hong Kong as their power base.'[72] By early 1967, 57 trade unions with a membership of some 60,000 came under the banner of the communist-dominated Federation of Trade Unions. They were perceived by Government as rather more akin to 'political associations' than organisations protecting the interests of the workers. Manifestly, engagement in the 'political indoctrination of their members by means of propaganda and by intensive courses of study of the works of Chairman Mao' encouraged the steady growth of a core of communist supporters.[73] Ongoing tensions were exacerbated by the views of the left-wing press, particularly the *Wen Wei Po*. 'It saw the police as a force intent on protecting management against "the legitimate grievances and complaints of the workers".'[74]

In this climate, and no doubt exacerbated by the events of the previous year, relations between workers and managements deteriorated. Demonstrations and pickets were the precursors to the rioting that followed in May 1967 and continued until the end of that year. Both the Government's and the police's view was that the rioting had been 'inspired and exploited' by communist elements of the community who 'encouraged the local population to participate in the ongoing conflict, attacking the police and government property'.[75]

In a short space of time, the demonstrations and rioting spread from Kowloon to Hong Kong Island. On 18 May, Government House became the focus of attention with petitions being handed in and demands to see the Governor, Sir David Trench. Several days later the police had the greatest difficulty in controlling the crowds, which succeeded in preventing traffic circulation. Any Europeans, including foreign press, found within this central district required police protection.[76] Contining disturbances were accompanied by a number of strikes and a period of 'token stoppages', the police's reputation taking a battering with rumours spreading of alleged brutality.[77]

One problem faced by the HKP was the population density within urban areas. Kowloon and Hong Kong Island were, in this respect, more difficult to police than the New Territories. In partial response to the previous year, numbers of HKP officers rose by 387 to 11,383 in 1967. (This was also in response to the number of crimes recorded, which rose by 11.8 per cent that year to 24,047, the highest figure reported for 11 years.)[78]

However, it was on the northern boundary of the New Territories that the police faced a more serious confrontation, resulting in the death of 5 officers and the wounding of 11 others. Historically, the border area required the presence of tactical support units and the nearby garrison of Ghurkha troops. Scott, who served in the New Territories from the early 1960s, noted the growing tensions. From numerous outposts along the border, the police provided the first line of defence: 'Essentially we kept a constant watch. It was incredible after a typhoon had blown away the foliage to see the number of field guns from the Chinese side pointing directly at you that we did not even know existed.'[79]

The Chinese side had paid close attention to the demonstrations of opposition within Hong Kong Island and Kowloon. Pro-communist propaganda through speeches and posters continued on the Chinese side, inciting local people to retaliate against the police and the Government. On 24 June, this escalated into violence, during the course of which the police made extensive use of tear gas to dispel the crowds. Shortly afterwards, the Peking Government officially protested to the Hong Kong Government that tear-gas shells had been fired into Chinese territory, and requested that the demands put forward by Hong Kong's Chinese residents and workers be met in full.[80] No doubt this constituted a threat aimed directly at the British and Hong Kong Governments, and indirectly at that of the United States. In response, Trench's statement purported to clarify the Chinese demands and to offer assurances to the Hong Kong people. These included 'the assurance from the Commissioner of Labour that the police do not and will not involve themselves in labour disputes but will only enforce the law when it is broken'.[81] Eates had already assured Trench that the police would act with as great a restraint as possible to prevent a worsening of events.[82] Contingency planning showed that the police should 'seize the initiative' wherever possible from an operational perspective and ensure 'vitally' that they won the hearts and minds of the public. During a state of emergency, all left-wing presses would be shut down and 'preventive arrests' undertaken.[83]

Despite the Government's previous encouraging noises, the backlash continued with over 100,000 people demonstrating within the New Territories. The army reported that machine-guns and an anti-aircraft gun had been sited within the Chinese section of the village of Sha Tau Kok. As the demonstrators filed over the border, the police fired tear gas and baton shells, and themselves came under machine-gun and rifle fire. The police retaliated with Greener guns. As police casualties mounted, the army was called in to relieve the police post and impose a curfew.[84] It appeared that cold war tensions between the global powers were being played out in the village of Sha Tau Kok. The British Government reacted by sending a delegation to Hong Kong to consider the overall situation, including a review of the security forces. The state of the police, the Government was informed, was 'excellent': the force had shown 'both restraint and vigour whenever necessary'. The unrest did, however, give rise to the problem of the employment of Chinese officers while retaining public confidence.[85]

By that stage, restraint was out of the question, and violence was spreading to many urban areas, as reflected in the increase in arrests. The police began to apply new tactics, making use of cordons and sweep-and-search operations. On 16 July, for example, police officers with soldiers from the Queen's Regiment and the 2nd Battalion of the 7th Duke of Edinburgh's Own Gurkha Rifles made almost 600 arrests in the Ma Tau Kok area of Kowloon using this technique. Following the arrests, searches for weapons and equipment were carried out, result-ing in finds of 'dummy machine guns and rifles, home-made spears, pitchforks and bottles of acid'. Subsequent raids the following day uncovered 'a vast number of weapons, some of which were described by Chief Superintendent E. P. Grace as "very nasty" ', including 'sharp-ened steel points embedded in wooden sticks'.[86] The HKP was aware that the disturbances were entering a different phase, as new methods of violence were used.

Bombing became the new method of virtually isolating the 300,000–strong population of Causeway Bay, North Point and Shaukiwan, the easternmost part of Hong Kong Island. Types of bomb planted covered a wide range and accounted for 1,420 incidents up until the end of December, by which point support for the communist cause had ebbed away, partly due to the general outrage at the use of bombs designed to harm children.[87]

A 'royal' aftermath

Overall the morale of the police remained unaffected by the events of 1967. Between May and December not one member of the regular or the auxiliary police was absent from duty without permission. Recruiting was easy and serving with the police began to take on a glamorous touch, as hundreds flocked to join the HKP's auxiliary force: a 2-day recruiting drive, for example, brought in 143 applicants.[88] Police morale no doubt was maintained through having sufficient officers within both the regular and emergency units to contain the situation. In Northern Ireland for example, during the 1969 'Battle of the Bogside', a physically and morally exhausted RUC failed to prevent the problem spreading to Belfast. Hong Kong's police force had, by contrast, learned lessons from the rioting of the 1950s, ensuring that sufficient training and numbers of officers were key to their success.

The HKP was awarded the title of 'Royal' and had acquired 'heroic' status, as reflected by the steady increase in recruits during the aftermath and generous public funding for police welfare schemes.[89] The public image of the *Royal* HKP greatly improved after the disturbances. In short, a riot aimed at destabilising British colonial rule had accomplished what the police could never have done in their own right, namely to win public support. In 1968, the Police Public Information Bureau was established, taking over from the Government Information Services,[90] and this would enhance police–public relations still further and, by extension, the practice of policing by consent. In this manner, the RHKP was seen as transforming its colonial image into a civil style of policing.

Yet the disturbances had prompted the Commissioner of Police to conduct a 'Secret Review' of the force to assess potential areas for reform. Eates noted that the ongoing emergency had disrupted the status quo in Hong Kong. The aim of the police was 'to restore normal life and prosperity in Hong Kong', and that relied on public support. Although the police were 'frustrated' by ongoing communist activities, particularly the bombing campaign, strikes, disruption of food and water supplies, border incursions, assassinations, and propaganda emanating from the media and locally erected posters. Eates nonetheless considered that the strength of the RHKP should be maintained, although this had not posed a threat to date. Morale too had not been a problem, with only a few resignations following serious incidents like that at Sha Tau Kok. Morale should be kept 'running high' on a 'sentimental' basis by offering awards and tributes, and 'financially' through a Police Education Fund, and additional pay and allowances. In essence, any real problem within the police would arise 'only if there is active intervention from China – it will be necessary to convince them that they will be taken good care of even if the British leave Hong Kong. This presumably would mean evacuation.'[91]

This fascinating review document revealed that there was real concern over the prospect of a premature British withdrawal from Hong Kong while the 'Cultural Revolution was in full swing'.[92] In an earlier confidential report, Eates had noted that though the combined strength of 'hardcore' communists stood at no more than 15,000, 'the speed with which they can reassert control depends on the unpredictable progress in China'. He added:

Although most Hong Kong people would prefer to live under [the] British Colonial Government than under C.P.G. [China's Communist Party] this is overborne by fear of supporting the losing side. Therefore to retain public confidence [the] Government must appear to be 'winning'. This the Special Branch perceived as key for physically C.P.G. is capable of snuffing Hong Kong out; this may be tempting because she is unable to take quick effective action elsewhere (Indonesia, Middle East, Vietnam, Mongolia, Bulgaria).[93]

There were difficulties for the RHKP to deal with during the aftermath of the year of conflict. A number of gazetted and inspectorate officers retired early from the force, never wishing to see another year like 1967. Corruption worsened and became more 'blatant'among both European and locally recruited gazetted officers: 'One way or another, the lustre of the Force began to dull.'[94] In some ways corruption may have been reflected by the soaring crime rates in the late 1960s and the 1970s; though rapid economic development no doubt contributed, as well as 'the break-up of the long-standing police–triad alliance', which saw a rise in cases of theft, assault and extortion: 'Residents routinely saw police openly approaching restaurants, bars and brothels to collect "tea money" '.[95]

There is inadequate space here to delve more fully into the world of HKP corruption. Corruption had always been endemic in Hong Kong and had involved the police from early on. 'Corruption money did what government funds were not available to do; it paid informers, kept an army of silent watchers on the alert and maintained eyes and ears in the underworld which monitored crime.'[96] It was not until April 1973 that Commissioner Charles Sutcliffe took steps to investigate Chief Superintendent Peter Godber on allegations of corruption. James Morrin, head of the Anti-Corruption Branch, was asked to prepare a case against Godber, having brought about the latter's dramatic flight back to Britain. During lengthy extradition proceedings, the Governor Sir Murray MacLehose took the matter into his own hands and established a new anti-corruption body, the Independent Commission Against Corruption (ICAC).

Heading a team that comprised many officers from the old Anti-Corruption Branch was John Prendergast, an experienced colonial policeman. The subsequent investigations led to the successful conviction of Superintendent Ernest Hunt, whose revelations allowed for extensive purges to take place within the police. 'As the ICAC impetus continued and extended to retired officers living overseas, the sense of disquiet in the Force grew . . . By 1977, police patience was wearing very thin indeed.'[97] As a direct result of the ongoing enquiry, many policemen in protest signed a nine-point declaration and called a meeting in October 1977 attended by 4,000 officers. They proceeded to march on police headquarters to present a petition signed by 11,000 of

[184]

the 17,500 members of the RHKP, including many senior officers and a large number of expatriates. To avoid an out and out confrontation between the police and the administration, MacLehose announced a partial amnesty for most corruption offences committed in the past and an investigation of police organisation headed up by James Crane, an Inspector of Constabulary. The RHKP's image as one of colonial policing's finest was tainted, despite the force's reputation for excellence within both regular policing and police intelligence systems.

In the case of both the Malayan Police and the RHKP, colonial practices were strengthened during the post-war years. Despite some successful attempts to improve community relations, and, by extension, a more *civil* side to policing – the 'hearts and minds' campaign in Malaya and winning public support in Hong Kong – complete transformation occurred in neither force. Both territories were faced with internal and external security issues brought about by the cold war, creating a demand for colonial-style policing and the development of semi-military auxiliary units, for example the jungle squads and mobile riot units. Moreover, the external threat from communism forced a reassessment of the intelligence-gathering capabilities of both colonies and brought the question of political policing to the fore.

Notes

1 Taken from an interview with Dick Craig (Palestine Police, Malay Police, Senior Assist. Comm., dec., 1946–64), January 2000.
2 Craig (interview), January 2000.
3 For an account of the 'shooting war' in Malaya see: Robert Jackson, *The Malayan Emergency: The Commonwealth Wars, 1948–66* (London: Routledge, 1991); Richard Stubbs, *Hearts and Minds in Guerrilla Warfare: The Malayan Emergency, 1948–60* (Oxford: OUP, 1989); Sir Robert Thompson, *Defeating Communist insurgency: experiences from Malaya and Vietnam* (London: Macmillan, 1966); Richard Clutterbuck, *Riot and Revolution in Singapore and Malaysia, 1943–63* (London: Graham Brash, 1984); A. J. Stockwell, 'Policing During the Malayan Emergency, 1948–60: Communism, Communalism and Decolonization', in Anderson & Killingray (eds), *Policing and Decolonisation*. For counter-insurgency, intelligence and the 'hearts and minds' policy see: Karl Hack, 'British Intelligence and Counter-Insurgency in the Era of Decolonisation: The Example of Malaya', *Intelligence and National Security*, 14:2 (summer, 1999), pp. 124–55; Karl Hack, ' "Iron Claws on Malaya": The Historiography of the Malayan Emergency', *Journal of Southeast Asian Studies*, 30:1 (1999); Susan L. Carruthers, *Winning Hearts and Minds: British Governments, the Media and Colonial Counter-Insurgency, 1944–1960* (Leicester: Leicester University Press, 1995). For a detailed political and social study see Tim Harper, *The End of Empire and the Making of Malaya* (Cambridge: CUP, 1999).
4 Arthur Young, *The Federation of Malaya and its Police, 1786–1952* (Kuala Lumpur: Charles Grenier & Sons, 1952), pp. 33–36.
5 Harper, *Making of Malaya*, p. 152. J. W. G. Moran noted that 518 members of the armed forces were killed. Up until the end of 1956, Communist casualties totalled 11,718 of whom 8,678 were killed by police jungle forces: J. W. G. Moran, *Spearhead in Malaya* (London: Peter Davies, 1958), p. 13.

6   Young, *Federation of Malaya*, p. 40.
7   Stubbs, *Hearts and Minds*, p. 66.
8   Moran, *Spearhead in Malaya*, p. 11.
9   Colonel Arthur Young, 'Appreciation of the Basic Situation', March 1952, RHL MSS
    Brit. Emp. s. 4863/1, notes, 1953, 2/1.
10 Mansfield, Memoir, no p. no., Family Papers.
11 Jackson, *Malayan Emergency*, p. 19.
12 Smith, 'General Templer', p. 68.
13 Stubbs, *Hearts and Minds*, p. 73.
14 Jones, *Postwar Counterinsurgency*, p. 82.
15 Moran noted that the communist insurgents were called 'bandits' or 'terrorists' by
    the police which may have denoted a lack of structure within their organisation.
    They were, however, well-trained and disciplined military force operating within
    their own regiments, each comprising four hundred men, and commanded by officers
    who took direct orders from 'Political Commissars'. Generally speaking they were
    also well equipped with up-to-date weaponry: Moran, *Spearhead in Malaya*, p. 10.
16 Craig (interview), Jan. 2000.
17 Mansfield, Memoir, no p. no., Family Papers.
18 Leon Comber (Malayan Police, rtd, 1945–54) in correspondence with the author,
    April 2001.
19 Godsave (interview), July 2001. Godsave served in 20 Jungle Company.
20 Young, *Federation of Malaya*, p. 39.
21 As many as 8,000 aborigines died as a direct result of the resettlement programme.
    Simon S. Smith, 'General Templer and Counter-Insurgency in Malaya: Heart and
    Minds, Intelligence, and Propaganda', *Intelligence and National Security*, 16:3
    (Autumn, 2001), p. 69.
22 Craig (interview), Jan. 2000.
23 Godsave (interview), July 2001.
24 Smith, 'General Templer', p. 69.
25 Godsave (interview), July 2001.
26 See for example: Moran, *The Camp Across the River* (London: Peter Davies 1963),
    pp. 78–79.
27 Service in a jungle squad for a period of 3 months, one month's administration work
    and investigating and solving 3 crimes during the emergency was sometimes con-
    sidered sufficient for promotion from NCO to gazetted officer rank: William P.
    Mathieson, *A Chequered Career* (London: Janus, 1994), p. 68.
28 Slim, 'Operations', 19 April, and Lt.-Col. Brownjohn, note 26 June 1950, NA CAB
    134/497 to E.Shinwell, MoD, 4 May 1951, NA CO 537/7263.
29 Home Secretary Fyfe, letter, 16 Jan. 1952, RHL MSS Brit. Emp. 486 4/4.
30 Allan Brodie with Roderick Grant, *Adventure in My Veins* (Farnham: Triple Cat
    Publishing, 1989), p. 147.
31 Brodie, *Adventure in My Veins*, p. 148.
32 Young, 'Notes on Malaya Police', 1952, RHL MSS Brit. Emp. 486 4/4.
33 Smith, 'General Templer', p. 65.
34 Gerald Murphy, *Copper Mandarin: A Memoir* (London: Regency Press, 1984), p. 69.
35 Young, *Federation of Malaya*, p. 35.
36 Smith has sought to overturn the 'stalemate thesis' regarding the controversy sur-
    rounding Templer's period in Malaya. He has reached the conclusion that Templer's
    role was 'central in turning the tide of the Emergency in Britain's favour . . . taking
    together improvements in intelligence and propaganda, his prioritizing of the civil-
    ian aspects of counter-insurgency, and the more vigorous prosecution of the war
    against the communists': Smith, 'General Templer', pp. 60–78.
37 Gurney to Creech-Jones, 25 Oct. 1948, 'Commissioner-General's Conference',
    Minutes, Bukit Serene, 12 Sept. 1948', NA CO 717/177/52849/41/48.
38 Harper, *Making of Malaya*, pp. 156–157.
39 John Cloake, *Templer: Tiger of Malaya* (London: Harrap, 1985), pp. 221–225.
40 Craig (interview), Jan. 2000; see also *The Times*, 28 Aug. 1952.

41   R. J. W. Craig, A Short Account of the Malayan Emergency (unpublished), pp. 16–20, Craig, Family Papers.
42   'Report to the Director of Operations, 20 Nov. 1951', NA CO 1022/22.
43   Jackson, Malayan Emergency, p. 20.
44   Brodie, Adventure in My Veins, p. 120.
45   Godsave (interview), July 2001.
46   Eates, 'Notes by Commissioner of Police', Visit of Mr R. Heath Mason, Under Sec. State, Commonwealth Office, 19 June 1968, Eates, Family Papers.
47   Eates (interview), May 2005.
48   Mark S. Gaylord & Harold Traver, 'Colonial Policing and the demise of British Rule in Hong Kong', International Journal of the Sociology of Law, 23 (1995), p. 29.
49   Eates (interview), July 2003.
50   Jeffries, Colonial Police, p. 84. In 1935, Dowbiggin had commented that the HKP were better equipped for crowd and riot control than many of their colonial counterparts; this included transport and weaponry available: Dowbiggin, 'Notes on Police Forces Visited in 1935', RHL MSS. Ind. Oc. s. 288/f. 24.
51   Jeffries, Colonial Police, p. 171.
52   Gaylord & Traver, 'Colonial Policing', p. 29.
53   Eates (interview), July 2003.
54   They included the constabularies of Devon, Bradford, Cornwall, Glasgow, Luton, the Metropolitan Police and the RUC: Confidential enclosure, 'Hong Kong: Reversion of Certain Metropolitan and County Force Policemen to Parent Forces in the UK 1949–50', NA CO 850/261/9.
55   Gaylord & Traver, 'Colonial Policing', pp. 24–26.
56   Taken from an interview with Michael Ko chun (RHKP, Sup. rtd., 1950–75), Aug. 2003. Ko chun was born in Wei Hei Wei, arriving in Hong Kong in 1950 as a refugee.
57   Hong Kong Gov. to Colonial Office, Telegram, 1 Sept. 1950, 'Recruitment Pakistanis for Police Force', NA CO 537/6044.
58   Acting UK High Com. Pakistan to Commonwealth Relations Office, 14 Sept. 1950, NA CO 537/6044.
59   Taken from an interview with Ivan Scott (RHKP, Sup. rtd, 1955–87), May, 2001.
60   Scott (interview), May 2001.
61   Khursid Ahmed and Mohamed Mawaz Malik, Pakistani members of the HKP, were killed at Sha Tau Kok: John Cooper, Colony in Conflict, The Hong Kong Disturbances May 1967–January 1968 (Hong Kong: Swindon Book Co., 1970), pp. 124–125.
62   Ko chun (interview), Aug. 2003.
63   Hong Kong & Pacific Monthly Reports by Special Branch Police, 1950, NA CO 537/6075.
64   C. L. Scobell (RHKP, Sen. Assist. Com. rtd, 1951–78) in correspondence with the author, Feb. 2000.
65   Scobell (interview), Feb. 2000.
66   'Kowloon Disturbances 1966', Report of a Commission of Inquiry (Hong Kong: Government Printer, 1967), p. 9.
67   'Kowloon Disturbances', pp. 30–53.
68   Scobell (interview), Feb. 2000; Eates (interview), July 2003.
69   'Kowloon Disturbances', pp. 66–67.
70   Commissioner of Police, Annual Departmental Report, 1965 (Hong Kong, 1966), p. 1.
71   Commissioner of Police, Annual Departmental Report, 1965 (Hong Kong, 1966), p. 1.
72   Eates (interview), July 2003.
73   'Hong Kong Disturbances 1967', Confidential Report, Colonial Secretariat (Hong Kong, 1968), pp. 1–3.
74   Cooper, Colony in Conflict, p. 59.
75   'Hong Kong Disturbances', p. 6.
76   Cooper, Colony in Conflict, pp. 20–24.
77   'Hong Kong Disturbances', p. 14.
78   Hong Kong Police Annual Report, 1 April 1967–31 March 1968, pp. 4, 8, 19.
79   Scott (interview), May 2001.

80 Quoted in Cooper, *Colony in Conflict*, pp. 63–64.
81 Trench quoted in Cooper, *Colony in Conflict*, p. 66.
82 During the disturbances, the Commissioner of Police, Tyrer, was on leave. Eates, as Deputy Commissioner became Acting Commissioner and was then promoted to Commissioner on 21 July 1967: Eates (interview), July 2003.
83 Acting Commissioner, Notes on Contingency Planning, Police Circulation, 16 May 1967, Eates, Family Papers.
84 'Hong Kong Disturbances', p. 33.
85 Eates, 'Notes for Meeting with Sir Arthur Galsworthy etc', 22 May 1967, Eates, Family Papers.
86 Eates (interview), July 2003.
87 Bombs caused the deaths of 16 people, including 2 police officers; there were 340 injuries, 74 to police officers: 'Hong Kong Disturbances', p. 45. There were 'explosive objects [planted] on the roads', where they could harm children. 'Another distressing feature was that school children were being urged by the left-wing press to help out as "planters" and on 13 October 9 bombs were set down by them in Mong Kok . . .': Cooper, *Colony in Conflict*, pp. 233–234).
88 Cooper, *Colony in Conflict*, p. 94.
89 Eates (interview), July 2003.
90 Scobell (interview), Feb. 2000.
91 'Secret Review' by Acting Commissioner of Police to Tyrer & Defence Secretary, Hong Kong Government, 1 Aug. 1967, Ref. CP/S/27/1, Eates, Family Papers.
92 Eates (interview), May 2005.
93 Eates, 'Appreciation by Acting Commissioner of Police', Secret, 10 June, 1967, Eates, Family Papers.
94 Scobell (interview), Feb. 2000.
95 Gaylord & Traver, 'Colonial Police', p. 231.
96 Kevin Sinclair & Nelson Ng Kwok-cheung, *Asia's Finest Marches On* (Hong Kong: Kevin Sinclair Associates, 1997), p. 51.
97 Sinclair, *Asia's Finest*, p. 53.

CHAPTER EIGHT

'Political policing?' Pawns in the imperial endgame

Winston Churchill wrote in 1954 that an 'efficient police force and Intelligence service are the best way of smelling out and suppressing subversive movements at an early stage, and may save heavy expenditure on military reinforcements'.[1] Despite IGCP Johnson's protestations in 1948 that intelligence systems empire-wide should be improved, it took colonial unrest and emergencies to force a gradual reassessment and reorganisation of the policing bodies concerned. The development of independent special branch units came comparatively late, echoing the familiar theme of a lack of police reform within the colonies.

After 1948, policing procedures acquired a different momentum indicating that the very nature of the colonial state had changed. The Special Branch emerged as an alternative and additional source of information-gathering and processing, dedicated to the pursuit of political and security intelligence, once the domain of the CID. Intelligence needed to be capable of assisting a colony in its 'vital "cold war" battleground'.[2] The concept of 'political policing' took on a more important role as colonial governments attempted to maintain control throughout the end stages of decolonisation. Political policing encouraged a closer surveillance of public organisations and prominent political figures ostensibly to ensure that appropriate individuals gained centre stage at independence. In this way, the colonial police became pawns in the imperial endgame.

It has been argued that there existed in colonial systems few distinctions between political and criminal misdemeanours, and the means by which they were controlled differed little: crime and political subversion appeared as much the same to a colonial government. A serious transgression of the law was perceived as an implicit defiance of state authority and a possible prelude to rebellion; political resistance was either a 'crime' or else was leading to one.[3] So however limited the police resource, the problem was faced in a similar manner.

[189]

Yet political policing acquired a greater importance only with the rise of nationalism within colonies seeking to break free of colonial rule.

Prior to post-war reforms, the Palestine Police had pioneered newer approaches in police intelligence work when dealing with either Arab or Jewish nationalism. The Palestine CID, which was used for the gathering of intelligence, had been set up under the leadership of Eugene Quigley following the creation of the Palestine Gendarmerie in 1920. In parallel with the setting up of a records' system and a fingerprinting branch for the collection of criminal intelligence, Quigley acquired a reputation for his development of a system for gathering political intelligence that resembled that of the Metropolitan Police Special Branch. The later use of 'pseudo-gangs' possibly stemmed from this period during which members of the Palestine CID would penetrate the villages and desert areas of Transjordan dressed as 'locals'. Their brief was to collect intelligence on drug-smuggling, as well as on local politics and security issues.[4]

Despite promising beginnings, the CID was described in Dowbiggin's 1930 report on the Palestine Police as the 'weakest spot in the Force' because it was seen as monitoring *political* rather than religious-inspired subversion and failed to distinguish adequately between the two.[5] Indeed the Shaw Commission of Enquiry had pointed to intelligence shortcomings in failing to reveal a worsening security situation. When Harold Rice took over as head of the CID in 1930, the number of CID officers in each district were increased to enable a channel of command from headquarters down to district level. Divisional headquarters became responsible for new departments, which included a specific 'political section'. District CID branches mirrored this, adding in newer sections that included immigration and emigration work. By late 1930, the number of CID officers at police headquarters had risen from 30 to 52. CID offices in the districts were also strengthened, each having a staff of fifty men which included SLOs.

More importantly, Rice carved out a new role for the CID. Alongside the investigation of crime, the CID became responsible for intelligence on *all* subversive organisations, including communists. In terms of external security, the CID was to liaise with the police forces of the Middle East, Egypt, Cyprus and India, and with Scotland Yard.[6] The activities of the CID covered the prevention and detection of crime, as well as surveillance of political movements, repression of seditious activity and the censorship of the foreign press. In addition, police intelligence was responsible for the prevention of arms' and drugs' smuggling, the entry of illegal immigrants, consideration of applications for naturalisation, arranging deportations and extraditions, and maintaining links with the appropriate authorities outside Palestine. Despite an increased role, the reliability of the intelligence gathered by the CID remained a source of concern. Dowbiggin's suggestions that British rather than Arab officers hold senior posts at district level was perceived to be the solution. He also proposed that the relationship between district commissioners and district officers be clearly set out within Police Orders. In 1932, the Chief Secretary stipulated the need for close co-operation between the administration and the police to improve public security. The police were to inform their district commissioner of 'anything which affects the good order of his District' and district officers were required to do the same.[7] Following the 1936 Arab revolt, the CID expanded its district investigation branches still further to encompass a Jewish Affairs section to gather intelligence on Hagannah and its breakaway groups such as the IZL.

A decade later, William Moffat, an RUC Inspector, accompanied Sir Charles Tegart on his 1946 mission to Palestine to recommend CID reforms. (Moffat had, in fact, been in charge of the Special Crime Squad in Northern Ireland for some years.[8]) In his report, Moffat argued that 'to combat terrorism, reliance must be placed chiefly on the CID'. To that end it was vital that the 'Political Branch' of the CID outweighed the 'Non-Political Branch' in terms of its size, calibre of officers recruited and allowances, which were to be on 'the generous side'.[9] Moffat's most important recommendation was that the CID should be an elite branch of the police. This would be reflected in the high quality of officers recruited and their length of stay within the force. In effect, Moffat was recommending that the Palestine CID, for the remainder of their short existence, encompass both CID and Special Branch duties.[10] Until the end of the mandate in 1948, the CID remained responsible for both sectors, handling their constant overlapping. The experiences of Palestine were not, however, passed on to other colonial police forces in the interim.

Early CID outfits

Following a posting to the Uganda Police in the late 1930s, Christopher Harwich wrote of how 'police work at Entebbe could not be described as either exciting or arduous. Apart from the almost routine murders, usually reported by the aggressor, the only other crime of consequence was petty larceny.'[11] Up until the Second World War, many colonies seemed to have had little need for a separate special branch unit. While the setting up of a discrete CID often coincided with the creation of a colonial constabulary, these units did not evolve into separate special branches until a much later stage. Overall the regular police and the CID provided sufficient resources to deal with crime and internal security.

CID units operating prior to 1939 were primarily concerned with serious crime and internal security matters that ranged from the investigation of smuggling to the confiscation of seditious literature. They were smallish outfits, often headed up by a single gazetted officer. In Uganda, for example, the CID was set up in 1906 but was not officially recognised as a separate unit until 1923. Thereafter, its activities focused primarily on the work of the Criminal Records Office and the Fingerprint Bureau at police headquarters under the command of a gazetted officer.[12] The CID of the Nigeria Police Force was set up as late as 1936. It had been loosely based on a unit known as the Eastern and Western Preventative Service, established in 1931 with the sole task of preventing smuggling.[13] (The regular police had been formed on 27 February 1930 following the unification of the northern and southern forces. Quite differently from other colonial territories, the Nigeria Police Force was headed by an Inspector-General, with two Assistant Inspector-Generals for the Northern and Southern Regions respectively. In addition, a Commissioner was appointed for each of the seventeen Provinces. By the Second World War the Nigeria Police Force numbered some 5,000 officers.[14]) When Alan Saunders was transferred from Palestine as Commissioner of the Nigeria Police, he increased the size of the CID through a network of district branches. Saunders also modernised the criminal records' system by adapting the Palestine model, which remained the basic system in use up until independence.[15] John Coles, who served as Acting Deputy-Commissioner on the Gold Coast, recalled that 'no internal security problems existed prior to 1948 [for] the disparate nature of the territorial and tribal composition of the country and particularly the constitutional differences made any countrywide rising improbable. [Besides] the chiefs of the Gold Coast Colony proper had, after all, invited British rule in 1844.'[16]

Throughout the Empire, provincial and district commissioners shouldered much of the responsibility for supplying central government with the intelligence needed. In British Colonial Africa, they were assisted by members of the NAP or tribal police. Former members of the colonial police have commented that the tribal police were living and working among their own people, and their reports were lacking in accuracy on occasions, particularly where family members were involved in criminal activity. Some officers preferred to deal directly with the loyal chiefs and headmen who could be relied on to provide accurate intelligence.[17]

Second World War influences

Intelligence-gathering within the colonies seems to have muddled along until the onset of the Second World War, when a real opportunity for change and modernisation occurred. The need for police intelligence increased and the focus shifted towards internment and increased security threats. In many colonies war brought rising crime and public discontent. In the Gold Coast, for example, a chronic shortage of consumer goods led to widening corruption and the proliferation of crime, often unchecked by the police.[18]

In some instances, new units were established to cope specifically with the registration and internment of aliens. From the available documentary evidence, it would appear that some of these 'new' police intelligence units were drawn from existing CIDs, while others were created as new entities. In many colonies, civil intelligence and security units were established to carry out wartime duties alongside the regular police in dealing, for example, with the internment of aliens and the supervision of prisons. Some colonial police officers even took to referring to these units as 'Special Branch' rather than CID: Michael Macoun described his posting to the Special Branch in Tanganyika in 1939, which had been redesignated under war conditions as the Department of Intelligence and Security;[19] similarly, in Nyasaland a Political Intelligence Bureau was set up to deal with enemy aliens and at the same time a 'small special force' was raised to guard key installations.[20] In Kenya, a section known as the Special Branch was created in 1940 and located within the CID. For the duration of the war, this small section became responsible for the collection of intelligence on the enemy, information regarding German and Italian citizens and various religious groups.[21] The police were expanded to help guard the Northern Frontier territories against the Italian armed forces. Their role was essentially to gather intelligence, act as guides and interpreters, and on occasion to serve as fighting units.[22]

The Second World War certainly influenced the creation of new police and civil intelligence systems in many African, Southeast Asian and Middle Eastern colonies. However, within other corners of the Empire, wartime intelligence-gathering was being seriously hampered by ineffective CID work and a lack of Special Branches. During a brief tour of the Caribbean police forces in 1942, Major R. H. Onreat reported that the 'control and direction of criminal investigation' within the Trinidad Police was barely in evidence. He recommended the prompt creation by the CID of an 'organised investigation unit' for every Caribbean police division to assist the wartime effort. Moreover, there was no Special Branch to carry out 'security duties' that would 'ascertain and maintain the changing history and development of political, social, religious, economic, racial and so on movements in the island and keep track of them throughout the years'. He noted that in terms of 'real' Special Branch work, 'the tail is wagging the dog': 'There is scope here for intelligence work for the brains are undoubtedly available', he wrote. The situation had become all the more urgent because of the need for security in the Caribbean area:

> Records, experience and money are required; the last named money if properly used is the most powerful. In this matter the records of the local police appear to me to be strangely niggardly. Perhaps the loan of a police officer with 'expert' knowledge of the Chinese or East Indians could be arranged.[23]

Borrowing officers from other colonial constabularies was nigh on impossible during the Second World War. Many CID units were faced with manpower shortages as officers were either posted to other units or seconded elsewhere for the duration of the war. In Uganda, for example, at the outbreak of war, local CID units were shut down due to lack of staff. So by 1941, an 'insufficiency of the present staff' made any prospect of dispersing CIDs[24] into the provinces unfeasible. With some of them being posted away from police headquarters at Kampala, CID officers were being used to undertake 'miscellaneous duties', having, for instance, to 'take their hand in traffic duties and as patrol officers', despite a reported rise in 'serious and intricate crime'.[25] This was also true of the Jamaica Police where, by 1945, a total of seventy-five CID officers had actually declined since 1929. Whilst inspecting this police force, Calver noted that however 'keen and dependable' these officers might have been they were simply not 'backed by a machine which is dependable and of sufficient capacity'. There was a real need to bring fingerprinting and criminal records up to date, to build up records and crime statistics, and to select and train CID officers, including probationers.[26]

This was also true of the substantially larger Nigeria Police. CID officers felt that their 'true task of detecting, preventing and suppressing subversive conspiracies and activity' floundered owing to a lack of time to collate and assess intelligence as a result of carrying out other police duties which took precedence.[27] Ian Proud, who served in the Nigeria Police, noted that police duties were 'out of place'. He described some policemen as 'revenue collectors' for 'motor vehicle licensing, testing learner drivers, inspecting vehicles for road-worthiness, weights and measures inspections etc. In fact revenue collection seemed to be of greater importance than measures for the prevention and detection of crime.'[28]

A noticeable increase in crime trends continued in the aftermath of the Second World War, particularly in colonies that had suffered social upheaval through enemy occupation or overall food shortages. In some African colonies, the continuing food shortages provoked general unrest and, as a result, increased crime, while in others the blame was placed on growing populations in urban areas in both local and European quarters. In Eastern Nigeria, the bloody 'Leopard Society' from 1945 to 1948 murdered 196 people. While these murders were perceived as neither political nor a threat to the legitimacy of British rule, they nonetheless forced the Commissioner to create a specific crime unit consisting of 4 Assistant Superintendents, 2 Inspectors and 95 rank and file. At the same time, John Hodge, who became Assistant Commissioner of the Nigeria Police, noted that by early 1946 the CID's headquarters in Lagos had acquired larger premises to accommodate growing fingerprinting and photograph sections. By the end of that year, CID records contained 127,000 fingerprint sets, with an average yearly addition of 16,000. A training team drawn from the CID was established to run courses in conjunction with trainers who were specialists in 'major' and 'complicated' crimes. To boost training, CID officers were sent to Britain to the Detective Training School at Wakefield from the late 1940s.[29] Austin MacDonald, who also served in the Nigeria Police, stated that regional CID units were provided with up-to-date equipment in 1945, with investigation squads formed to tackle serious crime outside the capital.[30]

Making use of the British security services

While Johnson was collating his reports on the Colonial Police Service and recommending reform, notably of police intelligence, Creech-Jones noted that here was 'someone who can speak with authority of the modern developments in police and Special Branch work'. Creech-Jones's view was that there were two main avenues through which a colonial government could collect intelligence, 'the Defence Security Officer and the Special Branch'. Creech-Jones explained:

> I do not wish to suggest that Colonial Governments should begin to regard the Special Branch of the police as their most important source of potential intelligence . . . They should co-ordinate two streams, the 'police' and the 'political', which should no doubt serve as a valuable cross check the one on the other.[31]

In the first instance, most colonial police forces needed to develop independent special branch units. Despite War Office recommendations to the Colonial Office in 1948 that intelligence systems should be in place to provide adequate warning of public disturbances, few steps had been taken to effect change unless prompted by an ongoing security situation. When the emergency was declared in Malaya, police intelligence was 'semi-independent' and 'grossly understaffed'. It had been set up in something of a hurry in 1945 to cater for both Singapore and Malaya; its role 'was poorly defined and its responsibilities nebulous'. Despite early warning of a 'Communist rebellion', the intelligence unit was disbanded in June 1948 and replaced by a new CID. Given a dual role to both collect intelligence pertaining to the emergency and to investigate crime, the CID was initially 'little more than a skeleton organisation, incapable of influencing intelligence-collection procedures at ground level'. Intelligence officers operating in the field were thus given free rein, and that led to 'the employment of excessive strong-arm measures to extract information, [including] much use of the highly-vaunted truth drug'.[32] A worsening security situation and a growing need to interrogate 'surrendered enemy personnel' forced the Government to reform the CID. By 1950, this police intelligence function was able to shed its CID mantle and to change its name to 'Special Branch'. The role of the new organisation was clearly defined as being both 'tactical and strategic', i.e. obtaining and processing information leading to operational planning.

In Hong Kong, where the police force was perceived to be on the A list, the tiny Special Branch had depended heavily on MI5 for support in weeding out Japanese collaborators, pro-KMT and pro-communist members who vied for the hearts and minds of the Hong Kong Chinese. Communist influences were spreading through trade unions, the media and cultural associations.[33]

In African colonies, the police were providing barely any intelligence of this nature. Andrew Cohen, Assistant Under-Secretary of State with responsibility for Africa, requested regular political intelligence reports to view 'the progress of political development . . . because of the very much greater interest in the Colonies now existing both in this country and internationally'. In the spring of 1948, Cohen noted that the 'African Affairs Fortnightly Review', which came from Uganda, was the 'only one we receive'.[34] Cohen asked colonial governors to differentiate *political* from *security* reports. The police provided political intelligence summaries that would include the 'general political situation . . . that is nationalist movements, tribal relations, activities of local societies, race relations, the attitude of the press and public to government policy and influential personalities'. The section dealing with external matters considered communist activities and relations with neighbouring territories.[35] The Colonial Office would then prepare a synthesis of the material, giving 'a really good birdseye view of political trends in the colonies'. The real change stemming from Cohen's proposal was that the Colonial Office was now in direct receipt of intelligence summaries rather than having to rely on other intelligence channels.[36] Relevant information concerning communist activities within the colonies would be passed on to the Foreign Office, which viewed the earlier Gold Coast disturbances as a clear signal that an 'overhaul of the security and intelligence arrangements' was needed in the colonies.[37]

This change in circumstances underlined the importance of the police in terms of their intelligence-gathering duties. Indeed, the following year, Henry Gurney, High Commissioner in Malaya, pointed to this while noting that 'good police work, as is well known, demands an intimate knowledge of individuals and of everything that goes on'.[38] Gurney, along with many colonial governors, believed in the police taking a more active frontline role, including intelligence-gathering, considering that the 'opposition' would have more to fear from the police than from the army. He explained:

> The Police are the only force possessing the information and intelligence necessary for the conduct of an underground war. An effectively trained Police Force takes a longer time than the formation, say, of a battalion of infantry and is not something that can be left to a late state. [Besides] without information the large sums spent on the police and troops will be useless.[39]

With these points in mind Gurney organised for some 200 Chinese detectives to be brought in on the recommendation of an 'expert' from Scotland Yard advising on all aspects of police intelligence work.[40]

But clearly reinforcement was needed in *all* territories to ensure that adequate police intelligence was provided. An immediate solution was the despatch of Alexander Kellar, head of MI5's E Branch, to West Africa to offer assistance.[41] On his return, Kellar recommended the permanent posting of an MI5 officer 'to provide ginger' to the local police intelligence services. The Colonial Office felt that this measure would offer some solution.[42] Many have been described as colourful and peripatetic characters, collecting intelligence within their vast territories in whatever manner they saw fit; they included 'Beetle' Williams, the SLO for West Africa during the 1950s, who came to be known for attending cocktail parties in a bid to 'gather' intelligence.[43] In Kenya, several years later, MI5 was to play an important role in the reorganisation of police intelligence with the onset of the Mau Mau emergency. Percy Sillitoe, head of MI5 and a former member of the British South Africa Police, was despatched to Kenya specifically to review the Kenya Intelligence Committee (KIC) structure and consider the reorganisation of Kenya's

Special Branch. This would allow Special Branch to have a link through the SLO, via the KIC, to the Governor. By 1955, Special Branch had developed a sophisticated network comprised of five main sections: 'X Branch', which had units working in surveillance and agent-running; 'Political Affairs', which monitored individual political parties; 'Counter Espionage'; the 'Mau Mau Bureau'; and the 'Divisional Headquarters Special Branch', which handled domestic security, personnel and funding.[44]

Despite MI5's often disparaging view regarding the use of police officers for intelligence work ('keep the boots to that side'), the KIC was rapidly reorganised to include Special Branch officers and members of MI5 and MI6.[45] MI5 officers, as a result, were posted throughout the colonies to assist in the development of special branches and their liaison with MI5 in London. In some colonies MI6 liaison officers also provided a link between the colonial government and London. In Hong Kong, both MI5 and MI6 provided 'political advisors' who worked closely with the Special Branch and other foreign intelligence agencies. A security meeting was held weekly to discuss ongoing relations between China and Britain, the activities of communists in Hong Kong in different political groups, the trade unions and schools.[46]

The 1948 watershed

From 1948, monthly intelligence reports were sent from every colony which, until the expansion of special branches, were often prepared by CID or defence security officers. Typically, intelligence was collated from reports sent in by a district or a high-level committee comprising senior members of the police, army and administration. Reports were sent from even the smallest colonies, such as the Falklands, although it was soon recorded that there was 'no political situation at all' in that area.[47] Cohen's request for monthly reports to be produced across the board highlighted the Colonial Office's increasing interest in political developments throughout the Empire. It also pointed to the Foreign and Colonial Offices' concerns about mounting cold war tensions.[48] The growing interest in the gathering and delivery of this type of intelligence contributed to the development of special branches.

On 5 August 1948, Creech-Jones, then Colonial Secretary, had despatched a circular to all colonial governors highlighting his particular concern about the security situation in Malaya and, to a lesser extent, the Gold Coast:

> You will be aware that in the Federation of Malaya and in Singapore the Governments are at present engaged in the defeat of a determined

attempt by organised dissident elements, through a campaign of terrorism and murder, to overthrow the establishment. It is essential that every
possible means should be taken to prevent similar happenings in other
colonial territories.

With some urgency Creech-Jones requested that a 'review of the
present state of efficiency, in numbers, organisation, equipment [and
the] Security forces' be undertaken. The governors were asked specifically to outline 'the existence or otherwise of intelligence and special
branches'.[49] This circular was followed by a despatch on 20 August,
stressing once more the need for intelligence organisations but suggesting that they be based on the needs of an individual territory.[50]

Johnson was expected to advise colonial governments and their commissioners of police on methods of improving and modernising their
police forces. He was also expected to advise the Colonial Secretary and
colonial governments on all aspects of intelligence-gathering and dissemination. The ICGP was most critical of the intelligence and security arrangements overall, despite the formal introduction of special
branch units in some territories. O'Sullivan noted that the Nigeria
Police CID's 'sparse intelligence coverage had not gone unnoticed' by
Johnson and that, as a result, funds were gradually made available to
increase personnel and equipment, and to provide more training.[51]
Thereafter, security and special branch courses at MI5 and Scotland
Yard were set up. By 1950 thirty-one colonial police officers had
attended these courses.[52] As more funds were made available so middle-
ranking special branch officers, both European and locally recruited,
were invited to attend courses in Britain.

Johnson's report was made available to all the colonial constabularies he had visited. Many senior officers were highly critical of its contents and considered that the Inspector-General had little grasp of the
realities in view of the turmoil that some colonies were facing.[53]
Overall, forty-two territories came under the Colonial Office's wing,
and intelligence networks could hardly be improved in them all
overnight. The need for a separate and efficient special branch in every
colony was recognised but would take time to implement, with those
facing colonial unrest taking priority. In Malaya, for example, in 1949,
the ongoing emergency increased the need to reinforce internal security. In a top secret report the Malayan Government expressed the need
for 'an efficient Special Branch which will in fact be the eyes and ears
both of the Government and the Police themselves. It must work in the
closest co-operation with other intelligence organisations and the intelligence branches of the armed forces in the territory.' However it was
noted that very few colonial Special Branches were proficient in

political intelligence-gathering 'or can be relied upon to draw the right deductions from [such intelligence] . . . the task now demanded of the Special Branch demands a very high standard and a great deal of research and study, but it must be attempted'. Without this, the huge sums spent on building up the police and the army would have been squandered.[54]

Essentially the building up of intelligence systems within the colonies depended on an increase in spending on police bodies to bolster their effectiveness in ensuring order. However, the Colonial Office was asking colonial governments to make 'a maximum contribution towards the costs of defence' at a time when they were struggling to resolve post-war financial issues, and to deal with ongoing security issues.[55] The 1949 Defence White Paper had stressed the need for Britain to assist in internal security arrangements 'as Colonial governments are feeling the draught when it comes to providing finance'. This would prevent political embarrassment and would 'leave no room for doubt [that] we were very willing to help'.[56]

In the event, the creation of Johnson's post coincided with the setting up of separate desks within the Colonial Office to co-ordinate matters of defence, security and intelligence. Colonial officials engaged in police intelligence matters collaborated with those working on legal and defence matters. The Home Office and MI5 were consulted whenever needed and provided considerable input into the development of special branches in many colonies during the 1940s and 1950s.

The development of colonial police special branch units

The development of police intelligence systems within the colonies centred on the partial translation of colonial office policy into working practice. In very few colonies were special branch units already in place that could be expanded and modernised. Hong Kong provided the principal example alongside the Malayan Police Special Branch, which was to develop rapidly during the emergency. Hong Kong's Special Branch became well known by British and foreign intelligence organisations by the early 1960s for its 'expertise on Chinese subversion and espionage'. Involvement in the 'Kashmir Princess incident' in 1955, which had considerable international ramifications, marked 'the first phase of the coming of age' for the Hong Kong Special Branch. During the 1950s it uncovered several networks of KMT agents working in and around Hong Kong.[57] 'From then until its dissolution shortly before 1997 it maintained a reputation with the Intelligence Community of the West for professionalism unlike any other special branch in the world.'[58]

Eates noted how both the CID[59] and Special Branch units became highly efficient in 'marrying criminal and political intelligence as the needs arose', particularly when dealing with the triads and narcotics. In Hong Kong, both units included officers who had started out their policing careers in Palestine and had brought with them an experience in security and counter-insurgency. In the case of the Special Branch, much was owed to the work of John Prendergast, who had served both in the Kenyan and the Cyprus Special Branch during the emergency periods. This was put to good effect in Hong Kong during the 1960s with the ongoing state of play with the Chinese Government.[60]

In most cases the creation of a special branch necessitated the disentangling of an existing unit within the CID in order to create a separate entity. These sections of CID had been known as the 'Political Intelligence Bureau', for example in the case of the Nyasaland Police,[61] or, in Nigeria, as the 'Intelligence Section', known within the force as 'I' Branch, an unofficial title that was not used outside the police owing to concerns of political criticism.[62] In Uganda, the guiding principle during the earlier period was that the so-called Special Branch section of the CID 'enquired but did not prosecute', this being left to the CID in order to keep Special Branch work firmly under wraps. The Special Branch of the Uganda Police had its origins in the Second World War as a section of the CID, which was expanded after the events in Uganda of 1945 and then the watershed of 1948. By the mid-1950s, Special Branch staff operated at all provincial and some district headquarters.[63]

However, in some territories, the development of a special branch took longer. A review of the Caribbean forces in relation to possible communist infiltration in 1948, revealed that the majority had no special branch, and many simply no intelligence-gathering capabilities whatsoever. The Bermuda Police, for example, were unable to provide a 'regular appreciation of current information' and badly needed a ' "trained Information Officer" to disseminate Government information and collect information of current trends of thoughts and feelings amongst the population, both coloured and white'.[64] The problem lay initially in selecting the right person to head up this type of unit. Candidates could be drawn from the Palestine Police, bringing considerable experience of gathering intelligence.[65]

Overall, the creation of separate special branch units ran parallel to the expansion, and often decentralisation, of CID branches. Urban unrest in Tanganyika led to the expansion of the CID into eight provinces and the subsequent creation of a Special Branch.[66] Denis Brockwell, a former CID officer who served with the NRP noted an increase from 2 gazetted officers and 16 Inspectors to 16 gazetted and 67 Inspectors by 1949; the number of African constables was augmented in line with these figures. Brockwell commented on how this increase in CID staff corresponded to its gradual relinquishing of Special Branch duties. Yet it was not until 1949 that a Special Branch officer was formally appointed. He described operations in 1948 and 1949 where CID duties were 'combined with a covert operation which required prolonged surveillance, including travel and sensitive screening of documents'. The NRP had uncovered a communist 'cell' set up by Simon Zukas and other Europeans who organised secret meetings. In the event, this proved to be the first communist cell in Central and East Africa, Zukas having joined forces with the banned South African Communist Party, and its activities helped trigger the creation of the Special Branch.[67] Douglas Cracknell, who served in Eritrea at this time, wrote of how 'terrorist activity in the urban areas began to occur. Young elements of the pro-Ethiopian Unionist Party directed attention to the Italian community with hand grenade attacks, shooting and one or two cases of kidnapping . . .'. This prompted the creation of the Special Branch in 1950 as a unit separate from the CID.[68]

Jenkins noted that on the Gold Coast the

> Convention Peoples Party pursued a vigorous and militant self-government campaign. Special Branch and the police were heavily committed to controlling large political meetings and demonstrations held with increasing frequency throughout the colony after 1948. Militant trade union leaders supported the campaign by encouraging unrest amongst organised labour and sporadic outbreaks of violence inevitably occurred. The authority of the chiefs was systematically undermined and their control of the youth was eroded . . . under these circumstances the need for a constant flow of reliable intelligence was paramount.[69]

In the police forces of the British Caribbean, which could be placed on a par with those of the West African colonies, disengaging the Special Branch from the CID was a lengthy process. Visits by the IGCP in 1952–53 found most police intelligence systems lacking in adequate staff and training, the result principally of under-funding. Muller visited the Jamaica Police in November 1952 and found that Special Branch and CID activities were still overlapping, although in a relatively 'well-organised' manner. He reported at some length on the practice of magic that took place on the island which the Special Branch had failed to contain:

> At Black River I was informed that Obeah men are still able to influence the cause of justice by such methods as intimidating superstitious witnesses. These men are practising the old methods of the African witch doctor and events in Kenya suggest that the Special Branch should keep their activities under careful and constant observation. Special Branch men must be posted to country areas and include this in their normal duties.[70]

Similar comments were made in relation to other territories in the British Caribbean. During a tour of the British Guiana Police the following month, Muller recommended that Special Branch keep a close watch 'on the activities of the "Obeah" men' even 'within the police force itself'.[71] The problems with developing special branch units within 'small police forces', as they were described by Muller, lay in 'persuading local legislators to agree funds to improve the police'.[72] Although the British Guiana Police Special Branch had been described as 'the most effective in the region', inadequate staffing led inevitably to ineffectual political policing. In 1955, following the despatch of British troops to the colony in aid of the civil power, the Colonial Office admitted that the 'weakness of the police' and the inefficacy of the Special Branch had been direct contributors.[73]

In general, the new roles of CID and Special Branch had to be clearly outlined. Typically, the function of the Special Branch was to procure, collate, assess and disseminate intelligence that potentially affected the security of a colony or the maintenance of public order. This involved the investigation of subversion, espionage, sabotage and other activities, deemed unlawful, unconstitutional or violent, which might endanger the safety of the state. Certainly the distinction between security and political intelligence became less than clear during this period, and the two frequently overlapped. This was further complicated by the setting up of 'intelligence co-ordination committees', to meet weekly at police headquarters. In many colonies, intelligence and security organisations comprised a *central* intelligence committee responsible to the administration, the police and the army, a security division of the Chief Secretary's Office, Special Branch and its district subsidiaries.

The police and 'political policing'

A change in policing priorities occurred in the final countdown to independence. It was at this time that the police–public relationship altered, allowing greater political intervention in setting policing priorities. The increase in trade union activity and political activity necessitated increased police action, whether through the Special Branch or the CID, to prevent or curb public disorder. Often the perpetrators of public unrest were given a certain amount of free rein before police action was taken. Thus rather than arresting the speakers and provoking violence, the police recorded political speeches and proceeded via the issue of a summons at a later date.[74] Former members of the Special Branch have also noted that some change in their policing priorities occurred during this period. The monitoring of political parties became more important, with particular focus on the rivalry between different political factions.[75]

Political policing developed at this time through the extension and strengthening of the Special Branch. Mervyn Manby, formerly Deputy Commissioner of the Special Branch in the Kenya Police, pointed to the effect that this might have on any semblance of police impartiality that existed at that time. He admitted that in theory a police officer was required to have no personal political views and to be clear in his own mind of the distinction between legitimate and illegitimate political activity. During the run up to independence in Kenya, Manby intimated that this viewpoint could be at variance with the wishes of the Government.[76] The role of the police in the management of *lawful* assemblies, political rallies and the arrest and release of political detainees became increasingly a bone of contention not only with the colonial administration but with local politicians. He commented that 'we kept the gunmen off the backs of the politicians and made it clear to the politicians that they would not themselves be able to further their aims with violence'.[77]

Aside from the Kenya Police Special Branch, the uniformed branches became more involved with issues centred on the future independence of the country. John Standring, then Superintendent and Divisional Commander in Nairobi, commented that the final four years before independence was a time of 'intense political activity'. Political parties held weekend meetings and rallies at which the police were expected to 'hold the ring' – according to Standring, the idea behind that phrase was that the police were non-political and were present 'to hold the ropes of the ring so that the contestants could fight the election by the rules'. He noted that uniformed police were expected to act impartially towards the different political parties: 'We were not supporters of one party or another, and although individuals might have personal preferences as to the outcome, I just do not recall it ever being of any concern at Divisional Commander level. I remember once being asked by a senior intelligence officer "Would my policemen be loyal to me if there was any trouble?" and I had to reply that I certainly hoped so.' From a policing perspective, the final years before independence entailed additional work. Meetings had to be overseen and crowd control undertaken to prevent riots or disturbances. The emphasis officially was on non-political intervention. Unofficially, the police were encouraged to support or restrain specific parties or political figures as the Government saw fit.[78] Akker, who was posted to Nairobi in 1957, saw a certain bias in the Special Branch's 'control' of political meetings and the procedures that existed to monitor politicians. He pointed to the lack of restraint in dealing with certain African politicians, including

Tom Myboya and Jomo Kenyatta.[79] Indeed, following independence, Kenyatta is said to have asked those former members of the Special Branch involved with his arrest and detention to leave Kenya; others were invited to stay and serve the new Kenyan Government.[80]

Generally speaking, political policing increased throughout decolonisation in CID as well as Special Branch. Public order disturbances and rising crime, partially triggered by growing nationalism, expanded the role of the CID. By the time events were getting out of hand on the Gold Coast in 1948, the Nigeria Police's Special Branch element of the CID was still struggling to produce a daily report of intelligence gleaned from newspapers articles, the odd contact with political and trade union activists and, for the most part, gossip acquired from government officials, police and military officers. On instruction from Whitehall, a 'Central Intelligence Committee' of police, military and administrative members had been set up, overseeing the developing Special Branch arm of the CID, the Security Division of the Chief Secretary's Office and their contacts throughout the colony. O'Sullivan, who would go on to head up the Special Branch, recalled that matters were dealt with reactively, rather than proactively, hence the general lack of success. The onset of the cold war meant that the perceived threat was Marxist infiltration. Prior to the formal creation of the Special Branch, the unit's size was progressively increased to meet intelligence requirements arising from self-government throughout the provinces, Africanisation of the government structures, political and tribal unrest, and penetration by perceived foreign subversives. However, it was not until as late as March 1959 that the CID and the Special Branch were officially separated within the Nigeria Police. The CID became 'D' Department and the Special Branch and 'Aliens' Branch' amalgamated as 'E' Department.[81] This was prompted, in part, by the appointment of a new Inspector-General, Kerr Bovell. The occurrence of an emergency situation in Nigeria may well have prompted the earlier development of a separate Special Branch unit.

The same was true in Kenya where, by 1954, with the onset of the Mau Mau emergency, the Special Branch consisted only of three Europeans, one Asian officer and a handful of rank and file, working solely within Nairobi. The Kenya Police Special Branch had been set up in the early 1940s as a unit of CID, but the two were separated in 1945 after it was found that 'this arrangement suffered from one fundamental defect. The detection of crime [is] urgent; the collection of political intelligence appeared less urgent and consequently suffered.'[82] The Special Branch also had a drawback in that it did not initially operate outside Nairobi and Mombasa and, therefore, had to rely on information supplied by local administrative and police officers. Much of the intelligence information was supplied by district intelligence teams, bodies which consisted of 'officers of all departments whose work brought them in contact with the people'. These teams were established in 1950 and were chaired by district commissioners as a result of the Kolloa affray in western Kenya, which caused the deaths of members of the public and the police.[83]

In some colonies, though, Special Branch units had still not formally been organised by the 1960s. This was particularly true of areas in the British Caribbean where certain colonies remained under British rule. However, in the case of British Honduras, the IGCP was still urging a radical overhaul of its existing Special Branch unit on the cusp of independence in 1966. Macoun, who visited the British Honduras Police as Deputy IGCP, strongly recommended the appointment of a 'security services officer' on a 12–18 month secondment, to provide 'expert assistance in an advisory capacity'.[84] One month later, M. L. McCaul, an SLO, visited the territory and stated that 'capable Special Branch' advisors were preferable to MI5 liaison officers, particularly in view of the approaching independence. The 'right' officer could be left in place after independence and his training could be continued at Bramshill if necessary.[85] This viewpoint was not dissimilar from one that pervaded the Colonial Office during the transition period. Attempts were made to leave a legacy of Britishness through reform of existing police systems and by leaving expatriate officers in place. However, in most instances, this clashed with the creation of covert police units undertaking intelligence work. The general idea of these units stemmed partially from the need to relieve Special Branch units of operational duties to allow them the freedom to concentrate on the political problems of subversion.

With emergency and public order situations worsening across the Empire, set against a backdrop of cold war tensions, police intelligence systems developed a colonial rather than a British style. In individual territories, this was typically a response to government needs. In some specific situations, where colonial conflict occurred, joint intelligence committee structures were put in place to oversee both police and army intelligence, which had the effect of developing police intelligence units and often the independent actions of their officers. Outside of emergencies, some colonies experienced a move towards a newer type of intelligence system. In the Federation of Northern and Southern Rhodesia and Nyasaland the Federal Intelligence and Security Bureau, a federal intelligence *coordinating* body, as distinct from the intelligence-*gathering* special branch unit, of each territory was set up in 1954. This left intact the powers of the territorial governments in the field of internal security but created an overseeing body. Following the UDI in 1964,

Rhodesia continued to develop its central intelligence organisation that increased police intelligence systems still further along distinctly *colonial* lines.

The development of colonial police intelligence systems originated in the Irish tradition of being the 'eyes and ears' of government. Most pre-war colonial police forces could rely, to some degree, on the local administration to assist in intelligence-gathering. In British colonial Africa, the NAP provided an additional back-up. The basic theme of 'too little, too late' also applied as much to the reform of police intelligence as it did to the uniformed police branches. The creation of special branches became a post-war necessity owing to rising political and security concerns at the end of the Empire set within the context of the cold war. While the principle of applying *Britishness* was demonstrated through the ad hoc loan of MI5, MI6 and Special Branch officers, to assist in the reorganisation of police intelligence systems, the end product had a distinctly colonial flavour, which continued in many territories after independence.

Notes

1 Churchill, 'Defence Policy', Cabinet Memo., 3 Nov. 1954, NA CAB 128/27.
2 Harold Macmillan, 'Internal Security in the Colonies', Cabinet Memo., 29 Dec. 1954, NA CAB 129/72.
3 Arnold, *Police Power and Colonial Rule*, p. 3.
4 Horne, *Job Well Done*, pp. 262, 465.
5 Dowbiggin Report, 1930, NA CO 733/180/1.
6 Horne, *Job Well Done*, p. 470.
7 Instructions issued by Chief Secretary, M. A. Young, 22 April 1932, quoted in Kolinsky, *Law, Order and Riots in Mandatory Palestine*, p. 101.
8 Wickham to Cunningham, 20 Aug. 1946, NA CO 537/3847/8.
9 W. Moffat, 'Criminal Investigation Department Report', 1946, NA CO 537/2269/54.
10 J. J. O'Sullivan, RHL MSS Afr. s. 1784, Box XVII, f. 3.
11 Christopher Harwich, *Red Dust* (London: Vincent Stuart, 1961), p. 7.
12 G. A. Anderson, RHL MSS Afr. s. 1784, Box XVIII, f. 49.
13 The *Nigeria Police Magazine* in 1938 recorded that the Eastern Preventative Service was concerned with tobacco smuggling: Clayton, *Thin Blue Line*, p. 34, p. 36.
14 The Nigeria Police was formed on 27 February 1930 following the unification of the northern and southern forces of the 1917 ordinance: Shirley, *History of the Nigeria Police*, p. 36.
15 Hodge. J. E., RHL MSS Afr. s. 1784, Box VII, f. 9.
16 Coles, J. F.G., RHL MSS Afr. s. 1784, Box I, f. 31.
17 Taken from an interview with Courtney Gidley (Nigeria Police, Acting Dep. Insp.-Gen., rtd, 1942–1963), Aug. 2003; Franklin (interview), Dec. 2004.
18 Coles, J. F.G., RHL MSS Afr. s. 1784, Box I, f. 20.
19 Macoun, *Wrong Place, Right Time*; p. 17.
20 Clayton, *Thin Blue Line*, p. 90.
21 Franklin (interview), Dec. 2004.
22 W. Robert Foran, *The Kenya Police 1887–1960* (London: Robert Hale, 1962), pp. 107–115.

23 Onraet, Trinidad Police Report, 8 July 1942, NA CO 295/627/5.
24 In fact the Uganda CID was not fully decentralised until 1960 when officers stationed in the districts were given the same powers as those at headquarters: G. A. Anderson, RHL MSS Afr. s. 1784, Box XVIII, f. 116.
25 Minutes, Meeting, Police HQ Kampala, 31 Jan. 1941, Anderson, RHL MSS Afr. s. 1784, Box XVIII/Appendix E, ff. 29–30.
26 Calver, Report on Adequacy of Police Force Jamaica, 23 Oct. 1945, NA CO 137/867/1.
27 O'Sullivan, RHL MSS Afr. s. 1784, Box VII, f. 9.
28 Proud, RHL MSS Afr. s. 1784, Box VII, f. 4.
29 Hodge, RHL MSS Afr. s. 1784, Box VII, ff. 9–12.
30 Macdonald, A. E., RHL MSS Afr. s. 1784, Box VII, f. 4.
31 Creech-Jones, Secret Circular despatch to Colonial Govts, 20 Aug. 1948, NA CO 537/2781.
32 Craig, *Malayan Emergency*, pp. 6–9, Family Papers & interview with author, Jan. 2000.
33 Scobell (interview), Feb. 2000.
34 The events that took place in Uganda in January 1945 had taken both the Government and the police 'completely by surprise': neither had been 'in possession of any information which would suggest the possibility of the disturbances': *Report of the Commission of Inquiry into the Disturbances which occurred in Uganda during January 1945* (Entebbe: Government Printer, 1945), para. 28. This contributed to the need for a 'Fortnightly Review'.
35 Cohen to all Governors in Africa, Secret despatch, 15 March 1948, NA CO 537/2686/1.
36 Colonial Political Intelligence Summaries 1948, Minutes, NA CO 537/2677.
37 Colonial Political Intelligence Summaries 1948, Minutes, NA CO 537/2760.
38 Gurney to Malcolm MacDonald, Colonial Secretary, 11 April 1949, NA DEFE 11/33/297.
39 Gurney to Arthur Creech-Jones, 30 May 1949, NA DEFE 11/33/2.
40 Report on the Malayan Police Force, July 1949, NA DEFE 11/33/169.
41 CO Minutes, May 1948, NA CO 537/2760; Sir M. Logan, 'Political Intelligence Report West Africa', Reports on Communism, 14 July 1948, NA CO 537/3653.
42 J. C. Mangan, Minute, 20 May 1948, NA CO 537/2760.
43 Gidley (interview), Aug. 2003.
44 A detailed breakdown of the Kenya Police Special Branch structure is provided at Appendix 1.3, Franklin, Family Papers.
45 Franklin (interview), Dec. 2004.
46 Eates (interview), July 2003.
47 Colonial Political Intelligence Summaries, 1948, Minutes, NA CO 537/2677.
48 'The Secretary of State for Foreign Affairs has called for periodical surveys of communist activities in countries outside the Soviet Union. The Foreign Office has asked that any material in relation to Colonial territories which may be relevant to these reports should be provided every fortnight': Lloyd, CO, to Gormusch, FO, 26 May 1948, NA CO 537/2677.
49 Creech-Jones, 'Colonial Police Forces', Circular Despatch, 5 Aug. 1948, NA CO 537/2770.
50 Creech-Jones, Circular despatch to all Governors, 20 Aug. 1948, NA CO 968/727.
51 O'Sullivan, RHL MSS s. Afr. 1784, Box XVII, f. 28.
52 Morton, *Just the Job*, p. 273.
53 Hadow (interview), Jan. 2002; Eates (interview), June 2001. 'Johnson had the grace to admit later, when he had been around more, that his criticisms were due to his ignorance at the very different conditions under which we operated': Ffforde, RHL, MSS Afr. s. 1784, Box XV, f. 177.
54 Malaya Federation, Despatch No. 5, NA DEFE 11/33/148.
55 'Financing of Colonial Defence', Cabinet Committee Meeting, 10 Dec. 1948, NA CAB 130/44.

56 G. T. Gavalan, Defence, to Mr Donaldson, Colonial Office, Minute, 18 Jan. 1949, NA DEFE 11/413.
57 For a detailed account see: Steve Tsang, 'Kashmir Princess Incident', *China Quarterly*, 139 (Sept. 1994).
58 Scobell (interview), Feb. 2000.
59 At this time the CID was divided broadly into three: the crime, narcotics and commercial sections.
60 Eates (interview), July 2001.
61 The Nyasaland Police was established in 1920; its CID was set up the same year, while the Nyasaland Special Branch was set up in 1949–50.
62 Gidley (interview), Aug. 2003. Sullivan, who worked in 'I' Branch, noted that its duties did not meet with the approval of the Police Commissioner, 'as it seemed the Government feared that there might be hostile reaction in the Legislative Council and the local press'. Indeed in some circles, this unit was referred to as CID (S), although 'nobody seemed to know whether the "s" meant "secret", "security" or "special"'. Duties after the Second World War were mainly taken up with producing a 'Daily Intelligence Report' to be dispatched to the Chief Secretary, the Commissioner and the General Officer Commanding: Sullivan, RHL MSS s. Afr. 1784, Box XVII, f. 8, f. 15.
63 Anderson, RHL MSS Afr. s. 1784, Box XVIII, ff. 60–68.
64 R. Leatham, Governor to Creech-Jones, 7 Sept. 1948, NA CO 537/2776.
65 Creech-Jones to Leatham, 30 Nov. 1948, NA CO 537/2776.
66 The Tanganyika Police was established in 1916, with its CID set up the same year; an independent Special Branch was set up in 1953: J. D. Blake, in Macoun, RHL MSS s. Afr. 1784, Box XX, f. 130.
67 Brockwell, 'Secret letter from CID HQ to Com. NRP', 11 March 1949, RHL MSS Afr. s. 1784, Box XV, ff.6–11.
68 Cracknell, RHL MSS Afr. s. 1784, Box X, f. 9.
69 T. Jenkins, RHL MSS Afr. s. 1784, Box XVIII, ff. 20–23.
70 Muller, ICGP Report on Jamaica Police Force, 1953, NA CO 1031/107.
71 Muller, IGCP Report on the British Guiana Police Force, Dec. 1952, NA CO 1031/103.
72 Muller, Secret Minutes, 22 Jan. 1953, NA CO 1031/103.
73 N. L. Mayle, minutes, 25 Jan. 1955, NA CO 1031/103.
74 Bailey in correspondence with the author, Nov. 2000. This point was clearly in evidence in an operation order concerning the Miji Kauda Union, African Social Centre, Tononka, Mombasa, 11 October 1959, from which a licence was issued to Ronald Agala, President of the Union: Bailey, Family Papers.
75 Franklin, 11 Oct. 00.
76 Manby, RHL MSS Afr. s. 1784, Box X, f. 24A.
77 Manby, RHL MSS Afr. s. 1784, Box X, f. 24A.
78 John Standring (Div. Com. Kenya Police, rtd, 1954–64) in correspondence with the author, 14 & 27 June 2000.
79 Akker, RHL MSS Afr. s. 1784, Box VIII, f. 8.
80 Franklin (interview), Oct. 2000.
81 O'Sullivan, RHL MSS Afr. s. 1784, Box XVII, ff. 22–33.
82 Corfield Report, ch. 3, 1940–52 (1960), NA CO 822/1222.
83 Corfield Report, ch. 3, 1940–52 (1960), NA CO 822/1222.
84 Macoun, Summary of Comments and Recommendations, British Honduras Police, 10 Nov. 1966, NA CO 1037/257.
85 B. Hood, Gov., to Sec. of State Commonwealth Affairs, Conf. Savings, 7 Feb. 1967, NA CO 1037/257.

CHAPTER NINE

Remnants of Empire

Inadequate provisions for the localisation of gazetted officers within most colonies prior to independence led to many expatriates being asked to remain *in situ*. Essentially, this preserved colonial traditions within police administration and practice. Paradoxically, it allowed also for aspects of Britishness to be retained simply because many officers were British-born, and some locally recruited officers had been on training courses in Britain. A decline in many colonial traditions would occur in part when the officers left their respective police forces.

Officers stayed on after independence for a number of reasons. Many quite simply preferred to work as police officers outside of Britain and were happy to 'serve a new master'.[1] Indeed, a considerable number of them never returned to Britain, settling predominantly in Kenya, South Africa, Australia and Canada. Some officers stayed on for a short time and then returned home, pressured it seems by financial concerns, often linked to pension issues. Police officers who had been recruited into the Colonial Police Service from the home police forces had their years of service at home discounted from the calculation of their overall pension. Changes to the British police pension scheme were slow in coming.[2] This matter had been raised at later colonial police commissioners' conferences as constituting 'disparate treatment of officers'. Catling, in particular, was concerned that members of the Kenya Police, recruited directly from the home forces, should not be penalised.[3] There were proposals to make regulations under the Police Pension Act of 1948 which would enable police officers 'in certain circumstances to take up permanent approved posts overseas and to retain "frozen pensions" rights in respect of their police service'. In this way, an officer who had previously served in the home forces would retire with an overseas pension *and* a UK pension.[4] For officers who had served solely within the Colonial Police Service, and had stayed for a period of service after independence, pension prospects were bleaker.

As the number of police forces in the Colonial Police Service diminished at the end of Empire, so the role of the IGCP was brought into question. Essentially the post had been created in line with the Colonial Office's idea of standardisation, which had emerged as policy following the creation of the Colonial Police Service. While *unofficial* CPAs had been around since Dowbiggin's time, the creation in 1948 of an *official* advisor to the Colonial Secretary brought the post into line with like advisory capacities – in respect of agriculture, law, medicine, and so on. Informing the Colonial Secretary on all overseas policing matters required of the advisor frequent overseas visits and liaison with colonial police commissioners. To clarify this relationship, the title 'colonial police advisor' was changed in 1950 to inspector-general of colonial police. At the same time, the post of deputy inspector-general of colonial police was created; assisted by two staff officers, the post was occupied during the peak of decolonisation between 1956 and 1960.

By 1961, most Colonial Office advisors had migrated to the Department of Technical Co-Operation (DTC; later the Overseas Development Agency), apart from the legal and security advisors, who remained at the Colonial Office. Any attempts to bring the serving IGCP, Ivo Stourton, into the DTC were met with resistance, and he bluntly refused to wear 'two hats', the one colonial, the other commonwealth.[5] A report by the Morton Working Party (the DTC's official think tank), concluded that the 'inclusion of police advisory services would savour too much of neo-colonialism presumably on the fallacious ground that police services are a form of imperial oppression'.[6] It pointed to the Government's view on leaving the right legacy in place, particularly as the 'work of the IGCP and of the Security Intelligence Advisors [was] so closely connected in the Colonial Office, with the political work of the geographical departments'. However, this also presented a problem when new Commonwealth countries were being encouraged to make both formal and informal contact with the IGCP on an ad hoc basis.

With the absorption of the Colonial Office into the Commonwealth Office in 1966–67, the title of the two police posts changed to overseas police advisor (OPA) *and* IGCP.[7] This too continued to pose problems as the Commonwealth Office were 'at first extremely sensitive to anything which seemed to smell of our colonial past'.[8] Would this new title be more palatable for new Commonwealth members or would they go on using IGCP? In the event, it was more the British who were concerned by its negative connotations, for OPA continued to be used by Commonwealth and dependent territories alike without a murmur of discontent.

Yet the use of the title IGCP remained a bone of contention until Michael Macoun became the final incumbent of the post. He brought pressure on the Foreign and Colonial Office to allow the title to drop. 'I consider it an anachronism that, when we no longer speak of our Colonial role, both my post and that of my Deputy should still bear the Colonial label', Macoun wrote in 1974 (although both posts were responsible for overseeing the remaining 15 dependent territories, in which approximately 15,500 police officers 'were still in direct service under the Crown'.)[9] Macoun's real issue was with the use of 'colonial' within Commonwealth countries where he offered 'a British advisory and support service [to restructure] man management and training in specialized and technical fields, and [give] advice on police developmental projects'.[10] All of this may have sounded decidedly British, but perhaps with a sense that 'colonial' echoed the guilt of Empire, that was creeping into government circles. An old Colonial Office hand Bennett, attempted to defend the use of the term 'colonial', however 'outmoded' it may have become. He suggested that Macoun deal with 'newly-independent clients' in an OPA rather than an IGCP capacity 'if that makes their *amour propre*'.[11] Besides no previous ICGP had encountered difficulties in the use of the title, even in territories like Tanganyika and Malaya that were not *real* colonies:

> Most of the surviving 'dependencies' *are* in fact colonies in the strict sense. Personally I have always felt that the term 'dependent territories' sounds *more* unpalatable than 'colonies', because it more explicitly denotes inferior status, besides being a bureaucratic multisyllable with no honourable historical associations.

Yet the hangovers of Empire persisted and all governors of dependent territories[12] were asked to examine their statute books to make appropriate amendments to any use of the title IGCP. In the event, IGCP did not appear in any legislation or regulations in any of the dependent territories and the recommendation was made to revert to the original title.[13] A sense of the colonial past, rather than a new era of commonwealth, was certainly present within post-independence policing.

Policing the postcolonial state

Imperial traditions were maintained to some extent within the policing of the postcolonial state – and can still be observed today – reflected in the work of CPAs, in the export of personnel, and in police training and procedures. In an attempt to crystallise the relationship between senior colonial policemen and their *British* counterparts, regular conferences and meetings had taken place since the first Conference of Colonial

Commissioners of Police in April 1951.[14] By 1983, a formal relationship existed between the Association of Chief of Police Officers (ACPO), dependent territories and commonwealth countries.[15] However, before the formalisation of this relationship, there had been a two-way process, and colonial methods had been tried and tested in Britain. Kenneth Newman, for example, brought his experiences as a Palestine policeman to the Metropolitan Police during the anti-Vietnam demonstrations in Hyde Park in 1968. Following his sojourn as Chief Constable of the RUC, he returned to the Metropolitan Police as Commissioner. During the 1985 Broadwater Farm riots, weapons and tactics borrowed from Hong Kong and Northern Ireland were used in line with policies adopted by ACPO in 1981. The Home Office subsequently 'urged' the case for plastic bullets, a modern day version of the wooden 'baton rounds' developed earlier in Hong Kong, and what the colonial police had used as tear gas, which had become known as CS gas.[16]

In Britain's former colonies there were numerous other examples. In a manner similar to that of the Palestine Police, the Israeli State Police became a highly centralised organisation that borrowed heavily from its predecessor.[17] Colonial police practices were maintained to some extent by Jewish and Arab officers who had served in the Palestine Police. Separated from the main body of the police were the Border Police and the Civil Guard. The Border Police, established in 1953, inherited the paramilitary traditions of the Palestine Police to guard the country's frontiers against guerrilla or terrorist incursions, traditions which have made the Border Police a controversial organisation, perceived in a light different from that of the regular police. The Civil Guard was established as a volunteer force after the 1973 Yom Kippur War. Its main function is the patrolling and guarding of public buildings, although it is responsible also for both anti-terrorist duties and crime prevention.[18]

In former colonies in Africa, British influences on policing were even stronger. The Kenya Police was a case in point, no doubt strengthened by the presence, both past and present, of Europeans within the population. Having taken office, Jomo Kenyatta wrote a personal letter to Richard Catling on 4 June 1963 saying that 'he looked forward to meeting members of the Kenya Police and seeing something of their work at close hand'. Kenyatta paid tribute to the work of the Kenya Police and the 'extra hours of duty which policemen of all ranks everywhere had to perform since the elections campaign began'. Indeed, he praised all members of the force, African, Asian and European.[19] Following Kenya's independence in 1963, the new Government preserved many of the colonial traditions within the 'new' Kenya Police, including the retention of expatriate personnel and senior-ranking

African officers, as well as the force's structure and organisation. At the same time, the Special Branch and the GSU were reinforced to protect internal security.

It has been estimated that several hundred expatriates stayed on in the Kenya Police following independence. Staff lists for 1957, for example, showed that of 183 Chief Inspectors, only 7 were African or Asians. By 1965, the number of European Chief Inspectors had dropped to only 7-5-, although there were still almost 50 ASPs.[20] The previous year, the first appointments of African police officers to the rank of assistant commissioner had taken place. Michael Arrumm and Bernard Nhenga Hinga were promoted rapidly through the ranks during the final years preceding independence. Hinga was to become, on Catling's retirement, the first African Commissioner of the Kenya Police.[21] The expatriates received financial incentives additional to their pensions and salaries.

In 1963, only a very few officers were 'weeded' out by the Government and asked to leave.[22] Most police officers left of their own volition. Some felt they could not countenance serving under African Officers, and others preferred to take the financial compensation package, fearing that if they stayed on their increased pension benefits might not be paid by the Kenya Government. At that time, Britain had not taken over responsibility for the payment of pensions.[23] After 1966, the police were transferred to an overseas allowance known as 'OSAS', paid by the British Government, which included a proportion for loss of pension rights, and the local salary paid by the Kenyan Government. While the local salary was taxable, the OSAS supplement was usually tax free, though for some officers the tax incentive was of lesser importance than 'the job and living in Kenya'. For others, the lure of a more secure job within the home forces prompted a resignation shortly after independence. David Hooper, for example, was encouraged to stay on as Inspector but feared that he would not easily secure a commensurable post in Britain as he was above the age of 30; he returned home in 1964, becoming a police constable in the Kent Police.[24]

The Kenya Police continued to maintain a link with Britain through the training courses undertaken by its officers. Prior to independence, only a limited number of locally recruited officers secured places on training courses. In 1960, only 23 officers attended a 5-month course at Hendon, including 6 officers from the Kenya Police, among them Inspectors E. M. Lusenak and S. F. Coutinho who were considered among the 25 'best ever' officers to have passed out of Hendon. Coutinho had been sent specifically to study 'modern methods of police detection', including practical work in forensic laboratories. Coutinho, an instructor at the Police Training School at Kiganjo, set up in 1948, was also interested in law and law court procedure.[25]

Meanwhile, British officers continued to head up the training school in Kenya, with David Hewson stepping down as late as June 1974.[26]

Importantly, the training of special branch officers had, prior to 1963, been a European preserve. Thereafter, training was opened to African officers who forged links with both MI5 and MI6. The Special Branch in Kenya itself soon underwent a name change, becoming the National Security and Intelligence Service, directly accountable to the President, rather than to the Commissioner of Police. With the gradual exodus of Kenya'a senior expatriate Special Branch officers, army intelligence officers were moved in to fill their posts. This had the effect of changing the nature of intelligence-gathering and operation: 'With the top echelons of the National Intelligence and Security Service being dominated by the military, they tended to adopt a soldier's attitude towards tackling a problem rather than that of a police officer.'[27] Expatriate Special Branch officers lamented the fact that control of the service was slipping away from the police, particularly after the initial post-independence period when European officers were still responsible for high-profile cases. This included, for example, the investigation by Allen Jenkins into the 'attempted' mutiny of the 7th Battalion of the Kenya Army (formerly the King's African Rifles), at the Lanet barracks in Nakuru on 24 January 1964, following attempted mutinies by military units within three East African countries: Zanzibar, Tanzania and Uganda. Working with the CID and the army's Special Investigation Branch, Jenkins concluded that there had been no 'outside' involvement, and the ringleaders were tried and imprisoned.[28] Special Branch officers were also involved in interrogating former Mau Mau who had been sent to an internment camp at Lamu just prior to independence.

The reform and strengthening of the Kenya Police in the light of the Mau Mau emergency had effectively paved the way for a strong arm of government after independence. Police experience of operating in Kenya's emergency situations led to several requests for their assistance during the early 1960s. Following the Belgian withdrawal from the Congo in 1960, a contingent of the Kenya Police was called in to help train the Congolese Police in Kivi Province. This followed on from the successes of the Nigeria Police in Leopoldville. Approximately 200 members of the Kenya Police would be funded by the United States, with $1.5 million being paid through the United Nations.[29] The services of the Kenya Police were subsequently requested in both Tanzania and Zanzibar. However, the most important security duties undertaken were internal to Kenya itself and focused on the auxiliary unit, the GSU.

The Kenya Police's GSU was used increasingly after independence to manage situations that threatened internal security. A growing concern for the new Government was the increased Somali *shifta* (insurgents) activity from late 1963 in the frontier areas, a concern heightened by allegations that Somali members of the Kenya Police and Army had 'gone over to the other side'. From this time, regular incidents were reported, with

> attacks carried out on Government camps and convoys. The Kenyan District Commissioner for Isiolo had been killed along with the Boran Chief Haji Galmo Deda. During the coming months the British District Commissioner for Wajir was shot outside his tent, the British District Officer for Mandera was ambushed and killed . . . Somali chiefs were also targets and a number killed. Towns were often ransacked . . . The gang had stolen items from the District Assistant's office, run down the new Kenyan flag from the flagstaff outside the Government offices in the centre of town, and destroyed the telephone exchange and post office.[30]

Repeated attacks by Somali *shifta* gangs resulted in the GSU being posted away to what was formerly the Northern Frontier District to protect police posts and carry out patrols. (The Northern Frontier had been important to Kenya in that it encompassed the borders with Somalia, Ethiopia, the Sudan and Uganda. This was complicated by the 'Ilemi Triangle', an area which was *de facto* Sudanese Sovereign Territory but *de jure* administered by the Kenya Government.) Problems with the Somali *shifta* had occurred since the 1950s and had forced the regular police in the area to operate more as a *gendarmerie*. Disputes arose, in the late 1950s, between Kenya itself and the Kenya-administered Sudan and Ethiopia concerning the border known as the 'Maud Line' which ran from Low Sand Hills to Kibish. This situation was exacerbated by the frequent border incursions by numerous nomadic tribes living in the area.[31] By 1964, it was assumed that the Soviets were assisting the Somalis in their bid to take territory from the Kenyan Government. The GSU, while being adequately trained, and equipped, were permanently under-strength and forced to use some regular and tribal police as back-ups.[32] Additionally, a lack of transport for both the police and the army contributed to the overall problem. As the situation worsened from 1965, outlying towns such as Moyale, Mandera, Wajir, Marsabit and Garissa had to be supplied by escorted convoys.[33]

Changes to the overall structure of the GSU were taking place throughout the so-called '*Shifta* Campaign'. Following Kenya's declaration of a republic in June 1964, Percy Wild noted that he remained the sole European within 'B' Company, with the other Europeans having been replaced by local officers.[34] With ongoing localisation of all Platoon Commanders and some Company Commanders, Europeans were transferred out of their units or given administrative or training posts. (Wild and Fred Mason were the last Company Commanders. Wild was eventually posted as an instructor to the Police College at Kiganjo before taking over GSU training at Embakasi from 1966 until 1968.[35] Despite this local emphasis, the GSU Commandant, Dick Angel, found it increasingly difficult to find local officers who were prepared to serve in the newly designated Northern Frontier Province (NFP). The problem worsened when two additional companies were formed and the training increased. Eventually the GSU would be made up of twenty companies which relied on British Army training. It served essentially as a back-up to the army to avoid possible coups which by 1968 had become so common in Africa. This was to be the old system of divide and rule adopted by the British and other colonial powers in the past.[36]

Thus it seemed that events had turned full circle. The GSU which had served to enforce the paramilitary side to policing during the Mau Mau emergency was being used to conduct the *Shifta* Campaign, 'a much bigger show' and a threat to Kenya's internal stability. Measures to install a more civilian style of police force in the *modus operandi* of Arthur Young had been foiled initially by lengthy emergency and subsequent events involving the Northern Frontier.

Policing the immediate postcolonial state relied on traditional colonial methods; it would be at a much later stage that interest in British policing would again come to the fore. The case of the Sierra Leone Police is revealing in a contemporary context. In July 1999, the Commonwealth Development Police Task Force brief to reorganise the police led to the appointment of Keith Biddle as Inspector-General of the Sierra Leone Police. (Biddle had been Assistant Chief Constable of the Kent Police.)[37] During Sierra Leone's civil war the police, had been targeted by the insurgents and army alike, and Biddle saw that he was dealing with a 'beleaguered' force that had lost 900 police officers during 10 years of civil war. At the time of his arrival, near chaos had replaced law and order. His brief was to reform the police and to extend police jurisdiction throughout the territory. Biddle perceived this as a way of 'changing police culture', decentralising the structures of command and improving police training.[38] During his period of office, he supervised just about everything relating to policing and law enforcement, trying initially to address the police's extremely low rate of pay and an overall lack of equipment.[39] Thereafter he adopted British methods of policing, prompting senior officers to adopt a new slogan: 'A force for good'. In essence, Biddle was trying to bring to the force some long-cherished police ideals in the manner of previous CPAs. Reform, he believed, necessitated an emphasis on policing *by consent*, and that would involve the introduction of community policing and a drive to restore law and order in what had become 'no-go' areas. Biddle also believed in diluting the paramilitary nature of the anti-riot squad, which he perceived as overtly political. In 2003, a Sierra Leonean, Brima Acha Kamara, was appointed Chief of Police with a brief to foster the improved relations between the public and police for which Biddle had worked.[40]

Hong Kong has offered an interesting case in terms of retaining both colonial and British policing traditions. The Hong Kong Government had always promoted knowledge transfers between its police and the home forces. Macoun noted that from a policing perspective

> Hong Kong had the advantage of being one of the last of the Crown Colonies and was therefore able to look back at history in other territories. We studied the internal security mechanisms of past colonies such as Malaya, Borneo, Kenya and Cyprus. They had a public order problem in each of those territories. So we were able to pick and choose the best from all of them and adapt it into the Hong Kong machine.[41]

Not only did the force borrow and adapt from the police of other colonies, but transferred its officers and its ethos to those police forces. In 1983, an agreement was reached between ACPO and the RHKP to permit regular 'formal' exchanges of operational officers. This followed an ACPO conference in September 1981, attended by Richard Quine, RHKP Director of Operations, who lectured on colonial police systems for dealing with public disorder.[42] The public order tactics used by the 1980s in Hong Kong had been tried and tested in former colonies for more than forty years. Overall the RHKP was the testing-ground for riot-control equipment and techniques throughout the decolonisation period.

The transfer of personnel, known locally as 'Cop Swop', saw cross-fertilisation taking place between the RHKP and British forces. Members of the RHKP could expect to be posted to the Metropolitan Police, Greater Manchester, Liverpool, Surrey and Sussex police forces, for example, for approximately two years, though many were keen to stay on for longer. The RHKP also continued to recruit expatriates until 1996: in November 1987, an advertisement in *Police Review* for British recruits noted that the RHKP was 'the proving ground for natural leaders'. By 2005, almost a decade after Hong Kong's transfer to Chinese sovereignty, there were still approximately 300 European officers serving in the RHKP, Assistant Comissioner P. Michael Dowd being the most senior.[43]

Notes

1 Franklin (interview), Oct. 2002.
2 'Pensions of Colonial Police Officers recruited UK Forces, 1960', NA CO 1037/78.
3 Conference of Colonial Police Commissioners, paper presented by Catling on pensions, Sept. 1960, NA CO 1037/185.
4 P. L. Taylor, HO, to C. E. R. Darby, CO, 16 Aug. 1960, NA CO 1037/185.

5   Sir Hilton Poynton, Minute, 14 June 1960, NA CO 866/118.
6   Confidential Minute, 'Department of Technical Cooperation – Police Services', to Armitage-Smith, Stourton, Williamson, Gidden & Anderson, 15 March 1961, NA CO 866/118.
7   The titles OPA and IGCP remained unchanged when the Commonwealth Office was merged with the Foreign Office to become the Foreign and Commonwealth Office (FCO) in 1969.
8   J. S. Bennett, Advisor on Colonial Affairs, to Mr Bickford, Legal Advisor, 'Overseas Police Advisor and IGCP', 30 July 1974, NA FCO 86/272.
9   Macoun to Long, FCO Personnel, 27 March 1974, NA FCO 86/272.
10 Macoun, *Wrong Place, Right Time*, p. 97.
11 Bennett to Bickford, 30 July 1974, NA FCO 86/272.
12 These were: Tristan da Cunha, Turks and Caicos Islands, St Helena, Pitcairn, New Hebrides, Hong Kong, Montserrat, Gibraltar, Cayman Islands, British Virgin Islands, Seychelles, Anguilla, Ascension Island Belize, Bermuda, BSIP and the Falklands.
13 R. G. Tallboys, FCO, to Mr Bellamy, Dept. OPA, 31 Jan. 1975, NA FCO 86/272.
14 Jeffries, 'Colonial Police Service', p. 78.
15 Northam, *Shooting in the Dark*, p. 127.
16 Northam, *Shooting in the Dark*, p. 62.
17 For an in-depth account of this transition see Joseph Caspi, 'Policing the Holy Land 1918–1957: The Transition from a Colonial to a National Model of Policing and Changing Conceptions of Police Accountability', PhD (City University, 1991).
18 John D. Brewer, Adrian Guelke, Ian Hume et al., *The Police, Public Order and the State: Policing in Great Britain, Northern Ireland the Irish Republic, the USA, Israel, South Africa and China* (Basingstoke: Macmillan, 1988), pp. 132–133.
19 'Prime Minister Visits Police', *Kenya Police Review* (Sept. 1963), p. 6.
20 Kenya Police Staff List, 1957, & 1 July 1965, Kenya Police Association.
21 'Promotion for Two African Police Officers', *Kenya Police Review* (March 1964), p. 23.
22 This scenario was echoed in most territories at the time of independence. Inadequate provision for localisation meant that European officers were frequently asked to stay on. Their length of service post-independence varied from one territory to another. In Nigeria, for example, officers were invited to stay on for a maximum of seven years.
23 In 1963, an inspector who had served in the regular police from 1953 would receive approximately £1,000 per annum. Franklin, 12 Oct. 02.
24 Taken from an interview with David Hooper (Kenya Police, Insp. rtd, 1955–1964), April 2005.
25 'East Africans praise British Police Methods', *Kenya Police Review*, Sept. 1960, pp. 15–16.
26 Hewson, 30 April 2001.
27 Franklin (interview), Oct. 2002.
28 Allen Jenkins, 'K.A.R. Mutiny at Lanet', *Habari*, 32 (March, 1999). Although Percy Wild, who had served as Chief Inspector in charge of 'B' Company GSU, maintained that 'all four insurrections had been planned with the probabe assistance of the KGB and Chinese. They had been timed to take place after the independence of Kenya, the last of the four East African Territories to achieve freedom from colonial rule': Wild, *Bwana Polisi:* p. 67.
29 D. M. H. Riches, Ambassador Congo, to K. M. Wilford, FO, Secret, 19 Feb. 1962. 'Kenya Police to help the Congolese, 1962', NA CO 822/2077.
30 Wild, *Bwana Polisi*, pp. 67–69.
31 Bailey (interview), Nov. 2000.
32 'We used to practice the anti-ambush drills regularly using live ammunition and figure targets set up in the bush. I found it good for morale and any band of shifta in the area would know that we meant business': Wild, *Bwana Polisi*, p. 81.
33 Wild, *Bwana Polisi*, p. 78.
34 'In fact I think that 'B' Company was the last all-European officered company in the GSU': Wild, *Bwana Polisi*, p. 82.

35 Wild, *Bwana Polisi*, p. 101. Wild left the Kenya Police in 1970 and took up a post in the Botswana Police, where he remained until 1976.
36 Wild, *Bwana Polisi*, p. 90.
37 Daniel Bergner, *Soldiers of Light* (London: Penguin, 2005), p. 138.
38 Peter C. Anderson, Interview with Police I-G Keith Biddle, 17 June 2001, http://www.sierra-leone.org/feature061701.html.
39 Bergner, *Soldiers of Light*, pp. 145–147.
40 Lansana Fofana, 'Two Sides of Sierra Leone's Police', 9 Sept. 2003, http://news.bbc.co.uk/go/pr/fr/-/2/hi/africa/3091518.stm.
41 Michael Macoun quoted in Northam, *Shooting in the Dark*, p. 135. Macoun was Commissioner of the RHKP for six years.
42 Northam, *Shooting in the Dark*, p. 134.
43 Taken from an interview with Keith Lomas (RHKP, Assist. Com., rtd, 1959–1997), June 2005.

Afterword

The British Government's long-term plan had always been to leave a *British* rather than a *colonial* policing legacy. This would have corresponded to the evolution described in Jeffries's three phases of colonial policing, the third being the transformation from a colonial to a civil police force.

Colonial forces have raised problems for our understanding of the term 'paramilitary', as well as in identifying differences with the 'civil' model. A 'paramilitary force' can refer to an organisation structured, administered and operating along military lines. Historically, paramilitary police forces were armed. However, in some territories – West African colonies and the Caribbean for example – firearms were available but were not carried on duty. In the Nigeria Police riot unit, which comprised 50 officers, only the 'rifle party' itself, consisting of 6 constables and a handful of gazetted officers, was armed. In theory, one of the differences that can be drawn is that in a civil police force the police officer can act as at his own discretion and on his own responsibility. This relates to the question of having the status of a constable at law, an issue so close to Young's policing ethos. In a paramilitary force, the police constable generally operates as a member of a group under the direct orders of his superior officer. Within this colonial context, constables were recruited locally and officered by expatriates. In the absence of emergency legislation, the law governing the use of force was the same for both a civil–British and paramilitary–colonial force; namely that the *intention* should be to use minimal rather than maximum force to restore law and order.

Attempts at reforming police forces along civil lines had occurred well before the Second World War. In the cases of Ceylon and Jamaica, however, they had been less than successful. In the post-war period, reforming the Colonial Police Service had been essentially an *ad hoc* process. In the main, police reform was triggered by Britain's entry into

[221]

its long era of decolonisation following the withdrawal from India in 1947. The manner in which the British went about this was far from consistent, since the policing demands of the end of empire conflicted with the ideal of exporting the British model. The policing of the post-colonial state was tinged with the remnants of both British and colonial models and this has continued to the present day.

Peel had not meant to create two different concepts of policing. Had the Irish model been acceptable to London's ruling classes, then it may well have been transplanted from Ireland rather than the form of *new* police that emerged in London (though, paradoxically, this centralised and hierarchical body of men was controlled by the Home Office, Irish-style, and was directly accountable to Parliament). Policing became part of the mechanism of government, its principal means of ensuring the security of the State. British- or Irish-style forces shared certain features. The Metropolitan Police's pattern of accountability certainly echoed colonial police traditions. By the same token, colonial police forces *borrowed* aspects of civil policing throughout their histories. This could be seen, for example, in the manner in which law and order were transported from Britain to its colonies, in methods of 'beat' policing and, in the final stages of Empire, in the use of 'hearts and minds' policing. Overall, the criminal justice systems used throughout the old and the new Empire 'broadly mimicked the English system in ideology and practice'.[1] Crucially, therefore, colonial and English–British models overlapped throughout their history.

This is clear from the case of Canada; and further consideration of the police forces of Australia and New Zealand would have revealed traces of both the Irish and the English–British police models. Dean Wilson, for example, has provided striking examples of how the Melbourne Police adopted the Metropolitan Police practices to 'confront uniquely colonial problems'. These centred on discipline, drill, uniforms and regular beat patrols to counter 'the tumultuous social climate of gold-rush Melbourne in the nineteenth century'.[2]

Yet colonial policing developed in ways different from those of its English–British counterpart. Designed to keep Ireland's population under what amounted to colonial subjugation, the RIC developed as a centralised body of armed men. In carrying out extraneous duties, the RIC effectively became the 'eyes and ears' of government and could provide a great deal of intelligence about the population it policed. To work efficiently, the rank and file were kept separate from the officer corps. In a divided Ireland this meant that Catholics were typically excluded from the upper ranks. In colonial police forces similar notions applied, enabling an expatriate gazetted class to oversee a locally recruited rank and file, these expatriate officers being trained, housed and managed separately from the indigenous officers, rather than alongside them.

To date, there has been limited debate surrounding the nature of the colonial model. Nevertheless, the *ethos* of colonial policing was essentially inconsistent, never more so than at the end of Empire. Colonial governments effectively condoned the use of force to enable the police to maintain control of particular territories. This clashed with any notion of retaining, let alone importing, quasi-civil styles of policing. Moreover, there were numerous examples of auxiliary police units operating independently, particularly during periods of colonial conflict. Considering, for example, how Farran's 'snatch squads' in Palestine and the KPR in Kenya became a law to themselves goes some way to illustrate the degree of their autonomy. There was a tendency on the part of colonial governments to turn a blind eye towards the more sinister policing aspects of end of Empire.

Following the Second World War, one colony after another challenged British authority. There would be no peaceful finale to Britain's long era of decolonisation. In territories with settled European populations – Kenya and Southern Rhodesia – the situation was complicated by the settlers' determination to retain their privileged position. Their police forces contained a higher proportion of Europeans, owing to the numbers of settlers who joined both the regular and auxiliary units. Generally the behaviour of the 'settler' police towards the local population was measurably harsher than that of expatriate policemen. Authoritative and repressive tendencies were exacerbated by the overtly political nature of colonial policing in the dangerous cold war world. Post-war reform included the development of police special branches, responsible for both internal and external security. These police units were encouraged to adopt a strong anti-communist stance. Guarding Hong Kong against a further influx of Chinese communism gave the police a role in *external* as well as *internal* policy-making. Ensuring that Cyprus remained British was certainly about the police preventing EOKA from gaining the upper hand. However, during the aftermath of the Suez crisis, it was also about keeping Britain's options open regarding Cyprus's future strategic role in the Mediterranean.

The French transported their policing model lock, stock and barrel to their colonies. The British allegedly created a brand new model.[3] Yet, in both instances, policing relied more heavily on coercion than on consent. Ultimately Waddington's core thesis on the importance of *who* is policed is applicable to both.[4] In the British case, the proposed standardisation of colonial police forces under the auspices of the Colonial Police Service in 1936 marked the beginning of the attempt to create a unified colonial force. Yet there had been no 'common establishment, no common fund, [and] no central direction'. Police forces, to all intents and purposes, *belonged* to the colonial governments they served and they developed as self-contained units. The Colonial Police Service was 'hardly a Service at all in the accepted sense of the word'.[5] Prior to the creation of the official post of inspector general of colonial police, any attempt at standardisation British-style had been made sporadically by roving police advisors, typically making their way home on leave or by inspired commissioners of individual police forces. Thus by 1948, when the Colonial Office had pressing reasons to carry out police reform, it was simply a case of too little, too late.

In a few cases, policing the new state in the aftermath of independence was decidedly *British* in nature. Some preparation had taken place during the transfer of power to ensure that this occurred. For example, in Aden, the Colonial Office repeatedly urged the local administration to consider the public service aspects of policing, and to ensure that a police commission was in place to oversee developments. Advice also hinged on 'insulating' the police from political influences and interference.[6] Public and police service commissions would theoretically provide a system of checks of balances in a similar manner to the local police authority system operating in Britain.

Yet, the nature of colonial policing during the transfer of power was not wholly conducive to a *civil* model. Prolonged unrest saw a strengthening rather than a weakening of colonial traditions. The emphasis had been on reforming and increasing the presence of mobile or riot units and police intelligence systems. At independence, there was little attempt to dismantle this framework. Indeed, the tendency was to build upon what was already in place.

Jeffries's theory of colonial policing outlined a three-stage evolution of policing from the formal era of colonisation through until the end of Empire. Starting out as paramilitary organisations to ensure the defence of a colony, the police essentially held the line. During the second phase came the possibility that the maintenance of law and order could take precedence over internal security. Yet during period of civil unrest, the police reverted to their earlier paramilitary role. It was only during the third phase, when British rule theoretically no longer required police protection against local subversion, that the police could shed their semi-military image. Yet, in practice, policing the end of Empire was more about holding the line to ensure that the process of decolonisation took place in an orderly manner. A refinement of the instrument of control and repression reoccurred; and it was this which was arguably the true legacy of British colonial policing.

Notes

1 Barry Godfrey & Graeme Dunstall (eds), *Crime and Empire 1840–1940: Criminal Justice in Local and Global Context* (Cullompton: Willan Publishing, 2005), p. 5.
2 Dean Wilson, 'Traces and Transmissions: Techno-Scientific Symbolisms in Early Twentieth-Century Policing', in Godfrey & Dunstall, *Crime and Empire*, pp. 108–110.
3 Robert I. Mawby, 'Models of Policing', in Tim Newburn (ed.), *Handbook of Policing* (Cullompton: Willan Publishing, 2005), pp. 17–19.
4 Mawby, 'Models of Policing', p. 22.
5 Jeffries, 'Colonial Police Service' p. 75.
6 'Police Service Commission Aden, 1960–62', CO Memo, March 1961, NA CO 1037/145.

APPENDIX 1

Colonial Police Service authorised regular establishment, 1948

Country/ region	Territory	Gazetted European	Officers non-European	European Inspectors	Other ranks	Total
West Africa	Gold Coast	68	6	–	3,368	3,442
	Sierra Leone	16	4	–	523	543
	Gambia	2	1	–	168	171
	Nigeria	106	9	–	5,784	5,899
East Africa	Kenya	70	–	164	5,114	5,348
	Tanganyika	85	–	7	2,309	2,401
	Uganda	29	–	33	1,334	1,396
	N. Rhodesia	28	–	143	1,138	1,309
	Nyasaland	10	–	17	543	570
	Zanzibar	6	1	–	486	493
	Somaliland	10	–	6	700	716
	Mauritius	4	21	–	708	733
	Seychelles	1	1	–	94	96
	St Helena	1	–	–	11	12
Mediterranean	Aden	7	–	–	678	685
	Cyprus	9	4	–	1,004	1,017
	Gibraltar	2	–	–	230	232
	Malta	–	10	–	1,025	1,035
Western Pacific	Fiji	13	–	12	414	440
	Gilbert and Ellice Is.	1		–	74	75
	British Soloman Is.	1	–	–	209	210
	Ocean Is.	1			67	68
	N. Hebrides	1		–	58	59
	Tonga	–	4	–	52	56
	Falkland Is					–
West Indies	Bahamas	6	–	4	270	280
	Barbados	7	1	–	556	564
	Bermuda	5	–	6	110	121
	British Guiana	21	3	1	1,040	1,065
	British Honduras	2	1	–	189	192
	Jamaica	24	7	–	1,779	1,810
	Trinidad	23	3	–	1,396	1,422
	Leeward Is.	6	2	–	257	265

Continued

Windward Is.	Dominica	1	1	–	107	109
	Grenada	2	–	–	140	142
	St Lucia	3	–	–	173	176
	St Vincent	–	2	–	93	95
Far East	Fed. Malaya	335	29	35	15,455	15,854
	Singapore	73	10	14	3,398	3,495
	Sarawak	10	–	–	1,108	1,118
	Brunei	2	–	–	165	167
	North Borneo	17	–	–	942	959
	Hong Kong	32	–	217	3,049	3,298
TOTALS		1,040	120	659	56,253	58,072
South Africa	Basutoland	14	–	–	286	300
	Bechuanaland	10	–	–	243	253
	Swaziland	10	–	–	159	169
TOTALS		34	–	–	688	722

Source: Report on the Colonial Police Service, 28 Dec. 1949, PRO CO 537/5440.

APPENDIX 2

Typical colonial establishment

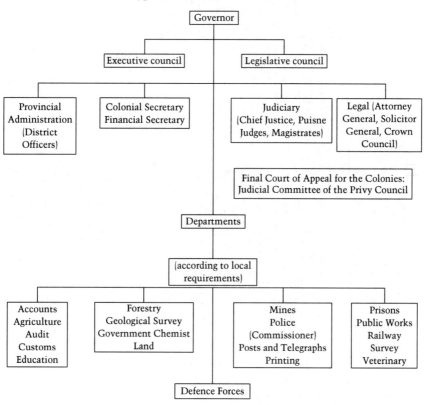

APPENDIX 3

Layout of Kenya Police Special Branch

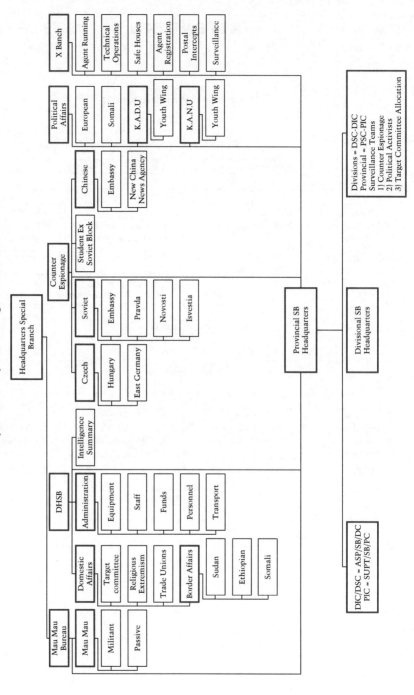

Key:

DIC = District Intelligence Committee, with the same composition as DSC. To discuss and take action on intelligence matters, i.e. political activities causing public disturbances, strikes, illegal meetings, Mau Mau activities, religious extremism and border affairs.

DSC = District Security Committee, comprised of District Commissioner, Police Commander and Special Branch officer. Met weekly to discuss and take action on issues affecting key-points in the division, i.e. airstrips, bridges, essential services. If necessary would invite others to attend, i.e. veterinary officers, immigration officers.

PIC = Provincial Intelligence Committee. Same composition as PSC. Met to discuss the overall intelligence assessment for the Province. Minutes of DIC and PIC distributed in similar fashion to DSC and PSC.

PSC = Provincial Security Committee, comprised of Provincial Commissioner, Provincial Police and SB officers. Meetings held following DSC meeting to provide an overall assessment of the province. Both DSC and PSC Minutes sent to Nairobi, i.e. to senior Administration, Police and Army.

Surveillance Teams = had their targets set by the Target Committee in Special Branch HQ. Main duties included surveillance linked to counter espionage, i.e. Soviets/Chinese, political activists, communists, agents causing suspicion, people considered for recruitment as agents, providing support to technical teams (bugging/tapping).

SELECT BIBLIOGRAPHY

Principal sources searched at the National Archives

Air Ministry

AIR 2/10228, 8/2186, 15/887

Cabinet Office

Cabinet memoranda and committees: CAB 128/27, 129/28, 129/72–6, 130/44, 134/497, 148/49

Colonial Office

CO original correspondence: geographical classes

Aden: CO 1015/166, 1015/379–80, 1015/1911
Caribbean: CO 111/742–96, 295/627, 1031/92, 1031/103–7, 1371/867
Ceylon: CO 54/789, 54/789
Cyprus: CO 67/218
Hong Kong: CO 850/261, 1023/106
Ireland: CO 904/174
Kenya: CO 822/1222–23, 822/1293, 822/2690, 822/2077, 866/118
Malaya, Sarawak, Borneo: CO 717/177, 1022/22, 1022/171–2
Palestine: CO 733/128, 733/180,733/355, 733/383, 733/451, 850/32–56, 850/267, 1017/34
East Africa: CO 1015/372, 1036/3–4
West Africa: CO 554/572–3

CO original correspondence: subject classes

Colonies supplementary ('Secret'): CO 537
A considerable amount of correspondence relating to colonial policing and security throughout the colonies is distributed across this class. The major groupings of files are as follows:
CO 537/1696–9, 537/2269, 537/2712, 537/2770–81, 537/3653, 537/3847, 537/4382–4, 537/5440–4, 537/5439, 537/5856, 537/5874, 537/5893, 537/5900, 537/6044–75, 537/6157, 537/ 6932–67, 537/7263, 537/2677–86, 537/2712, 537/2768–81
Colonies supplementary ('Police Departments and Successors'): CO 1037
CO 1037/2–39, 1037/78, 1037/110–11, 1037/145, 1037/156–8, 1037/175–8, 1037/185, 1037/192, 1037/200, 1037/224–6, 1037/520–53, 1037/257, 1037/ 856–67

Other classes

CO 111/818, 321/425, 323/1916, 537/968/286, 850/189, 850/210, 850/261/9–10, 852/1109, 866/118, 877/43/1, 885/60, 885/124, 968/272–8, 968/283–4, 968/498, 1017/262, 1017/275, 1017/467, 1021/7

Ministry of Defence

DEFE 11/33, 11/413

Record of the Royal Mint

MINT 20/1708–9, 20/1255–6, 20/2098–102, 20/2705, 20/3133, 20/3232

Foreign Office and Foreign and Commonwealth Office

FO 371/185311
FCO 53/373, 63/235–48, 86/272, 371/1851–3

Home Office

HO 35/66, 45/24727, 287/122, 287/250, 287/250, 287/303

Metropolitan Police Records (to 1969)

MEPO 2/6093, 2/7555, 2/7925, 2/11464, 2/279611

Prime Minister's Office

PREM 8/1406, 11/2616

Treasury

T 164/180, 213/632, 213/631–2, 213/685, 333/34, 333/57, 333/161, 333/164

War Office

WO 106/5720

Principal sources searched at the Public Records Office, Northern Ireland

Cabinet Memoranda and Committees: PRONI CAB 9G/56

Principal sources searched at the National Archives Canada, Ottawa

These are indicated in the text by the following abbreviations: RG 18 (A-1). RG 18 (B-1)

Papers of other individuals and organisations

(Family papers are not currently available for consultation by the general public.)
Papers of John Biles, Family Papers
Papers of J. D. Bryant, Family Papers
Papers of R. J. W. Craig, Family Papers
Papers of Sir Herbert Dowbiggin, Rhodes House Library, Oxford, MSS. Ind. Oc. s. 288
Papers of Ted Eates, Family Papers
Papers of Derek Franklin, Family Papers

Papers of Neil Hadow, Family Papers
Papers of Peter Hewitt, Family Papers
Papers of Howard Mansfield, Family Papers
Law Enforcement in Former British-African Territories: Gold Coast, Nigeria, Kenya
Northern Rhodesia, Nyasaland Uganda (Oxford Development Records Project), Rhodes House Library, Oxford, MSS. Afr. s. 1784
Papers of the Palestine Police Association, Edward Horne, Private Papers
RUC Archive, Police Service of Northern Ireland, Belfast
Papers of George Robins, Rhodes House Library (RHL), Oxford, MSS Medit. s. 9
Papers of John Rymer-Jones, Family Papers
Papers of Sir Arthur Young, Rhodes House Library, Oxford, MSS. Brit. Emp. s. 486

Unpublished manuscripts

Jack Binsley, Autobiography, 1910–1984, Book 3, 1930–1948 (Palestine)
R. J. W. Craig, A Short Account of the Malayan Emergency (2000)
Derek Franklin, Memoirs of a Colonial Police Officer, 1953–1981 (2003)
Howard Mansfield, Memoir, Palestine Police

Interviews

Since 1999 interviews have been conducted and correspondence exchanged with approximately 400 former colonial police officers, colonial administrators and members of the armed forces. The following interviews formed the core of the oral and written testimonies used directly in this book:
John Bailey (Kenya Police, Div. Com., rtd, 1954–66), 16 Nov. 2000
John Biles (Palestine, Nigeria, the Gambia, Cyprus, Zanzibar, Com., dec., 1936–63), 30 March 2000
John Burton (Kenya Police, Div. Com., rtd, 1954–66), 4 Aug. 2000
Bob Bradney (Nigeria Police, ASP, rtd, 1953–64), 6 Nov. 2000
George Briffett (Nigeria Police, ASP, rtd, 1951–64), 13 March 2000
Sir Richard Catling (Palestine Police, Malayan Police, Kenya Police, Com. dec., 1935–63), 2 June 2000
Don Clarke (Kenya Police, Chief Insp., rtd, 1953–64), 11 Sept. 2000
James Colquoun (Kenya Police, District Officer, rtd, 1954–56), 29 Jan. 2001
Leon Comber (Malay Police, rtd, 1945–54), April 2001
Dick Craig (Palestine Police, Malayan Police, Senior Assit. Comm., dec., 1946–64), 12 Jan. 2000
Roger Dracup (Palestine Police, Kenya Police, ASP, rtd, 1947–1960), 23 June 2000
Ted Eates (Nigeria Police, Gambia Police, Sierra Leone Police, Royal Hong Kong Police, 1946–69), 25 & 28 June 2001, 21 July 2002, 25 June 2003, 2 May 2005
Ted Evans (Kenya Police, Special Branch, rtd, 1954–73), 17 July 2000
James Forster (Kenya Police, Insp., rtd, 1954–56), 29 May 2000

Derek Franklin (Kenya Police, Bahrain State Police, Lesotho Police, Botswana Police, Dep. Head Special Branch, Sen. Sup., rtd, 1953–81), 23 March 2001, 7 Dec. 2004

Courtney Gidley (Nigeria Police, Acting Dep. Insp.-Gen., rtd, 1942–63), 28 Aug. 2003

Jim Godsave (Palestine Police, Malayan Police, Dep. Sup., rtd, 1946–60), 30 July 2001

Neil Hadow (Ceylon Police, Gambia Police, Sierra Leone Police, Uganda Police, Comm., rtd, 1935–58), 10 Jan. 2002

Peter Hewitt (Kenya Police, Cyprus Police, Nyasaland and Papua New Guinea Police, rtd, 1953–72), 30 July 2002

David Hewson (Kenya Police, Chief Sup., rtd, 1951–75), 11 March 2000

David Hooper (Kenya Police, Insp., rtd, 1955–1964), 25 April 2005

Edward Horne (Palestine Police, Metropolitan Police, Act. Insp., rtd, 1941–74), 2 May 2001

Peter Kingsley-Heath, 20 May 2002

Michael Koo (Royal Hong Kong Police, Sup., rtd, 1950–75), 18 Aug. 2003

Colin Limb (Nigeria Police, Nyasaland Police, Acting Chief Sup., rtd, 1950–71), 20 Aug. 2000

Avtar S. Matharu (Kenya Police, Assist. Sup., rtd, 1953–64), 2 June 2002

Philip Milton (Nigeria Police, Assist. Sup., rtd, 1955–66), 25 July 2000

Ronald G. Postlethwaite (Palestine Police, 1945–48, RSM, rtd, Royal Signals, 1950–72), 26 Nov. 2004

David Rowcroft (Kenya Police, rtd, 1955–63), 25 Nov. 2000

John Rymer-Jones, 29 Oct. 2005

C. L. Scobell (Royal Hong Kong Police, Sen. Assist. Com., rtd, 1951–78), 22 Feb. 2000

Ivan Scott (Royal Hong Kong Police, Sup., rtd, 1955–87), 21 May, 2001

John Standring (Kenya Police, Div. Com., rtd, 1954–64), 14 & 27 June 2000

E. G. Wells (Palestine Police, Hong Kong Police, Kenya Police, Chief Insp., rtd, 1946–65), 30 May 2000

George Willis (Nigeria Police, Chief Sup., rtd, 1954–66), 5 Sept. 2000

Official publications

Kessing's Contemporary Archives, 1952–55

Aden Police, Annual Reports, 1950–59

'Hong Kong Disturbances 1967', Confidential Report, Colonial Secretariat (Hong Kong, 1968)

Hong Kong Police Annual Reports, 1964–69

Kenya Police, Annual Reports, 1945–1960

Colonial Office, Historical Survey of the Origins and Growth of Mau Mau (London: HMSO, 1960), a report written by Sir F. D. Corfield

Report of a Commission of Inquiry into the Kowloon Disturbances (Hong Kong, 1967)

Report of the Commission of Enquiry into Disturbances in Aden, December 1947 (HMSO, 1948)

Journals and newspapers

Habari (Kenya Police Association journal)
Kenya Police Review
Nigeria Police Review
Palestine Police Old Comrades' Association Newsletter
The Times

Books and articles

Anderson David M. & Killingray, David, *Policing the Empire: Government, Authority and Control, 1830–1940* (Manchester: MUP, 1991)

Anderson David M. & Killingray, David, *Policing and Decolonisation: Politics, Nationalism and the Police, 1917–65* (Manchester: MUP, 1992)

Anderson, David, M., *Histories of the Hanged: Britain's dirty war in Kenya and the end of the Empire* (London: Weidenfeld & Nicolson, 2005)

Annieson, Anthony, *The One-Eyed Dragon: The Inside Story of a Hong Kong Policeman* (Moffat: Lochar Publishing, 1989)

Arnold, David, *Police Power and Colonial Rule, Madras 1859–1947* (Oxford: OUP, 1986)

Bayley, David, H., *The Police and Political Developments in India* (New Jersey: Princeton University Press, 1969)

Bickers, Robert, *Empire Made Me, an Englishman Adrift in Shanghai* (London: Allen Lane, 2003)

Boritch, Helen, 'Conflict, Compromise and Administrative Convenience: The Police Organization in Nineteenth-Century Toronto', *Canadian Journal of Law and Society*, 3 (1988)

Brogden, Mike, 'The Emergence of the police: the Colonial dimension', *British Journal of Criminology*, 2:1 (winter, 1987)

Brown, Judith M. & Louis, W. R. (eds), *The Oxford History of the British Empire*, Vol. 4: *The Twentieth Century* (Oxford: OUP, 1999)

Burton, E. A., 'The Policing of Bermuda from the Earliest Times', *Bermuda Historical Quarterly* (1955)

Clayton, Anthony, *The Thin Blue Line: Studies in Law Enforcement in Late Colonial Africa* (Oxford: Oxford Development Records Project, 1985)

Cooper, John, *Colony in Conflict: The Hong Kong Disturbances, May 1967–January 1968* (Hong Kong: Swindon Book Company, 1970)

Curry, J. C., *The Indian Police* (London: Faber & Faber, 1932)

Darwin, John, 'British Decolonisation since 1945: A Pattern of a Puzzle?', *Journal of Imperial and Commonwealth History*, 12 (1984)

Dep, A. C., *A History of the Ceylon Police, 1866–1913*, Vol. 2 (Colombo: The Times of Ceylon, 1938)

Dunn, P. W. D., 'The Role of the Police in a Democratic State', *Journal of African Administration*, 4 (1952)

Elkins, Caroline, *Britain's Gulag: The Brutal End of Empire in Kenya* (London: Jonathan Cape, 2005)

Ellison, Graham, & Smyth, Jim, *The Crowned Harp, Policing Northern Ireland* (London: Pluto Press Ltd, 2000)

Emsley, Clive, *The English Police: A Political and Social History*, 2nd Edition (Harlow: Longman, 1996)

Farran, Roy, *Winged Dagger, Adventures on Special Service* (London: Collins, 1948)

Fedorowich, Kent, 'The Problems of Disbandment: The Royal Irish Constabulary and Imperial Migration, 1919–29', *Irish Historical Studies*, 30:117 (May, 1996)

Fitzpatrick, David, 'Ireland and the Empire', in Andrew Porter (ed.), *The Oxford History of the British Empire*, Vol. 3: *The Nineteenth Century* (Oxford: Oxford University Press, 1999)

Foot, Sir Hugh, *A Start in Freedom* (London: Hodder and Stoughton, 1964)

Foran, W. Robert, *The Kenya Police 1887–1960* (London: Robert Hale, 1962)

Franklin, Derek, *A Pied Cloak: Memoirs of a Colonial Police (Special Branch) Officer* (London: Janus, 1996)

Gaylord, M. S. & Traver, H., 'Colonial Policing and the Demise of British Rule in Hong Kong', *International Journal of the Sociology of Law*, 23 (1995)

George, Boyce, D., '"Normal Policing": Public Order in Northern Ireland Since Partition', *Eire–Ireland*, 1 (1979)

Godfrey, Barry & Dunstall, Graeme (eds), *Crime and Empire 1840–1940: Criminal Justice in Local and Global Context* (Cullompton: Willan Publishing, 2005)

Griffiths, Percival, *To Guard My People: The History of the Indian Police* (London: Ernest Benn, 1971)

Hack, Karl, '"Iron Claws on Malaya": The Historiography of the Malayan Emergency', *Journal of Southeast Asian Studies*, 30:1 (1999)

Hack, Karl, 'British Intelligence and Counter-Insurgency in the Era of Decolonisation: The Example of Malaya', *Intelligence and National Security*, 14:2 (summer 1999)

Hanson, Robert, Warchol, Greg & Zupan, Linda, 'Policing Paradise: Law and Disorder in Belize', *Police Practice and Research*, 5:3 (July, 2004)

Hickinbotham, Sir Tom, *Aden* (London: Constable & Co., 1958)

Hillman, Richard, S., & D'Agostino, Thomas, J. (eds), *Understanding the Contemporary Caribbean* (London: Lynne Rienner, 2003)

Hiscox, Chistopher Lawrence, *The Dawn Stand-To* (Bideford: Lazurus Press, 2000)

Holland Robert, *Britain and the Revolt in Cyprus, 1954–1959* (Oxford: Clarendon Press, 1998)

Horne, Edward, *A Job Well Done: A History of the Palestine Police Force 1920–48* (Tiptree: Anchor Press, 1982)

Imray, Colin, *Policeman in Palestine* (Bideford: Edward Gaskell, 1995)

Imray, Colin, *Policeman in Africa* (Lewes: Book Guild, 1997)

Jackson, Robert, *The Malayan Emergency: The Commonwealth Wars, 1948–66* (London: Routledge, 1991)

Jeffries, Charles, 'The Colonial Police Service', *Police College Magazine* (Sept. 1951)

Jeffries, Charles, *The Colonial Police* (London: Max Parrish, 1952)

Jenkins, Arthur Hughes, *A Long Beat: Service to the Crown, Home and Abroad* (Denbigh: Gee & Son, 1994)

Jones, Tim, *Postwar Counterinsurgency and the SAS 1945–1952: A Special Type of Warfare* (London: Frank Cass, 2001)

Kolinsky, Martin, *Law, Order and Riots in Mandatory Palestine, 1928–1935* (New York: St. Martin's Press, 1993)

Lang, Michael, *One Man in His Time: The Diary of a Palestine Policeman 1946–48* (Lewes: Book Guild, 1997)

Lapping, Brian, *End of Empire* (London: Guild Publishing, 1985)

Lord, Cliff & Birtles, David, *The Armed Forces of Aden 1839–1967* (Solihull: Helion & Co., 2000)

Macleod, Rod C., *The NWMP and Law Enforcement 1873–1905* (Toronto: UTP, 1976)

Macleod, Rod C., *The North West Mounted Police 1873–1919* (Ottawa: Canadian Historical Association, 1978)

Macoun, Michael J., *Wrong Place, Right Time: Policing the End of Empire* (London: Radcliffe Press, 1996)

Marquis, Greg, 'The "Irish Model" and Nineteenth-Century Canadian Policing', *Journal of Imperial and Commonwealth History*, 25:2 (May, 1997)

Mathieson, William P., *A Chequered Career* (London: Janus, 1994)

Mawby, Robert I., *Comparative Policing Issues: The British and American System in International Perspective* (London: Unwin Hyman, 1990)

Moran, J. W. C., *The Camp Across the River* (London: Peter Davies, 1963)

Morrison, William R., *Showing the Flag: The Mounted Police and Canadian Sovereignty in the North 1894–1925* (Vancouver: UBCP, 1985)

Morton, Geoffrey, J., *Just the Job: Some Experiences of a Colonial Policeman* (London: Hodder & Stoughton, 1957)

Murphy, Philip, *Alan Lennox-Boyd: A Biography* (London: I. B. Tauris, 1999)

Newburn, Tim (ed.), *Handbook of Policing* (Cullompton: Willan Publishing, 2005)

Northam, Gerry, *Shooting in the Dark: Riot Police in Britain* (London: Faber & Faber, 1988)

Orrett, W. A., *The History of the British Guiana Police* (Georgetown: Daily Chronicle Ltd, 1951)

Paget, Julian, *Last Post: Aden 1964–1967* (London: Faber & Faber, 1969)

Palmer, Stanley H., *Police and Protest in England and Ireland 1780–1850* (Cambridge: CUP, 1988)

Pippet, G. K., *A History of the Ceylon Police, 1795–1870*, Vol. 1 (Colombo: Times of Ceylon, 1938)

Rawlings, Philip, *Policing: A Short History* (Cullompton: Willan Publishing, 2002)

Reiner, Robert, *The Politics of the Police*, 3rd Edition (Oxford: Oxford University Press, 2000)

Reith, Charles, *British Police and the Democratic Ideal* (Oxford: Oxford University Press, 1943)

Ross, Jeffrey Ian, 'The Historical Treatment of Urban Policing in Canada: A Review of the Literature', *Urban History Review*, 24:1 (October, 1995)

Rotimi, Kemi, *The Police in a Federal State: The Nigerian Experience* (Ibadan: College Press, 2001)

Ryder, Chris, *The RUC: A Force Under Fire, 1922–2000*, 4th Edition (London: Arrow, 2000)

Segev, Tom, *One Palestine, Complete: Jews and Arabs under the British Mandate* (London: Abacus, 2000)

Small, N. J., 'The Northern Rhodesia Police and its Legacy', *African Social Research*, 27 (1979)

Smith, Simon S., 'General Templer and Counter-Insurgency in Malaya: Heart and Minds, Intelligence, and Propaganda', *Intelligence and National Security*, 16:3 (Autumn, 2001)

Stonier-Newman, Lynne, *Policing a Pioneer Province: The British Columbia Provincial Police 1858–1950* (Madeira Park, BC: Harbour Publishing, 1991)

Storch, Robert D., '"The Plague of Blue Locusts": Police Reform and Popular Resistance in Northern England 1840–57', *International Review of Social History*, 20 (1975)

Stubbs, Richard, *Hearts and Minds in Guerrilla Warfare: The Malayan Emergency, 1948–60* (Oxford: OUP, 1989)

Talbot, C. K., *The Thin Blue Line: An Historical Perspective of Policing in Canada* (Ottawa: Crimecare Inc., 1983)

Talbot, C. K., Jayewardene, C. H. S. & Juliani, T. J., 'Policing in Canada: A Developmental Perspective', *Canadian Police College Journal*, 8:3 (1984)

Talbot, C. K., Jayewardene, C. H. S. & Juliani, T. J., *Canada's Constables: The Historical Development of Policing in Canada* (Ottawa: Crimecare Inc. 1985)

Thompson, Robert, *Defeating Communist Insurgency: Experiences from Malaya and Vietnam* (London: Macmillan, 1966)

Tobias, John J., 'The British Colonial Police', in Philip J. Stead (ed.), *Pioneers in Policing* (Montclair, NJ: Patterson Smith, 1977)

Waddington, P. A. J., *The Strong Arm of the Law: Armed and Public Order Policing* (Oxford: Clarendon Press, 1991)

Waddington, P. A. J., *Policing Citizens: Authority and Rights* (London: UCL Press, 1999)

Wallace, Gerald F., Higgins, William & McGahen, Peter, *The Saint John Police Story: The Clark Years 1890–1914* (Fredericton, NB: New Ireland Press, 1991)

Wild, Percy, *Bwana Polisi: Under Three Flags* (Braunton: Merlin Books, 1993)

Willis, John Mathew, 'Colonial Policing in Aden, 1937–1967', *Arab Studies Journal*, 5:1 (Spring, 1997)

Young, Arthur, *The Federation of Malaya and its Police, 1786–1952* (Kuala Lumpur: Charles Grenier & Sons, 1952)

Theses

Ahire, P. T., 'Policing Colonisation: The Emergence and Role of the Police in Colonial Nigeria, 1860–1960', PhD (Cambridge University, 1985)

Allgood, John William, 'Britain's Final Decade in South Arabia: Aden, the Federation and the Struggle Against Arab Nationalism', PhD (University of Texas, 1999)

Caspi, Joseph, 'Policing the Holy Land 1918–1957: The Transition from a

Colonial to a National Model of Policing and Changing Conceptions of Police Accountability', PhD (City University, London, 1991)

Clark, David, J., 'The Colonial Police and Anti-Terrorism, Bengal 1930–36, Palestine 1927–47 and Cyprus, 1955–59', DPhil (Oxford University, 1978)

Hewitt, Stephen, Roy, '"Old Myths Die Hard": The Transformation of the Mounted Police in Alberta and Saskatchewan 1914–1939', PhD (University of Saskatchewan, 1997)

Morrison, Hamish, '"Quis Custodiet Ipsos Custodes?" The Problems of Policing in Anglophone Africa during the Transfer of Power.' PhD (University of Aberdeen, 1995)

Rotimi, Emmanuel, K., 'A History of Native Administration Police Forces in Nigeria, 1900–1970', PhD (Obafemi Awolowo University, 1990)

Sinclair, Georgina S., ' "Settlers" Men or Colonial Policemen? The Ambiguities of Colonial Policing, 1945–1980', PhD (University of Reading, 2002)

INDEX

Lightning Source UK Ltd.
Milton Keynes UK
UKOW031141290512

193514UK00001B/8/P